BEYOND
BOUNDARIES

BEYOND BOUNDARIES

The Adventures of a Seer

Foreword by
Willis W. Harman

Louise Platt Hauck

Lamplight Publishing Company
New York, New York

ISBN: 978-0-9769205-4-0

Lamplight Publishing Company
511 6th Avenue, Ste. 234
New York, NY 10011

For Adrianne and Dylan—
My greatest teachers.
In memory of Ruth and Les Hauck—
who lit the lantern I carry.

Contents

Foreword   11
Preface   21
Acknowledgments   27
Introduction—If I Had a Dime   29

Part One

How It Appears

Chapter One   **Beyond the Present**   37

   The Filmstrip and the Projector   39
   Synchronicity   42
   Strong Future Events   43

Chapter Two   **Viewing Timeless Spaces**   45

   Background   45
   About the Readings   48

Qualifying the Presentation of Future Information   49
Meeting Ben   53
Ben's Reading   54

Chapter Three   Changing the Past, Influencing the Present and Future   59

In the Judge's Chambers   60
Alone in Her Room   64

Chapter Four   Overlays of Concurrent Life Spaces   69

England   69
David, the Light Technician   74
A Transcendental Soiree   77
I'll Give You a Sign   85

Chapter Five   Passing Over and Re-entry—Conditions Favorable   92

Choosing Parents and Conditions   95
Anticipating Returns   100
Conditions of an "Almost Child"   105

Chapter Six   Replaying Old Themes: Choosing New Outcomes   108

The Stockbrokers   113
The Power of Old Themes   116

Chapter Seven   Meeting Ourselves   124

The Minister   130
Mother Superior on my Couch   136
Return to the Slave Plantation   139
Replay in Spain   142
Meeting a Guru   150

Chapter Eight   Meeting Old Friends   160

"Please Help Me Die"   164
Tending the Gardens   168

Chapter Nine   Intersecting and Repeating Paths   177

   Train in China   182
   Soulmates and the Holographic Partner   187
   The Girl with the Cane   190
   Suicides   196

Part Two

The Other Side— What They Communicate

Chapter Ten   Not So Far Away   207

Chapter Eleven   Gratitude   216

   The Scientist and the FBI Agent   220

Chapter Twelve   Awareness   225

   Mountain Man   229
   Proof of the Continuum   235

Chapter Thirteen   Resolution   238

   Your Sister Got the Pearls   243

Chapter Fourteen   Gifts to Give   245

   "She's Looking Beautiful"   251
   Relief from Guilt: The Twin's Twin   255
   You're Just as Smart as Billy   259

Chapter Fifteen   From "Famous" Entities   263

   Amelia   268
   The Guru   290
   Fritz Perls   292
   Ernest Hemingway   294

Chapter Sixteen   Caught Between Dimensions   298

   Zorro   306

Part Three

The Light and The Homeward Journey

Chapter Seventeen White Light   315

    Surrounded   317
    White Light and Chuck E. Cheese   322

Chapter Eighteen What Keeps You From Going Home 331

    Finding the Pain   336
    Believing the Illusion   342

Chapter Nineteen The Rewards   350

    Epiphany   358
    Free Time   362
    New Life Experiences in Responseto Clearer Choices 363

About the Author   369

Foreword

Some who read this book (and many more who would never read it) will wonder about the experiences described. They are fascinating; they certainly seem like reports of available information which the informant had no physical way of knowing, of plausible memories of past lives, of communication with persons who are physically "dead." But such things don't happen in the world described by modern science. Do they?

This discrepancy between the world of science and the mysterious happenings we hear about—and, in many more cases than are commonly talked about, experience directly—is puzzling to say the least. Many in the modern world have been willing to deny their own experience because "science says" it couldn't have happened. Yet these denied experiences are of the sort which persons in other "pre-scientific" societies held to be of the utmost importance.

Louise Hauck has done us a service with her "stories." We are tempted to believe in them. I would like to contribute a few thoughts as to why we might well yield to that temptation.

There is a public misconception about science, not shared by really good scientists: that is, that science describes reality. The activity of science is basically a way of understanding based on making models (e.g. H_2O, $E=mc^2$) or choosing metaphors (e.g. electric current, stream of consciousness) to represent certain aspects of reality, and then testing those models and metaphors through empirical inquiry. We use metaphors to understand or communicate about the unfamiliar in terms of the familiar. No one thinks that electric current is really some sort of fluid flowing down the wire, but the term represents certain aspects of the phenomenon in terms of something easily visualized.

In some respects science is like the well-known story about the blind men examining the elephant. Western science has been insistent that the "elephant" of ultimate reality is really "fundamental particles" and interacting fields. Eastern thought has held (much longer) that it is consciousness. Modern quantum physics has examined the "elephant" in finer detail and decided there are no such things as separate particles, and no phenomena without observers. But we have tended to miss the real point of the story.

When the blind man feeling the leg claims the elephant is a tree trunk, and a second, feeling the tail, claims it is a piece of rope, both are using metaphors. Rather than argue over who is right, they need to explore together in what sense the elephant is like a tree, and in what sense like a rope.

Simple enough with elephants, but the lesson has been harder to grasp with regard to science. Great mischief can result when the models and metaphors of science are mistakenly taken to be the "true" description of reality. Because when they are, then people feel a necessity to defend them, and to stamp out competing reality claims. Many of the conflicts in the history of science, as well as the conflict between science and religion, have been battles between groups who each insist that their metaphors are "really" how reality is.

As with the story of the blind men and the elephant, some aspects of experienced reality are like the world known to the physical senses; some are like our knowledge of ourselves as whole organisms. Some, however, are like our inner knowledge or our own minds. (For example, it has often been remarked that social insects such as termites display characteristics that suggest a "group mind" which responds as a whole to an intrusion, even though the individual insects could not be in physical communication with one another.)

The implicit or explicit epistemological position of the "hard" scientist is that we know what we know through the empirical observation of quantifiable, replicable interventions in the physical world. A less positivist scientific attitude holds that reality has many aspects, and is never fully captured in any model or metaphor. Thus various kinds of metaphors may be employed, with appropriate ways of testing their fitness and range of applicability—since they each may help us to understand and communicate about certain aspects of a fundamentally mysterious reality.

Mainstream science, characterized by an obsession with prediction and control, has almost exclusively employed physicalistic metaphors such as "mechanisms," particles, waves, or fields. It has been very dubious about more holistic metaphors such as organism, personality, ecological community, or the Gaia metaphor for the Earth and its biosphere. Scientists have typically insisted that these whole-system descriptions can or will be understood in terms of their parts.

Mainstream science has tended to disallow a third kind of metaphor, a *consciousness metaphor*. It has tended to be very uncomfortable with explorations of the ways in which experienced reality might resemble our experience of our own minds.

My own consciousness is my most direct experiencing of reality. Perceptions of the world through the physical senses are far more indirect, being mediated by the unconscious mind in ways only recently appreciated.

Looking into my own mind, I find, first of all, that mind is not something that exists in the space-time world. To the contrary, my experience of the space-time world is constructed within my mind from vast numbers of physical-sense perceptions.

Among the most fundamental aspects of consciousness are awareness, volition, and creativity. I find there are levels of awareness, from subliminal or subconscious, to what feel like "higher" or "supraliminal" levels. I also find that there are "partitions" in my mind; there are parts that seem somehow separate from other parts, what C. G. Jung called "autonomous complexes"—multiple personalities being an extreme case.

In my experience, consciousness is both something experienced *and* the experience—that which I consider my "self." Myself is that which thinks my thoughts, feels my feelings, participates in the choosing of my actions, generates my insight and my creativity. The self is surely real in some sense, for it has real consequences. For example, in the well-substantiated placebo effect, the fact that my self holds a belief regarding the medicinal qualities of a sugar pill results in real physiological effects, unrelated to the chemical composition of the pill. In the field of psycho-neuro-immunology the efficacy of the body's immune system appears to be affected by images and thoughts held in the mind of the self.

To some extent I am able to refer to specific processes or contents of consciousness—such as ideas, or images, or emotions—but these are never really divorced from the whole; the fundamental reality is that, as the quantum physicist Erwin Schrodinger put it, "Consciousness is never experienced in the plural, only in the singular." Consciousness is not something to be subdivided, measured, or quantified.

Even so, the "partitioning" of the mind produces apparent separation. For example, in research on hypnosis it appears that there is a "hidden observer," not accessible to ordinary conscious awareness, that does not believe the suggestions of the hypnotists which another part of the mind has so readily accepted. In dissociative experience, the conscious part of the mind is experienced as separate from the body and other aspects of the self. In the experience of creativity, the conscious ego-self becomes aware of products generated by some other, out-of-awareness part of the mind.

Those are some of the characteristics of our own individual consciousness; let us now try to think of nature using the metaphor of consciousness as experienced in the individual mind. Thus nature is experienced as one whole, with many aspects. Characteristic of the whole are awareness (pervasive consciousness) and volition (most evident in organisms). Like the multiple personalities sometimes found in an individual, there is an appearance of multiplicity—different organisms with different consciousnesses for instance—yet at another level consciousness is one. *Within this metaphor* (making no ontological claim), things of the physical world are analogous to the images in a dream in the individual mind (images which in the dream state pass certain "reality tests" that they fail to pass in a higher state of awakeness). Within this metaphor it is not surprising that all organisms exhibit some characteristics or extent of consciousness, nor that "separate" organisms (like the cells of a slime mold, or the birds of a flock) seem to have a collective consciousness. Within this metaphor it is not surprising that the evolutionary process seems to show apparently teleological aspects, movement toward "higher" levels of consciousness, bursts of "creative experimentation" (such as the bursts of new genera and even new phyla at certain geological periods). Within this metaphor the fact that a migrating bird "knows" its destination is less surprising, and we have less compulsion to search for a physical "mechanism." Within this metaphor one can easily imagine that the oriole's knowledge of nest-building resides in a sort of species-collective mind, "higher level" than the individual bird-mind (something perhaps like Rupert Sheldrake's concept of a morphic field built up through "habits").

Vast ranges of extraordinary human experience are far more easily accommodated in a consciousness metaphor than in the reductionistic metaphors of mainstream science. For example, research on creativity and intuition reveals interesting characteristics of the behind-the-scenes part of the mind. Not only does this part of the mind regularly come up with creative solutions to problems, aesthetic creations, and deep wisdom; it also on occasion has available to it knowledge which appears not to have ever been learned through the physical senses. Furthermore, the more it is trusted and turned to, the more competent it seems to become.

In research on cases of multiple personality disorder, the person's mind is partitioned more than with so-called normal persons, to the point that there may be a number of near-complete personalities with different self-identities, gestures, carriage, voice characteristics, memories, allergies, body chemistries, ocular characteristics, and so on. These different ego-states, which sometimes have no awareness of one another, may alternately take over the body and conscious awareness. They have different life histories, many or most of which appear to be related to early childhood sexual or physical abuse. But one—called the "inner-self helper"—is unique. It claims never to have been born, nor to die; when the physical body dies and decays, and the other personalities disintegrate, "I remain," it reports.

The research literature of parapsychology, and that of the earlier field of "psychic research," is full of apparent instances of telepathic communication, clairvoyant "remote viewing," psychokinesis, out-of-body experiences, and near-death experiences, all of which tend to leave the experiencer with the conviction that mind is more than simply brain functioning, and that personal consciousness in some sense can exist independently of the body and that it in some sense persists after physical death.

If one is entranced with the physicalistic metaphors of mainstream science, many of the above sorts of reports—like the anecdotes in this book—have to be viewed with skepticism; nay, with incredulity. They have to be the consequence of undiscovered "mechanisms," illusion, or fraud, since in that paradigm there is no other possible way of accounting for them. Within the consciousness metaphor, on the other hand, since one is imagining one universal mind (with levels and partitions), none of these kinds of reports has to be presumptively explained away. The reports need not all be accurate, but they are not intrinsically more mysterious than the more commonplace phenomena that go on within my own individual consciousness.

It is not really necessary to turn to the "outrageous" to make this point. Our everyday experiences of conscious awareness, memory retrieval, volition, intention, quest for meaning, aesthetic sense—none of these fit into the physicalistic metaphor any better than the most outlandish psychic phenomena. Scientists have attempted for generations to ignore that fact in the faith that someday everything in our mental and physical behavior will be explained through our knowledge of cranial neurocircuitry and the DNA. It is time to recognize the need for a different metaphor.

William James urges that scientists adopt a criterion of "radical empiricism," by which he meant that we should refuse to exclude from our scientific picture of reality any elements that are regularly directly experienced. Any class of inner experiences that have been reported, or of phenomena that have been observed, down through the ages and across cultures, apparently in some sense exist and have a *face validity* that cannot be denied. Such is the case with the kind of "stories" found in this book. It doesn't mean, of course, that one must believe any particular report; only that the entire class of reports cannot be denied simply on the basis that they don't seem to fit comfortably into the scientific worldview.

What I am arguing is that admitting the consciousness metaphor allows us to return to ourselves *the authority to interpret our own experience.* Although the present reductionistic science, based largely on a particle-interaction metaphor, continues to be useful for many purposes, it no longer need have the authority in our lives to imperiously insist that we humans are here solely through random causes, in a meaningless universe. We are free to explore the possibility that the highest human ideals *are* more than the capricious choice of a fortuitous product of physical evolution; that our consciousness and all of its products *are* more than the chemical and physical processes of the brain; and that the "stories" such as Louise Hauck relates here *can* be used to inspire and enrich our lives.

Willis W. Harman
Institute of Noetic Sciences
Sausalito, California
October 1992

Preface

I recently had the thought to create a new edition of *Beyond Boundaries*. Authors usually revise published works when subsequent research or pertinent events will update or enhance the content.

That idea carried me back in time—it comes with the territory in my work, the way I go forward and backward through time when I 'merge' with the timeless consciousness of my clients. I found my younger self seated at her Mac Plus computer in the converted Murphy bed closet office in her small apartment located on Lake Merritt in Oakland, California. Louise in the early 90s didn't know where the book would lead her, but she felt driven to document her tales.

As I merged further with my past self, those moments began to expand. Her children had left the nest sooner than anticipated, and her financial situation changed overnight. She was forced to downsize and relocate immediately. She didn't know how she was going to stay afloat.

I felt her fear; I could tell that at times she felt alone and adrift at sea. I felt protective of her. I wanted to rush to intervene and show her the life I live today. But I recognized in her the robust and undying faith in God that I have continued to embrace. That faith and trust have served us both well throughout difficult times.

I watched her for longer and observed her tactics for coping with those sudden changes. She'd meditate every morning. She'd take a break from writing and go for a walk around Lake Merritt to clear her head. Now and then, she would treat herself to a matinee at the Grand Lake Theater, located halfway around the Lake—once she permitted herself to catch a movie *on a weekday afternoon*.

When haunting uncertainty crept back in, she would allow in the fear and observe it, feel it, and then resist the urge to run from it. However, sometimes, fear caught her off guard, she'd seriously consider 'logical' (versus *intuitive*) solutions, such as seeking employment at the US Post Office or Nordstrom. There she might earn a predictable income, hopefully with benefits.

And then I saw how that Louise would turn toward gratitude and pull herself out of fear. One thing she was the most grateful for was her work. And the stories of her clients' awakening. And evidence of wonderful synchronicities showing up in their lives.

My past self didn't feel regret. Her choices were her own. he felt like she was moving forward. The serendipity of finding the apartment, driving by on Lakeshore Drive, looking up, seeing the number to call posted in a window. She called. They answered right away.

She'd also had a series of auspicious and affirming meetings with visionaries, such as Willis Harmon and Peter Russell in the Bay Area, and Gary Zukav in Mt. Shasta. All road signs signaled it was right to pursue her life's work.

Merged with my past self, I could tell that Louise was doing her best to maneuver through unexpected circumstances. In those scary, fearful moments of the unknown, I knew she was running on pure faith that things would work out.

However, I did have a gift for her. In the way that I reposition and empower clients in their past, once merged, I did this with my own past self there in her closet office. I transmitted to her a very different view of the future that she could embrace in moments of doubt, a future filled with wonderful, unexpected adventures with plenty of serendipitous synchronicities ahead.

I sent her the message that she need not slide into 'survival mode' that would prompt her to make more non-intuitive, impulsive choices motivated by fear. Nor did she need to embrace the perception of a future that might, by default, prompt her to look for a ho-hum job for some degree of security.

I passed on an additional tool to my past self, one I've practiced since the 90s and still offer to my clients to help them through their challenging times. It's a life-shifting technique that encourages them to 'zoom out' for a view of the much larger landscape of their lives. It served as a reminder to my past self that this whole lifetime *is just one big adventure.*

These days, from that larger 'zoomed out' view, I'm usually able to chuckle at the ironies, give thanks for the synchronicities, and appreciate the learning I signed up for in this lifetime.

Still merged with my past self, I felt her compelling need to document the collection of stories gathered from her work with clients over the years. Those accounts were no longer simmering on the back burner but felt ever-present in her heart and mind with an urgency to be shared.

The metaphysical truths and principles shared in *Beyond Boundaries* continue to serve me. Likewise, clients report that they've assisted them as well.

We all love stories, and the value and variety of metaphysical truths told in *Beyond Boundaries* haven't changed. To honor my past self and her determination to move forward during unforeseen changes, I decided to keep her efforts alive. They remain just as she wrote them in her present time, nearly thirty years ago, along with her hope that they might assist others on their journey through unpredictable challenges, and perhaps illuminate their paths along the way.

Much love,
Louise Piatt Hauck
March 2020

Acknowledgments

It takes a lot of courage to trust and support a friend/ counselor/mother/sister/spouse, whose work and continual reference point in life involves the unseen and the unproven. I am blessed to be loved and embraced by many such courageous souls. Their faith in me and my explorations has been a cornerstone in the foundation that supports this book.

Throughout and before the book's conception, Dylan and Adrianne Ponath never hesitated to extend their sustaining unconditional love and belief in their mother's unconventional adventures, and Adrianne later added her precocious critiquing to the project.

And, my thanks to clients and friends who made themselves available—both in physical and non-physical form—contributing and allowing me to recount their stories. Some will recognize themselves, though their names were changed to respect their personal paths. It is through their contributions that I'm sincerely grateful and confident that growth and insights in some measure will be gained by the reader.

If I Had a Dime

"When did you first learn that you had these gifts?"

I've been asked this question hundreds of times. I can feel it coming when I meet someone and they ask what I do. I try to respond with different answers, to sound more interesting to myself, but it still comes around to pretty much the same answer. Since so many people ask me the question and are curious about the same thing, it must be important to answer. So here is my response to that most-often-asked question.

At first, I thought everyone had the same gifts, so I didn't identify my gifts as unusual until they started getting in my way. I grew up with stories from my father about his grandmother, "Mamo," who would awaken in the night and command her husband to hitch up the buggy, because so-and-so was ill and needed help. He never questioned her, he always complied, and her precognitive "knowings" were usually accurate. She would also announce when it was time to go into town to rescue another young woman who had been tempted towards employment at the town brothel.

My mother was a very radiant soul, a concert pianist who for several years earned extra money playing the organ at church. People used to say that angels sang when she played. She and I had a very loving, spiritual bond. We often discussed life with an emphasis that I can now define as spiritual (not religious) depth. I saw a few visions as a child and even called to her to come share one with me once, but when she ran to me, it was gone. She said, "It must have been just for you."

So I was blessed with a mother who reflected back to me my own spiritual awareness and priorities, rather than one who might have made me feel strange or wrong in all that I was learning to trust about life. She once felt that she had written a whole symphony in her sleep, and often woke up with a precognitive awareness about one of my three brothers or me, but we never discussed things in terms of "psychic."

I remember when I was very little telling her that when she "went to heaven we would write letters." I think that I "knew" that she would pass on relatively early and that I would be able to communicate with disincarnated souls who were "on the other side." (Both my parents passed over at age fifty-one, within four years of each other.)

My daughter Adrianne, also very intuitive, came down the stairs one day when she was four years old and announced, "Your mom talked to me today!" I had found that metaphysical principles gave me a sound and consistent moral framework within which to raise my two children, but I was always vigilant to keep physical and non-physical awareness in balance, and not "get weird" about it.

"Oh?" I responded, somewhat cautiously, "and where did she talk to you?"

"I was playing in my closet and she told me about you scratching in the bushes!"

No one knew that when Mother and I used to go for brisk walks, circulation increasing in the legs, we would jump into bushes to scratch all over, laughing ourselves silly.

Both my son and daughter were born after my parents passed over. Their lives didn't intersect with each other in the physical, at least not this time. I knew that Adrianne was very intuitive. In addition to the normal childhood friends ("Don't shut the door on Jennifer!"), she spent time communicating with lost souls of little children who had died but were still "stuck" on this plane and hadn't made it to the light. She played "school" with them, setting up all her dolls around the room, as if talking to them. At times, I could see them as well.

One day I picked up Adrianne at her friend's house and the housekeeper came to the door looking wide-eyed and flabbergasted. I found that Adrianne had "read her palm," telling her about her boyfriend and other details about her life. On the way home I asked Adrianne how she had done that, and she replied she just knew things and thought she ought to tell the lady. She didn't know a whole lot about my work, but what she did know was never learned in the context of fortune telling. She received a gentle but firm lecture that evening about invading others' lives by telling them what she "knew."

So it seems that there is an element of inherited abilities present in my case; but I believe that we all have the potential, that such gifts are part of our true, whole selves, and that they were once quite natural to us all before we got so stuck in this physical dream or illusion. Our attachment to this illusion separates us from our true identity, our natural gifts, and from Home.

I never teach classes in "How to Get Psychic." I believe psychic abilities are awakened as the soul urges the persona to become alert and attentive to all the experiences and teachings that are presented in life.

With the awakening comes certain gifts, such as the ability to trust that which is perceived from beyond the five senses, to know much that circumvents intellectual reasoning, and to remember more and more of all that the soul carries, which is never forgotten. Some seem to come into this dimension able to remember what others are better at forgetting.

There came a point in my early adult life when I would sit on a bus, look at those around me, and unknowingly slip into their consciousnesses. I'd know that she plays tennis, he's having a hard time with his marriage, and that business man over there is very discouraged about his job. Then I would get off the bus with their emotions: "What's the use!" I'd feel so negative walking from the bus stop, after having started out with very optimistic feelings.

Or, when in a restaurant, I would know that the waitress taking my order was having a hard time with her teenage son. I knew I just couldn't keep going around being such a ready receiver to everyone's "stuff."

About that time, my mother-in-law was coming for a visit and I was in a quandary as to how to entertain her. Knowing she was interested in psychic explorations and such, I found a metaphysical church in the yellow pages and arranged to take her for a "reading." She emerged from her reading with a smile, announcing that she had paid for me to have one also. I hesitated, but my curiosity and certain other strong influences, I know now, led me to accept.

My mother came through in the reading, from the Other Side, confirming that we were indeed in communication, saying that she loved and was aware of her precious grandchildren. She said that she had caught my thoughts weeks before when I had longed for her presence while rocking my son to sleep. Finally, she laughed at Adrianne's awareness of her while playing in her closet.

The woman who gave the reading that day turned out to be a very helpful teacher to me. From then on, my mother-in-law seemed to be serving a definite purpose, sending me the right book or source at just the right times.

I took meditation classes to help me awaken to deeper levels of awareness, to become acquainted with a very quiet place within myself, and to learn to hook up with higher consciousness. I also learned to be a receiver for only positive or preventative information, learned how to refine as well as turn off the gifts, and have now conditioned myself to "tune in" only when I am in the setting of doing a reading—much to the chagrin of friends and the relief of new or casual acquaintances.

I suppose that if I had a dime for every time I've been asked that question, I could feed the homeless. But again, I guess it wouldn't be asked so frequently if people didn't wonder a great deal about their own abilities and experiences, or about their own potential to receive the gifts. It must be a question worth answering.

PART ONE

How It Appears

Chapter One

Beyond the Present

Proof

Early in my work as a psychic, I tried to investigate how
it is that I am able to do what I do in readings. I searched
for explanations in science and new physics, having the
need to validate my work with some sort of concrete
evidence.

While preparing this book, I received a letter from
Dr. Willis Harman, president of the Institute of Noetic
Sciences, who mirrors the conclusions I reached from my
search through traditional science and physics:

> I am wary of trying to make too much out of the
> new physics; I fear that quantum physics jargon

is often used in an attempt to legitimize knowledge to which it is, in fact, quite irrelevant.

What the new physics does do is demonstrate the contradiction between a science fundamentally based on principles of separateness, and the ultimate demonstration in the new physics of connectedness. That is valuable, but it is a delusion to think that laboratory physics is going to lead us to an understanding of our own inner experience.

What we must do, and what the new physics will not help us with, is confront the need to extend science to include our subjective experience as valid data, and contemplatives and other trained "inner explorers" as scientists in their own right.

I have recently become comfortable accepting the use of my gifts as a valuable experience that needs no proof; it simply must be trusted. Gary Zukav writes clearly in his book, *The Seat of the Soul*, about the necessary shifts occurring with our species as we evolve from five-sensory beings to multisensory beings. He makes this distinction:

The five-sensory personality accepts every impulse and insight as his or her own, as originating within his or her psyche. The multisensory personality knows that this is not always the case. Impulses, hunches, sudden insights and

subtle insights have assisted us on our evolutionary path since the origin of our species. . . . The
multisensory personality . . . honors intuition in
a way that the five-sensory personality does not.
To the five-sensory personality, intuitions are
curiosities. To the multisensory personality, they
are promptings from, and links to, a perspective
of greater comprehension and compassion than
its own. The multisensory personality strives to
increase its awareness of this guidance.

It is crucial for our survival that we become multisensory, that we begin to trust our internal, intuitive
understanding of all that goes beyond concrete, scientific, or intellectual reasoning, and to use the resulting
abilities.

I have come upon a few ideas that help clients understand and feel more comfortable with the information
and scenes that I view clairvoyantly and which exist outside of this three-dimensional reality where time and
space are nonexistent.

The Filmstrip and the Projector

The first idea is a helpful analogy to understand that the
past, present, and probable future all exist simultaneously
rather than in linear and sequential order. Picture yourself holding the filmstrip of a movie you're about to put
through a projector. As you hold the filmstrip in both

hands, you can see that there is a beginning to it—close to where your right hand is holding it—which represents the past. Directly in front of you appear all the frames of the movie that represent the present; at the end of the strip—in your left hand—appear the frames that show the future.

If one frozen moment in time is observed, there seems to be no action, just as in viewing one frame of a filmstrip. But when you put a series of consecutive frames together, then you can see the frozen moments as if they are animated, and they create the movie. Einstein referred to this as a time-continuum.

Past-present-future all exist at one time, on that single strip of film. But, simply looking at that long strip of celluloid, there's not much to see. So you thread it into the projector and turn it on. The projector shines a light through each frame of the filmstrip and projects an image onto the screen that you can see, clear and enlarged.

As the frames on the screen appear, what you experience and view is your present life. The before and after portions of the filmstrip still exist, but you only focus on the frames being illuminated. Those few frames constitute the space in which you live out your present-moment life experience. But your perceiving and experiencing only that one space doesn't mean that the other life-spaces don't exist.

In fact, if you walk behind the projector to the white light in back of it, you can look at the entire film at once. This is what we do when we pass over and leave our physical bodies to go to the light: we look back and reflect on our whole life.

Just as all frames of the movie exist simultaneously, so do all moments in time. This "continuum of time" is an illusion. Time itself is an illusion.

So, when I "read" people, I view and "freeze-frame" a segment of the filmstrip, perhaps a portion that hasn't yet run through the projector, one which they would perceive' as "future," because they haven't yet focused on it. And I might be equally able to see a particular frame that has already run through it—a scene perceived by a client as being from the past. I go to a frequency in myself that allows me to view other frames of people's filmstrips.

Why are most people only capable of viewing and trusting that one, present frame? I like to quote John Boslough, from his article in the March 1990 *National Geographic,* "The Enigma of Time." He had seen graffiti on a cafe wall in Texas that attempted an answer: "Time is nature's way of keeping everything from happening all at once."

Boslough went on to remind us that children before the age of two have little sense of the passage of time and that it may have been the same for our early ancestors. Some scholars believe that people once lived in a state of "timeless present" with little or no sense of past or future.

Boslough also mentions an old Hopi Indian woman in northern Arizona who talks of a close friend, dead for several years, as if he just stepped out the door. Hopi verbs make no distinction between past and present. All time runs together into an ever continuing present.

Synchronicity

The second application that helps clients understand what I see is by understanding synchronicity. It is "the seemingly psychic timing of events," a term coined by Carl Jung, the famous Swiss psychiatrist who founded analytical psychology. There's the story about Jung's listening to a patient relate a dream about a scarab beetle. In the area where this was taking place there were no scarab beetles, but something very similar to one landed on Jung's office window sill at that very moment. That's when he came up with the term "synchronicity."

Synchronicity, the meaningful order of "coincidences" in our lives, is one way that we can know that we will always be where we're supposed to be. Your Higher Self—your connection to the God-force—guides you there and influences the choices you make that help you follow your path. You can be led by that guidance and perceive how things come about as mystical or coincidental, or you can start to recognize the sensations of the Higher Self guiding you and moving through you. When you re-orient to being led in this way, life becomes a whole new kind of adventure; every experience takes on a new flavor.

For one thing, you become much more conscious of synchronicity. All "future" frames of the filmstrip already exist. As you start to develop an awareness of what you are creating in your future, you will also gain an awareness of simultaneous time by being totally awake in your present. You will strongly sense what connects you to and manifests in your future, so that you won't fear being in the "wrong" place at the "wrong" time. If you have sensed yourself in a future moment, while still here in the physical plane, all moments that appear to come between the present and that future moment will have to synchronize.

Strong Future Events

Another helpful interpretation of synchronicity was given to me by a physical chemist who developed the concept of Strong Future Events (he refers to them as "SFEs"). He agreed that crucial future experiences already exist, and added that these events create pathways from them to us, to where we find ourselves in our present. As we clear up and heal current issues and challenges in our lives, we become more strongly "pulled around the bend," so to speak, by these SFEs. Thus, this interpretation of synchronicity has been very helpful to me and to my clients: when we start to get pulled by the almost magnetic attraction from SFEs, "situations" (which some might view as "coincidences") start to tumble into place.

I visualize this process as if I'm holding a magnet under a table, which I use to pull along particles that are scattered on the table's surface. As I pull the magnet faster, the particles start to form a line, and all of them move forward with the pull. The magnetic pull is the Strong Future Event; the particles are the events or moments between the present and the SFE. We've all heard stories like this: "And there I was, sitting on the bus, when the man sitting next to me mentioned such and such a person, who was leasing this place that turned out to be my next apartment, and next door happened to be the person who turned out to be my connection to. . . ." These are the kinds of stories we love to tell, when new events seem to speed up and magically fall into place.

Chapter Two

Viewing Timeless Spaces

Background

One particular client's reading stands out as an example of experiencing different concurrent time spaces. I had flown down from northern to southern California to begin a monthly series of classes and also to meet with old clients whom I'd known for over ten of the seventeen years that my ex-husband and I had lived in Newport Beach.

For a short time when I began exploring the use of my gifts, I worked at a magic club in Newport where my husband had bought us a membership. I had decided to experiment with the use of my psychic gifts, thinking that working there would help me sharpen and refine my skills and help me decide how best to use them. It was one of those experiences that let me know how I felt about it, clearly thrusting me in an opposite, new direction.

I worked at the club a few evenings a week, tucked in an armchair, way back in the corner of the central lounge. People convened there to meet and socialize before and after dinner and magic shows. I was Louise the Clairvoyant. Across the room from me was Jim the Astrologer and, in the other corner, Retha the Tarot Reader. Each of us tried in our own way to project the dedication and integrity that we gave our work.

Our talents went well beyond parlor entertainment or New Age mystification. We did attract a certain element who were able to appreciate that and sought what more we had to give, while others most definitely made my resolve stronger with regards to how I would and would not use my gifts!

It eventually became too compromising for me—entrepreneurs asking me for personal information about their mistresses (sometimes in front of their wives), sports heroes wanting me to guess their identity, women asking if I saw them meeting someone rich and famous.

Several too many of these undignified encounters pulled me back toward influences from my background in psychology, music therapy, working in the mental health profession, and from having lived with my husband, a psychiatrist, for so many years. My commitment was deepened to use my gifts in ways that would counsel and empower others rather than to entertain or disempower them by telling their fortunes.

I was, however, intrigued by some of the readings with people who were very successful in the business world and had obtained a great degree of material success that left them with a distinct lack of spiritual depth. That isn't to say that it isn't possible to have both, if that's in line with what a soul is seeking on its path. But this particular region of California seemed to attract souls who had many lessons in the areas of material and spiritual balance.

Some of the more rewarding readings enlightened a customer, sometimes grabbing his attention and turning him around to some realization. He might suddenly see that there is more than meets the eye—much more—to life. I remember the real estate mogul who dropped by my "station" on the way to his limousine idling in front of the club. He wanted "a quickie." As I tuned in, I first saw piles of a white, chalky substance. These had appeared before in readings, and a few brave clients had eventually identified them to me as cocaine.

Next, I viewed the man's grandfather, who suddenly showed up beside him, projecting himself literally "flicking his Bic," trying to ignite a flint lighter. The grandfather had passed over several years before and was projecting a memory to which his grandson could relate.

Sure enough, that was one of the fondest memories the man had of his grandfather, smelling the lighter fluid in his lighter when his grandfather would light up his cigar. He looked at me, shocked. "You mean we *don't die??*" he shrieked. He continued on briskly out to his car, looking a bit glazed. The manager of the club, who had been leaning on a pillar, surveying the lounge, eyed me cautiously, probably concerned that I might not be pleasing the customers by telling them other than what they wanted to hear.

About the Readings

As my dedication to giving readings increased over the years, so did my intention and desire that they be done responsibly and with integrity. I am continually monitoring what and how information is presented. I've therefore asked certain questions—and have received answers—that help me resolve important issues about my work and assist me in guiding my clients.

I never receive ominous or foreboding information, because I believe that the information "comes in" neutrally; it's the interpretation of the scenes that gives them positive or negative qualities. There are those who will interpret intuited information negatively. People who are very involved in their own sense of drama will be drawn to readers who deliver information with a dramatic flair.

I always seek to attract clients who have taken, or are ready to take, responsibility for their lives, who choose to see their challenges as opportunities for positive and necessary growth and expansion.

Qualifying the Presentation of Future Information

I have become careful and judicious about present-ing future information, mainly because anticipation of the future *does* take a person out of the present and, I believe, can slow down one's personal evolution. If a person continually leans out of her present, anticipat-ing her future, she's not fully present. If she's not living in her present, she won't attend to and expand from all of the current experiences in her life. Moving through the challenges that she finds before her in her present will cause her to access new aspects in herself, which will then enable her to grow and shift about in new and different ways.

The result of all this shifting will naturally allow her to present a new "collage" of self into her external world. She then starts to attract new situations and people who will represent reflections of these inner shifts, those who will respond to this new combination of herself as if she's always been this way.

I caution clients at this point that they might feel a little like a fraud, wanting to say to new relationships, "Wait a sec, I just became this!"—often more trusting, more intimate, more definitive, or more focused. They start to trust new aspects of themselves; the new reflec-tions help strengthen them. In this way, a person who obsesses about her future actually pushes away change and new situations.

I used to have an immediate, almost reflexive reaction to a particular (fortunately rare) type of client who would sit on my couch asking, "So do you think this means that I should get a job?"

"Do you *want* a job!" I would quickly reply, whenever I'd sense that the client was rendering himself a powerless vacuum in wanting to know his future, as if he had very little to do with it.

I was wary of the tendency for people to manipulate their present lives to fit future scenes. For example, a woman feeling powerless in an unhappy marriage, given a future scene of herself packing linens from a closet into boxes indicating a move, might try to make spring cleaning "a sign" that she's about to be magically extricated from her marriage.

Eventually, I resolved my hesitation about presenting future information in a couple of ways. The first was to acknowledge that relating future scenes can give people hope. I remember describing a scene to a recently divorced woman in her early 50s, with children raised, who was fearful and anxious about having to seek employment with no formal training.

I connected with a future moment one particular day, watching her sitting in her light blue bathrobe, at the table by the phone in her yellow-flowered kitchen, trying to decide between three jobs! Clients such as this woman can take heart that their lives are unfolding in new unseen ways, no matter how stuck they're feeling in their present.

The more outrageous a future scene seems to the client at the time, the more it pleases me, which brings me to the second reason I allow myself to present future information. The perspective we hold of ourselves in our reality is extremely limited and limiting. We evaluate and judge ourselves in our present by our past teachings, experiences, and the influences of social consciousness.

The latter is what I refer to as what we see "up on the big screen"—how people should be acting, looking, being in a relationship, and what we should expect from those relationships, what we should strive for and attain in our lives, what gets rewarded and applauded, what gets the world's attention, and what gets ourselves validated.

We are also programmed with an almost obsessive attachment to outcomes, to have a good story to tell. "SO. Are you still going together?" "SO. Are you not speaking to each other anymore?" "SO. Did you tell him off?" "SO. Did you quit your job?" "SO. What's the deal?" "SO. What is it?" This programming actually influences how we see ourselves in our lives, how we manipulate situations to achieve the desirable outcomes to have a good story to tell. Then we can see ourselves up on the big screen.

When we're so affixed to outcomes, we lose patience with our own gradual, extremely important process. We lose patience with the slow interweaving of plots in books and movies. We're motivated only to see the blockbusters, the instant winners. We lose the seasoning, the texture and depth from all that our experiences can hold for us.

We also develop a very rigid fix on the outcomes that we anticipate in our futures. We hold very definite ideas about how we expect future events to come about, exactly what and who they must contain, and how it all should look. Again, these future anticipations are only projections from our limited perception of past experiences and learning—what we've been taught to expect—and from the influences of social consciousness.

Fixed expectations don't keep us receptive to the unlimited and remarkable ways in which future events and opportunities can transpire in our lives. Our resistance to trusting that things will work out, even though out of our range of perception, is what causes so much frustration and pain.

So when a client is unable to calculate any visible bridges from where he finds himself in his present to the future scene, it forces him to loosen his grasp on his present reality, as well as his rigid expectations of his future. Since he can't even come close to sizing up what's available on down the road, why worry about it? That's when he becomes a more receptive "receptor" to probable future events.

That often brings the client to deduce for himself that he'll experience those new adventures sooner by being fully in his present. By living in this fully present fashion, his life will become richer, and he'll depend less on his future. Such was the case with the woman who was skeptical of the future scene of herself pondering three job offers.

Meeting Ben

I met Ben at the magic club. He stood out the first time he sat before me as a guest. I'd seen him there often, entertaining pretty ladies, but as he waited with anticipation for me to "tune in," I was reminded that I could not generalize about people. Similar exterior trappings did not mean the same lessons or degree of character development. He joked with me a bit nervously, but I had the (by now) very familiar feeling that I was reuniting with an "old friend."

He was going through a challenging divorce settlement, trying to do the right thing with his daughter, a young adult and only child, and find his way through relationships with young, beautiful women. At that time, the attention from these girls was flattering to him.

Ben eventually hosted the first of my metaphysical classes at his lovely home near Newport Beach. We met weekly at his place for a few years, whether he was there or on one of his exotic trips with an attractive companion. The class members progressed rapidly in becoming conscious and aware of new ways to view and live their lives, to take responsibility for them, and to change them in positive ways.

He seemed to be searching for an explanation to the game of life, which he'd played quite successfully, but was perhaps also apprehensive that it might not contain the substance to carry him around the bend. When the class moved on to new locations, Ben branched off into other pursuits, though he usually called for a reading once or twice a year.

Ben's Reading

This time it had been about a year since I had seen Ben. I had no reason to anticipate that his reading would be any different from the others, although each one usually brought something new and interesting to me, as well as to the client.

He arrived at my hotel suite with the warm greeting that always acknowledged a very dear connection between us. I began, as usual, with my invocation, then started to view the scenes as they were presented to me. My continual challenge in viewing these non-linear vignettes is to bring them down into this physical dimension and present them in a linear, sequential framework that the client can comprehend. The scenes are all there, with no space, almost as if condensed into a dot—yet expansive—with very clear themes, symbols, texture, nuances, and messages.

What I view is not limited by time, whether they are significant scenes in the client's past, glimpses of relevant past lives, or a moment in the client's future consciousness which he or she is already acting out. I would love to be able to directly transmit these scenes without words.

So much is lost in relating and perceiving in the ways by which we are so limited in this space, necessitated by the need to focus and communicate in the time period we seem to be experiencing.

Each time that I read Ben, it was as if the camera pulled farther back to reveal more pieces of the puzzle. In this respect, I can trust that a person is always given, just as I always ask in my invocation, "that which is for his highest good to receive, and for my highest good to give." The depth and scope of the scenes in the readings seem to parallel the growth or evolution of the client.

Since I often hold the scenes I view for long periods of time, I'm able to thoroughly explore them. This can be quite instructive to the client as well as to myself. However, I transcend to such a deep level (or to a much higher place in my consciousness) that after the reading I can usually remember only flashes of scenes. But the details of the scenario that I locked into, a moment in Ben's future consciousness, remain quite vivid.

The multi-dimensional scene appeared to me as a moving picture. At first I could only focus on one little piece of the picture at a time; however, the more I let myself be in the scene, the more I could comprehend and retain it.

First, I recognized a familiar piece of the picture that I'd presented to Ben before in several readings, involving Ben and an unknown woman cooking dinner together, but now in greater depth. His daughter Lisa and her (future) husband had just come to the door with their eighteen-month-old baby, Ben's future grandson. In Ben's present, Lisa was recently divorced and not dating anyone.

He was sautéing mushrooms in a copper pan, standing beside the lovely woman in a well-lit kitchen. Ben has yet to meet the woman who appears in that recurring future scene, but that kitchen in the "house by the water that he'd get through a fallen escrow," once viewed as a future moment, was now in his present.

Next, I became aware of Ben's father, who had passed over at least seven years before. He often made an appearance in his son's readings, having "gone to the light," and came simply to lend another perspective. He had been a hard-working man with old country values who, with his wife, had raised Ben in New York.

It seemed as if the father was standing on the other side of this scene (or hologram), watching it with me. He and I started to telepathically comment on what we viewed. I had to remember to pause to give Ben a play-by-play account of our conversation.

Lisa and her husband were dropping the baby off for the weekend before going on to the desert. I studied and commented on all the nuances of Lisa's relationship with Ben's wife/lover—whatever she had become—who reached out to hold the baby.

It was evident that Lisa and the lady had a past-life connection, and that the woman lovingly met some needs in Lisa's life that had not been met by her own mother. I could have gone on about that for at least an hour, but I made the effort to go to other parts of the picture.

Ben's dad's thoughts came in strongly again, so I went to them. He gave me a detailed account about why it had already been decided that *he* would be back as *that* grandson. *He* was going to reincarnate as Ben's daughter's son! *He* was watching himself in this "future" moment, as the eighteen-month-old grandson, now placed on a blanket in Ben's living room, looking up at his grandparents.

He indicated, as he watched himself watching them interact—they were talking about preparing lunch—that he looked forward to learning new ways of relating to women "next" time around. He was intrigued with the independent, warm, and loving nature of the woman standing beside Ben. He commented that *he'd* been waiting for Ben to find the right woman, now that he'd moved on from some of "those bimbos—like the redhead at the drug store!"

Ben responded that he was referring to a redheaded girl they had both known years ago who worked at the perfume counter at the neighborhood drug store where Ben grew up. (Souls who communicate from the Other Side are obviously not limited by time; memories are perceived as if they are still occurring.)

Finally, Ben's dad went into detail about some of the pulls that he knew would exist in this upcoming incarnation: to complete higher education at some academy, to gain special training relevant to a strong curiosity that had gone with him when he passed over. He looked forward to the growth and insights he would gain, this time as Ben's grandson.

At this point, with many more details to explore, I moved on to help Ben reframe some current challenges in his life. He chuckles at these ever enlarging future glimpses. Each time we meet, I caution him not to take the audio tape of the reading home to play for any present love-interest or to try to make her fit into this future reality.

Ben seems to be able to handle the specific information that I give him. I ordinarily wouldn't take the time to go into such detail about future information, but then again, I don't usually receive future scenes with so much depth. I also trust the information I receive in the readings, always invoking,

"That I be given that which is for the client's highest good to receive, and for my highest good to give...."

Chapter Three

Changing the Past, Influencing the Present and Future

We still exist in "our past in two ways. The first is an existence outside of this three-dimensional reality, outside of time and space. As I have explained, we are alive and well, *still* in our pasts, and are already experiencing probable futures. When I view a significant scene from someone's past, a hologram of that past self moves forward to communicate with me about what the self was/is feeling. For example, if the scene was/is from childhood, then the events served to awaken the memory of misbeliefs carried into this current space. Present life scenarios only exaggerate those perceptions that hold a person back, forcing him to choose new ways to react to experiences this time around.

I find that most childhoods are a re-creation of old themes which we come back to resolve. Parents serve as either a reflection of our own past selves or as catalysts—in positive or negative ways—to force us to make the choices that will release us from old themes.

Second, we are still in our past insofar as it exists in our perceptions of it. Our perceptions of our experiences create our realities (past, present, or future). Furthermore, our realities exist *only* through those perceptions. If we change our perceptions of the past, we change our past, and that will shift our present and future. It is crucial to work with your past to view it from new angles, to free yourself from playing the victim; carrying a victim-belief will create victimizing situations in the present and future. One of the most important aspects of my work lies in helping clients to change their pasts. A client will remember and continue to experience his past in whatever way he perceives it to have been. If he sees himself as the victim, his past will continue to feel painful. If he is able to piece together the possible reasons he might have chosen the challenges he came to, thereby changing his perceptions and shifting his emotions, then the past won't hurt anymore.

In the Judge's Chambers

I was approaching the end of a reading, about to summarize all that we had covered after looking at the past, present, and probable future of the woman who sat on my couch. Mary looked at me through sad eyes, cleared her throat and asked, tentatively, "So you think that I'm worth having a few adventures?"

The reading had begun with her present situation. From what I viewed, I could see that she was coming out of a divorce and was trying to take better care of herself by making more conscious choices in her life, particularly where men were concerned. Since Mary didn't feel that she could trust herself, this proved to be quite difficult for her.

It's meaningless to encourage someone to trust her feelings when she has disconnected from them to the extent that she doesn't even *know* what she feels.

Playing the part of pathfinder, I pointed out some significant steps that I could see she had taken; she had accepted a new job, where she happened to attract some very old friends from other (past) life spaces. They had appeared as if ready to acknowledge and respond to the new, trustworthy aspects in her, just as she herself was awakening to them.

Since her divorce, my client had also extricated herself from the beginnings of an abusive relationship. I went on to present future evidence; the path she was consciously choosing would lead her through many more positive adventures. But I felt there was still something holding her back, something in her consciousness that contradicted her best intentions to move forward.

It was the past scenes that played such an important part in this woman's reading. All through the reading, it seemed I was addressing two parts of the whole of Mary: when I related to her true essence and reflected back that light in her soul, she lifted her head and straightened her back and shoulders, a posture that displayed her body as if it were providing a frame for carrying and housing something cherished.

Then, when I related the scenes that I viewed from the past in which she had played the part of an unworthy victim whose life was an obstacle course of continuous hurdles, she slumped over, looking helpless, insecure, and sadly resolved to grab any leftovers that life might serve her. She was still so very present in her past, even with her intentions and attempts to move forward.

When Mary asked the question about being deserving of adventures in life, I turned to my left, where I view the past, and saw a very clear, revealing scene from her childhood. I watched Mary at three years old, wearing a little yellow dress with a lace collar and black Mary Jane shoes. She was seated between both her parents in a paneled room.

As I described the scene, my client sat bolt upright and exclaimed, "That was in the judge's chambers, when my parents were divorcing! I was asked to choose which parent I wanted to live with. To this day I have felt that I made the wrong decision and feel very guilty about it."

Since that day, Mary felt that she couldn't trust herself. I encouraged her to go back, visualize, and feel herself as that little three-year-old, and then to change the scene.

I suggested that Mary, as the three-year-old, stand up and face both of her parents, stating that she has something very important to say to them. I asked her to tell them, loudly and clearly, that she wants to remind them that she is only three years old and that they have many grown-up matters they need to resolve. I also suggested that she ask *them* to come to some understanding about the best place for her to live, so that she will have a strong sense of security in them, and to inform them she will wait outside, playing in the sandbox, while they decide. While on her way out, I added that she *might* inform the judge that he has no right to burden a three-year-old with such a decision.

In these cases, I give sample scripts as to how a client might change the past. Many times as I relate such an example re-orchestration of their perceptions, they're instantly "there," feeling themselves back in that past scene, ready and receptive to re-experience it with me.

I looked over at Mary, after relating the sample reconstruction of her past scene. Tears had reached her broad, beautiful smile. She looked radiant, as if the past had shifted and immediately hooked up with the more whole, emerging Mary who was making inroads into a new present and future. The Mary I now watched had no doubts about all the good things she deserved, and she was beginning to know where she could go inside herself to find the feelings that she could trust.

As Mary left, I encouraged her to ask her Higher Self to show her more of those past scenes, such as demeaning abusive relationships, and to continue to empower herself by changing those scenes. I asked her to then follow along or imagine the new outcome, and to visualize where that might bring her in the present. Meditating regularly on the outcomes that result from changed past scenarios *will* create a new alternate reality, which will start to influence the present one. This is a rather simple technique to produce such profound results.

Alone in Her Room

Clients often feel so alone, trying to find their way through the dark shadows cast from their pasts. I'm grateful for the occasional scenes that reveal locked-away vignettes of humiliation, shame and loneliness, representative of all that these clients have carried into adulthood. Such childhood scenes are usually reflections of beliefs they've lugged along for lifetimes.

When the clients are receptive to my relating such scenes, and are able to remember particular "past" situations and place themselves there, then I go further. I give examples of how they might change these scenes, replacing words, actions, or characters that will heal and illuminate their pasts. This in turn will empower them in their present as they flow into new self-perceptions.

The most common of the past scenes that I view involve alcoholic parents who are out of control. I view them raging at my clients in their childhoods, attacking them physically, berating them, pulling their hair, screaming words of humiliation, mocking them, locking them outside the house or in their rooms, and giving, then removing, very conditional gestures of love and affection.

These clients have inevitably grown up believing there is something very wrong, unlovable, and undeserving about themselves. They accept all the abuse that they attract into their lives as being exactly what they deserve. Clients often feel strong emotional shifts as together we recreate painful past scenes. This frequently becomes a strong positive influence on what they create in their futures. Nancy's reading demonstrates how an emotional shift in the past can change the future.

The past I viewed was similar to that of too many women for whom I read who continue to attract unhealthy relationships with men. I view a line-up of the men in their pasts, who have all been abusive verbally, emotionally, or physically, or in all three ways. I see these women defining themselves through the perceptions of these men, who actually projected their own self-scorn onto them. They take the abuse to be confirmation of their unworthiness.

Nancy sat slumped on my couch, looking like a sad puppy, her eyes searching mine, hopeful that I'd see any good news about her life. I described a scene that I was viewing of her in her past, when she was about twelve years old. She stood in a cream-colored hallway, facing her father. Red-faced and intoxicated, he was screaming at her. I watched her as she then walked down the hallway to her room, head bowed. She quietly entered her room, shut the door, and went to sit in her safe place at the back of her closet.

Nancy indicated that she was following all that I was describing, remembering many such occasions. I asked her to try to go back into the emotions of that girl. Then I said that it was important for her to change that scene. She needed to see herself walk back out of the closet and down the hallway to stand before her father.

I further encouraged Nancy to feel herself telling her father that *he* is the one with the problem, and that *he* needs to go to *his* room and calm himself until he can pull himself together! I asked her to tell her father some of the dreams that she plans to fulfill, the adventures that *she's* here to experience, and all that *she* is going to discover, learning to trust her *true identity* this lifetime. (I suggested that she remind him that it's *her* turn to talk, should he interrupt.) Then I asked her to see herself walk into their living room and seat herself on the couch there, feeling her dignity and her true self-worth.

I looked up at Nancy, now sitting very erect on my couch, looking proud and relieved, and visibly moved. Something had shifted. Then I went on to uncover some other issues in her present life. Towards the end of her reading, I viewed some new future relationships, personal and professional, that she would attract—a much more accurate reflection of who she is, and of what she deserves.

When Nancy got up to leave, I told her to try not to analyze all that had transpired in her reading, but rather to simply let it shift about in her consciousness. When we are awake, everything that comes into our path pushes us towards our healing, towards the integration of our whole true selves, and towards the light.

Linda was another client who projected a similar demeanor of very low self-esteem. She had come for a reading, seeking encouragement and direction for her life. She had gained several pounds since her divorce and was having difficulty in finding a fulfilling job.

I viewed Linda as a teenager, standing behind the counter in a room that had a damp scent to it. I saw a man come through the door, and as he did so, a bell rang. When I mentioned the sound of the bell on the door, Linda exclaimed, "That's the laundry where I worked one summer for my father! He yelled at me for everything that I did wrong. He said that I couldn't do anything right, and he finally threw me out."

Then I suggested ways that Linda might reconstruct the scene of her working for her father in his laundry plant. She came up with even better ideas and went on to relate other examples of similar types of humiliation that she had experienced with her father and later in her marriage.

It was distressing for Linda to relive the emotions from the past. I assured her, as I do other clients who feel the emotional shifts from changing strategic past scenes, that she wouldn't have to keep going back to them. Creating and sensing a different outcome in the concurrent reality that exists in her past would suffice. The past dissolves at it becomes healed.

When it is difficult for clients to remember a scene of this type, I go ahead and give them examples of how they might recreate the one that I've viewed, but ask them to go home with the information, to go into meditation and ask that they be shown for themselves a scene that will give them what they need to work with to change.

Some clients are unable to identify the past scenes that I present to them. In some cases, they are people who are very much "up in their heads," processing and understanding life through analytical reasoning, relating very little to the nuances of emotions and abstract ideas. Other times, people cannot place past scenes because of the protective mechanism of the psyche, which has blocked out pain from the past.

The feet that clients come for readings in which they are shown these past—often painful—glimpses means that they are ready to (and will) remember and receive on a conscious level all they need in order to heal the memories of inaccurate perceptions by which they've come to define themselves.

Clients report back that, indeed, they do begin to experience evidence of the effects from the inner shifts resulting from the unveiling of those painful vignettes. Once secreted away into dark corners, more of the past receives exposure to the light.

Chapter Four

Overlays of Concurrent Life Spaces

When I read for my clients, I'm seeing past lives and giving necessarily condensed descriptions. I, myself, have experienced past life spaces simultaneously with my present—an awareness which can continue for days. My senses are heightened and I'm very attentive to details because I have experienced them more than once, or because they have held a particular significance in a "past" time.

England

It had been a week and a half since my arrival in England, where I was treating myself to a short post-divorce getaway—after relocating with my two teenagers from southern to northern California, getting them through a couple more years of school, family counseling, and many challenges. I was enjoying my daily train trips into London from Beckenham, Kent, sitting next to silent commuters coming in on the same line each morning.

I stayed with Jane, a friend of my niece, in her little upstairs flat, along with her twenty pet gerbils. She was a gracious, jovial, young girl in her twenties who was happy to let me come and go as long as I kept the heat turned up for the little ones. She was gone much of the time, preparing for a trip to Thailand, a very popular travel spot for the British.

I had always felt a pull to northern Europe and had seen several past-life overlays of life experiences in and around England, so I was thrilled to be finally returning "home" for a visit.

The dominating emotion that I felt as my stay progressed was relief that I'd been able to move on from incarnations in that country. I was often distracted by a very clear awareness of concurrent past-life spaces which appeared like holograms over my adventure; these reminded me how much I had yearned/was yearning for spiritual freedom in other times and places.

My first dramatic recall came when a new friend escorted me to the Tower of London on his way to other business. He guided me through the right underground line and, after climbing up the stairs that led out of Tower Hill Station, I looked directly to the right and gasped at the sight of the looming fortress. He asked if I was feeling all right, commenting that the moment I looked over at the Tower, my face went from blushed and enthused to pale and cautious.

I toured the Tower alone and felt the past-life overlay of male guards walking on either side of me. I could hear the sound of their shoes on gravel but couldn't see their faces. I had a strong present sense of fear and risk involved with telling the truth. I don't know if I was reliving an experience of incarceration at this specific spot, or if I was remembering one from a similar setting. I also knew that there had been a jailer who had been good to me, bringing me food and conversation.

Stonehenge and Woodhenge also triggered distant memories of sacred ceremonies at those locations, or places like them. I felt sad about so much spiritual understanding, lost and suppressed with Roman invasions, but was encouraged when I reminded myself of all that is being remembered in these times. I shivered when the distant Viking burial mounds on the perimeter of these sites were pointed out to me.

I was taken with the verdant countryside and awed by the historical continuum that was so evident everywhere in that country. I visited a Norman church in Avebury where a wooden plaque on the stone wall announced the names of clergy from medieval to present times.

I met Harold, a past husband ("lord and master") of mine, at an after-work gathering to which I'd been invited at the Prince of Prussia Pub. He worked at a large bank and was known for his diligent efforts and perfectionism, and also for taking good care of his employees. I was talking to a bank consultant about his grandmother who had lived nearby in the West End, the neighborhood that had been victimized by Jack the Ripper. He was divulging the details of the murders and the "real" murderer when Harold and his entourage arrived.

We connected immediately, and Harold talked of his cave-spelunking adventures in Wales and of the sight of a 360-degree rainbow (called a brokenspector) in the Lake District. At the end of the evening he invited me for a drive to the country.

Harold picked me up the next morning at Charing Cross Station in his Rover. Dressed in slacks, with a bright green sweater over a pin-striped shirt, he looked as natty in his Saturday clothes as he had in his business attire. A friend had given me the delightful book *84 Charing Cross Road* the night before I left for London. It had become a useful and humorous guidebook, preparing me for just such unexpected adventures.

The author, Helene Hanff, in detailing her own long-awaited trip to London, emphasized that one must definitely wear a skirt on such outings. I had developed a practical and efficient routine of taking my ambitious tourist walks in slacks and high-top Reeboks, with flats and skirt rolled up in my shoulder bag, ever ready for afternoon matinees and tea.

He didn't see me as I exited the station; he was watching the pigeons in his rear-view mirror. As I reached his car, he looked up and smiled, greeting me with a proper, cheery "Hel-low!" Harold felt very familiar, and we talked and traveled in an easy, relaxed style. As we drove, he played a favorite tape on his player, Richard Harris reciting from the book *Jonathan Livingston Seagull*, with soft background music.

Winding up and down and around one-lane roads, I spotted little villages, tucked away and protected by gentle hills. The ones we drove through seemed to present to the outsider first church-with-spire for praying, then pub for congregating, then tidy homes with lace-curtained windows for peering.

The day that followed was idyllic and romantic, only imaginable in fairy tales: lunch at Le Talbooth Inn in Constable country, an elegant, quaint country inn, with a special coffee afterwards, sitting in a window-seat overlooking the surrounding pond, graced with demure white swans. Then a tour of Constable's home, a gallery of his paintings, and a walk through a lush country park at South Weald, a short distance from Harold's home in Essex.

I knew that we had walked together just as were doing then, hand in hand, through meadows and forests; we had walked so many times, every square foot of our own land, in another time. We ended the day with an early evening supper at a cozy pub nearby. As we parted, he invited me to spend the next weekend driving out to Oxford, Marlborough, Avebury, Stonehenge, and Woodhenge. I was thrilled to cancel my reservations for the bus tour that I had arranged, which in turn allowed me to purchase tickets to two more matinees.

I had left my camera in his car and regretted not taking pictures of our unforgettable walk through the park, but a few weeks after I returned home, I received a complete set of pictures from his loving efforts, he having retraced our steps to document the memory of each special spot. He made notes on the back of each picture, such as, "and here I found these lilacs placed on this rock—do you think they were left here, in memory of us?" Oh, sigh.

David, the Light Technician

I'd been waiting outside Buckingham Palace for an hour, and it was starting to drizzle. For nearly half of that hour I was entertained by a delightful elderly man who made it his business to accompany all of us who stood at the authoritative wrought-iron gate awaiting the Changing of the Guard.

The man served as unofficial British spokesperson to tourists, purveyor of royal gossip, historian, and commentator. "An' thaat's wier ther Queen irself oft times peers aut aufta 'ir m'ning tea! See? Raut thea! See?" he pointed upward, instructing with enough enthusiasm for this to have been his first day on the job. But his sing-song routine led one to suspect that this clearly could not be so.

Finally, the procession began, a distant sound of drums, trumpets, and bagpipes, getting louder as the guards approached the front of the palace, marching up from around the back on Buckingham Palace Road. They turned slowly in front of the Queen Victoria Memorial, began a new tune, and proceeded to file in through the front gate.

I wouldn't have thought that it could take over two hours to change guards. I'd grabbed a quick scone for breakfast, not thrilled with the dearth of breakfast eateries in London, even less thrilled each time I was referred to McDonald's, and was missing my customary apple or bran muffin.

I diverted my attention from my growling stomach to the guard who stood at attention directly in front of me, looking straight through the high black gate. He was facing towards me but couldn't have really been focused on anything that moved. I don't think he was even blinking.

By this time I had registered my initial reaction to the impressive and well-ordered event and slyly dedicated myself to the task of coaxing this guard before me to smile. He had red hair that looked fresh from the barbershop, green eyes, a thin face, long nose, and a mouth that slanted downward on one side. I decided to focus my energy on a point just between his two eyes. I was successful in my attempt; he flashed me a lovely split-second grin, then resumed his expressionless demeanor.

The guards turned on their heels, the sound of hundreds of shoe taps clicking in unison, and faced back toward the gate. I started thinking about where I would go next, and settled on a walk to Harrod's. I'd been told not to miss the hanging fowl in the Food Hall in the basement. It was my appreciation of a gift that came from there years before that lured me, more than the promise of displayed killed pheasant and quail. The gift that I still treasure is a delicate pair of tiny sewing scissors in the shape of a stork.

Trusting that I was heading in the right direction, I walked across Constitution Hill to Green Park and stood by the street light to consult my guidebook. That's when I met David. He was leaning against the light post, and as I took notice of him, I felt that he had been watching, almost waiting for me, as I crossed the street. He was dressed in a business suit, dark hair falling down his forehead, which he kept pushing over to the side. He smiled and spoke with a now rare, authentic cockney accent, asking, "Cud aey 'elp eue, miss:

I asked if he could direct me to Harrod's. "Jes dowen thes wey, 'yon ther paark 'ere," he offered, pointing further down Constitution Hill toward Knightsbridge, "an weil, since eim 'eaded dowen they wey meself, wuy don' eye just walk wit' eu, wuy naut, ey?"

I accepted his kind invitation to show me the way, and hurried to keep up with his long strides. He lectured me about walking through parks alone, and again, I felt that I was meeting another very old friend. I was distracted by another concurrent past-life overlay of this man whom I now knew had been the jailer who had brought me food. We stopped outside the Paxton Pub, a long block from Harrod's. He said, sounding very protective and concerned, that I looked hungry, and might I join him for lunch and a lager?

I agreed, but reminded him that I would then have to resume my day's walking tour. We talked and laughed through lunch, and he described his job to me, managing a lighting crew for an advertising company. He was a light technician and seemed resigned to carry on his inherited station in life as a working class citizen. He asked me about life in the United States and about what I did. I answered him in general terms, and he nodded and smiled.

After lunch we walked out onto the sidewalk; he pointed toward Harrod's, shook my hand and said something that to this day I find remarkable. As he turned to walk back in the direction we had come, he said to me, "Bye now! See 'eu in a 'nuther two hundred!"

There are times when I find myself in communication with a part of people's selves with which they don't seem to be consciously connected—as if a timeless, awake part of them comes through. When this happens, I'm astonished at the things they say—maybe a quick, soft remark—that I doubt they would even remember having said. I smiled and waved good-bye to David, wondering if we *would* meet again, in another two hundred.

A Transcendental Soiree

Viewing our lives and lifetimes as a continuum creates an illusion, as all of our life spaces exist simultaneously outside of this present dimension. I'm able to understand this better when I think about the gravitational pull of the earth. I envision the effects of no gravity on the astronauts, secured in their little space quarters, with orange juice packets and straws, razors and toothbrushes floating around. All that we've ever been or experienced is still floating around out there in other spaces that are still existing. It's as though earth's gravity also pulls time and lifetimes down into what we perceive as a linear sequence.

This dimension, within which we experience one time period, can also be seen as a hologram into which each of us projects our own perceptions, which we then view and experience as our own particular reality.

At times, there are those whose awareness expands beyond fixed time-oriented perceptions and allows them to experience themselves as existing in two time periods at the same time, non-linearly. Evidence of other realities existing in time segments outside of this hologram is felt when a present self runs into (what is viewed as) a past self that is still existing. I call this "meeting yourself."

Sometimes this is experienced as a concurrent past life overlay. The observer has an awareness or vision of himself—perhaps as quick flashes of a transparent movie—in another time period that exists simultaneously, laid over this reality in which his present consciousness is focused.

I often experience these scenes as overlays, other times as holograms, existing off to the side of my present space. This happens when I meet a person with whom I have had one or several past connections. I catch glimpses of scenes in which we act out a past drama or relationship from a past space (that is still occurring), while finding myself relating to him or her again in a new but often very similar way.

People also meet themselves when they are drawn to a particular location that feels strangely but unmistakably familiar. They often know the names of streets or location of specific buildings. On occasion, pulled to a foreign country, they begin to speak the language of that county, unknown to them in their present reality. A couple of the following stories are examples of this type of "meeting yourself."

Anna is a client who used to come regularly for sessions. Sometimes we "reframed" present situations in her life in order to put into a new context the challenges and growth she was experiencing. Other times, Anna would regress spontaneously to a past life and I would join her, viewing exactly what she was experiencing.

Experiencing past life scenes through hypnosis, meditation, or past-life regression is another way that people meet themselves. In Anna's case, we both went to "where" that other life space still existed. By "being there" with my clients, I can sometimes confirm experiences that they might tend to discount, thinking, "It's just my imagination!" or "This isn't real—I must have made it up!" That I'm seeing what they see helps them trust and explore the scene further.

One day Anna arrived for her session and settled in as I began the invocation, relaxed, and deepened herself as I did the same. After a few silent moments, I found myself watching a young woman on a beach, gathering driftwood. She wore a long dress; her hem was tucked into the waistline, exposing white legs and bare feet.

"Where are you?" I asked Anna.

"I'm gathering firewood to take back into the house," Anna responded, without hesitation. "I'm the last to leave, so I have to replace what we've used."

"Who is 'we'?" I asked.

"There are several of us, a group of women. We meet out here, outside town," she answered.

"What do you do there?" I asked, watching the young woman as she walked through sand dunes towards the house.

"I'm here to do some writing. Others come to do other things, creative endeavors. One is a painter, another a writer. The woman who owns the house makes beautiful pottery," Anna reported, speaking for her "other" self, who was now in the house, packing a carpet bag.

"What's happening now?" I continued.

"It's time to go. I have to catch the wagon," she answered. I watched her put two tortoise-shell hair combs into her bag.

"What are those?" I asked.

"They're from my father," she said, reflecting. "We have a close relationship."

The woman walked outside with her bag and stood in front of the beach house, looking down the road to the left.

"What are you waiting for?" I asked.

"The wagon," she answered. "I'm looking for the milk wagon. The driver brings it around to pick us up and take us back to town. He's not supposed to, but he doesn't mind giving us rides."

Anna and I watched the woman riding on the milk wagon, seated next to the driver on the front seat. Now he stopped to let her off at the house of a special friend, with whom she worked, and his wife. Anna added she and his wife both belonged to a select group, a soiree that met regularly on certain evenings. She said that this was in Massachusetts, at the time of the Transcendentalists.*

The last scene showed the woman handing some papers to a man in a shop, something that she had written with great care and diligence. I could see a printing press in the room and got the name Horace Greeley.**

---

* Transcendentalism was a philosophical and literary movement that flourished in New England around 1835–1860. Transcendentalists took their inspiration from German idealists such as Kant and from Eastern mystical philosophies. They believed in the divinity and unity of man and nature and the supremacy of intuition over sense-perception and reason as a source of knowledge. Ralph Waldo Emerson, Margaret Fuller, Henry David Thoreau, and Amos Bronson Alcott were major figures in the movement.

** Horace Greeley (1811–1872) was a journalist and reformer, the founder and editor of the popular *New York Tribune*. One of the most influential figures of the pre-Civil War period, he endorsed abolitionism, helped found the Republican Party, and was instrumental in the candidacy and election of Lincoln.

At the end of Anna's session, I reminded her that in past readings I had viewed a potential future where she would do some significant writing. We took this replay of a past life simply as an indicator that she had once used creative talents in a way that was again available to her. It was intriguing to her to think that she might have some buried talents that she could tap into. We left it at that.

A few weeks later, Anna called, sounding very excited, and asked if she could come over later that day. I invited her to come on ahead. When she arrived, she dashed in through the front door and seated herself in her customary place on my couch.

"Look at this!" she exclaimed, thumbing through some photocopied sheets on her lap. She stopped, took a deep breath, looked up at me and laughed, saying, "Wait a minute. I'd better start at the beginning!"

Apparently Anna had been reading a novel that she had checked out from the library. The book referred to a woman, a writer, who lived in Italy at the time that the novel took place. The woman's name was Margaret Fuller. Anna had never heard of her, but when she saw the name, she became obsessed to know more about her. She knew that she had been that woman.

She said that she took the book back to the library, adding with a chuckle that only with great effort had she refrained from asking the librarian to help her find information about the woman she had been in the 1800s. She calmly asked for references about Margaret Fuller.

"This is what I found!" Anna continued, handing me the sheets of paper. She showed me the information that she had collected about the life of this woman. It was the young woman we had observed in her last session.

Margaret Fuller (1810–1850) was an influential American critic and advocate of female emancipation. She was a member of a women's group that brought forth many ideas and support concerning women's causes. There was mention of a special relationship that she had with her father.

A friend of Ralph Waldo Emerson, she edited the Transcendentalist magazine, *The Dial.* She became a literary critic, working with Horace Greeley for the *New York Tribune* in 1844, and in the following year, published *Woman in the Nineteenth Century.*

She became interested in Italian politics after traveling through Europe, and she lived, married, and continued her writing there. She maintained correspondence with her friend, Henry David Thoreau, with whom she had edited the Transcendentalist magazine.

I interrupted Anna, saying that the energy of the one who had been Thoreau had just projected himself beside her. I told her that he was nodding in agreement, and was adding something about a child. "He's projecting the thoughts that 'they knew about the boy'," I added.

Anna looked up from her papers, smiled, then looked back down, continuing with her report: "Returning from Italy, Margaret Fuller was drowned with her husband and son in a shipwreck off Fire Island, New York. None were found."

"Well, Thoreau wants you to know that the body of the little boy was found, and they gave him a service. Thoreau will be around to help with ideas again, if you decide to do some writing."

After the excitement of having "met herself," Anna began to feel a little crazy, having met another self that was *still existing* in another time period. I encouraged her to focus on the present in which she finds herself, to integrate the awareness that this life represents the cumulative total of all her life spaces, experiences, and "selves."

The gift in Anna's re-experience was the awareness of talents that were still a part of her, from that (and all) lifetimes. She had only to trust and access the creative potential from within herself. It was clear to me why other life spaces are available to those who are open and receptive. It was also clear why we generally aren't able to view all life spaces at the same time. Present life experiences usually provide more than enough on which most people need to focus.

Awareness of other, concurrently existing "selves" can add depth to the understanding of our vast, multi-dimensional identity by acquainting us with subtle characteristics. It can also assist us in discovering and trusting our untapped gifts and potentials. However, that awareness can also distract us from the life space in which we are presently focused, just as Anna was momentarily distracted from her present.

As with the astronauts and all their "stuff," it's all floating around out there. We do need to be selective about what we pull in, asking to receive that which is for our highest good. Then again, I do trust that we're given only as much as we can handle.

I'll Give You a Sign

It's often quite confirming and even amusing to see how repetitious we are in some of our incarnations—we are not that original in how we rewrite the script for the dramas that pull us back in. Often a grandparent has been the parent, a parent has been the child, a wife has been the mistress and the mistress has been the wife. A loving neighbor has been a caring aunt, or a boorish husband is now the abusive step-father. The priest may now be the psychiatrist, and the land baron, a real estate mogul.

I've mentioned that there are times when I also feel that another part of a person with whom I am interacting is responding from a timeless place in himself, relating to me from another time, but not through his conscious mind-awareness. If the other person trusts his or her intuitive abilities, often a mutual identification may occur in which we both slip into a timeless space or time warp of sorts. For a moment, we both relate to each other from another time/space when we knew/know each other. As in Anna's case, I refer to this as *spontaneous regression*.

I experienced this phenomenon for the first time when my son Dylan was three years old. At bedtime, he and his five-year-old sister, Adrianne, both called to me from their separate bedrooms, "Tuck *me* in *last!*" They had figured out that the one who got the hugs and bedtime chat last usually got my exclusive attention longer.

This particular evening Dylan "got me last;" after "poofing" his down comforter, I sat on the side of his bed, about to lean over to kiss him goodnight. At that moment, he reached up, pulled my head down, and kissed me on the forehead. It wasn't the feeling of a three-year-old doing this.

On occasion I had chuckled to myself that this little person *had* to have been my father in another time, when I felt the loving concern he would show for me, almost off to the side of the drama we were presently acting out as mother and son. "You okay?" he'd turn back to ask, on his way outside to play. "Hadn't you better set the alarm earlier, to make sure you get us up on time in the morning, Mom?" or, "Don't you think this would be a better place to store our toys?" or my favorite, "You look like you need a hug!"

However, the moment Dylan kissed my forehead that night, we *were* in old England; he was my beloved father, he had white hair, he was dying, and I could see everything in the room. I rocked him in my arms, whispering, "Oh, father, please don't die!"

My father looked up at me and said, "Don't worry. We will be together again, another time. I'll give you a sign."

Dylan's fatherly kiss revived the soul memory of a relationship that existed between us on a very deep level and that never ended. Years later, I asked him what he thought of this story that he had heard me tell my friends. He answered, "You forgot to tell them that when I was dying, I wore blue pants."

Spontaneous regressions also occur in groups, and I recall a dramatic example of this during one of my first classes. There were only about five of us assembled this particular evening, and we were meeting at Ben's elegant condominium.

It was a chilly evening, and as we had all decided that a fire would be nice, Chris volunteered to help me figure out how to operate Ben's gas fireplace. I lit the match while he fiddled with the handle on the wall, adjusting the chimney flue. Thinking that all was ready, I struck the match just as he turned the handle downward—closing the flue instead of opening it. Just as the lit match connected with the gas flame, the combustion pushed the flame out onto me.

I thought I had come through unscathed until all the others started hitting me, smothering little embers that had caught onto my sweater. I checked for damage in the powder room and found that I had scraped by with singed hair and eyebrows.

I began our class with a meditation, asking for the significance of this opening little drama to be revealed. I relayed the response that what had transpired was not an accident, but was to serve as a catalyst for us all to remember what had come before, when we were together as a group over two hundred years ago. It was purposeful that we had reincarnated into these times to express and live by our beliefs openly and freely. I personally was meant to know that I need not fear being burned again (hah!) for what I knew, even if others I might encounter are responding from their own fears, again challenging my beliefs.

The others in our group were also deep in meditation, as we were quite accustomed to meditating together. One of them began to speak up, describing where she found herself, in another time, and the rest of the group acknowledged that they were "present" there also. We found ourselves together, meeting somewhere on the east coast of America in a clandestine way. We had agreed to meet there, on the other side of the ocean, after escaping religious persecution in Europe.

We could all see clearly the roles we played. Cindy was male at that time, but with traces of a few traits we could identify in her now. Back in this overlay, he (she) was a woodsman and a neighbor of Chris'. We saw them both coming out of the woods for a meeting, much in the way we met in the present moment. Jan worked in the town as a server in a pub, knowing and attentive to much more information that passed by her than one might have suspected.

Sandy was some kind of liaison, and Judy, a male, had just come into our campsite on horseback. He (she) was a spy from a military regiment and had slipped away to our meeting. I was there, female, and found myself jumping around, waving my arms and looking a little eccentric, trying to pull the group together.

Details came through about our purpose in coming together again, as before, but the significance for all of us was that in our present we had rejoined in better times to share what we knew and felt about spiritual matters. The synergistic effect of all of our separate energies combining brought about a magnification of that knowledge and awareness which we were now safe to trust and integrate into our lives.

Another spontaneous regression occurred a few years later, when some of the women in another of my classes spontaneously "went" to a time when they, as pioneer women, had escaped from a minister in the east. He had covertly molested these women in the name of God. Fearing that they would betray him to his congregation, he tracked this small group all the way to Colorado, where he shot them as they camped beneath the protection of the towering Rocky Mountains. One of the women suspected that in her present life space, the minister had been her abusive ex-husband.

Another time, in a meditation class I attended a few years before I started doing readings, one man, an aggressive lawyer, always sat across from me. He would look away whenever I tried to make eye contact. One evening, in meditation, we both re-experienced a deathbed scene where we were ending a miserable lifetime together. We could see that he had bought me from a tribe of American Indians among whom I had been raised, although I was not a member of their tribe. He had been a fur trader who paid for me with some of his pelts.

I was controlled and suppressed by this boorish man and ended my unhappiness with one of the few options I had available to me, to exit with a fever. I looked at the bucket at the foot of my soiled bed, and at him as he sat beside me, rocking back and forth, lamenting how he had treated me. I couldn't *wait* to check out—a familiar theme with me, I've come to discover—dying out of compromising, unhappy marriages. In the present life I took the option of divorce when it came time in my evolution to learn about coming into my own power as a female.

I am in a writers' group in the building where I live while writing this book. Madalena and David are extremely sensitive and intuitive members of the group, and this is clearly demonstrated in the screenplay and the book of short stories that they are writing, independently. We caught ourselves one evening, all having slipped into another time period, and commented on what we were seeing. Dressed in Victorian garb, we were reading poetry and prose to each other in a parlor, waiting to be called in to Sunday dinner.

We were either living there together, boarding house-style, or were meeting there on a regular basis, to share and support each others' creative endeavors. We couldn't help laughing as we recognized the odd fellow clipping the hedge outside the window of this lovely house. He kept peering in through the window, feeling very much like the neighbor who now lived below David.

This neighbor had objected profusely when David and his roommate installed a hummingbird feeder out on their fire escape, even putting up boards and towels around the fire escape to protect his windows from potential runaway drops of sugar water. More than once, David and his roommate, Jerry, had observed him peering through their windows. But again, the point was for us to recognize that we had agreed to meet again, to benefit from the loving bond that we share, and to further develop the use of our creative energies which are intensified by our coming together.

Soul groups do reincarnate together to further a cause or to facilitate each one's creative expression of the God-force. It becomes less and less surprising when one happens to view these overlays in personal or communal ways. These viewings confirm the existence of concurrent experiences, still existing, that connect us to each other and to all of our experiences in meaningful ways.

Chapter Five

Passing Over
and Re-entry—
Conditions Favorable

Closing the Bank Accounts

Some readings confirm to me that life contains no accidents. Loved ones who have passed over often come into a reading to describe ways that circumstances directed them toward their "exit" from the physical life, which they're now in the process of reviewing. They tell how we are gently awakened on the other side—if a rest is needed after our passing—then oriented and guided to reflect back and review our life experiences. All is in view, and we remember all the challenges faced and the choices made, as well as all that we accomplished and all that still remains to be learned.

Detailed descriptions from these souls demonstrate that some part of their being carried an awareness that their time of passing was near. This awareness had unconsciously guided them to prepare.

"Your grandfather's here," I said in the middle of John's reading. I suddenly noticed the visitor who, having left the physical plane, was involved in that process of reviewing his life. "He's showing me a scene of a white car coming towards him, then of his car going over a cliff."

"Yes," John answered, "that's how Gramps died. He was hit by an oncoming car. He went over the side of the mountain road and plunged down a steep ravine."

"Now I'm watching him cross a business street, after walking out of a bank," I continued, relaying it as I saw it, unable to make much sense of what I was viewing.

"He's saying," I said, trying to put it all together, "'Why do you think I closed the bank accounts the day before I was hit by the white car? I know now that part of me knew my time was coming.'"

"Ah," said John, sounding like he understood. "The day before the accident he closed all his bank accounts. My family wondered about that."

I find it very interesting when souk come forward with messages such as these. They really want to convey that their passing was not a haphazard occurrence, that they had unknowingly prepared for it.

Once a message came through from a son to his mother, acknowledging the letter or diary that she found in his bureau drawer during the aftermath of his passing.

That son, in his journal writings, had conveyed the feeling of an imminent passing, days or weeks before the motorcycle accident. In another instance, a soul attempted to confirm that he knew the loved one had found the receipts for paid bills and unfinished business that he had completed before he was hit by a drunk driver.

Other types of specific information can prove to be practical, but the most beneficial gift from these types of "transmissions" is the feeling of peace with which clients are left. Often they have a new sense of the purposefulness of the loved one's life and of his passing.

Such messages help heal the anger and feelings that many hold, perceiving another's fate as unyielding, unpredictable, or unjust. The client sees that the circumstances that brought the dearly departed soul to his end weren't random and senseless after all.

Another message that souls seem compelled to convey from the other side concerns their awareness of the agony their loved ones feel for them. This agony of family and friends is often a projection of their own emotions about what they think that *they* would have felt had they been the ones crushed in the car accident or had other violent endings. The liberated souls most often emphasize that they left their bodies before the moment of impact and that their loved ones need not continue to mentally replay such violent scenes.

Sometimes the soul transmits the memory of pain from injured limbs or malignant organs which lingered after his or her body's death. In those cases, the soul happily reports that the pain continued only as a thought form and disappeared as those thoughts dissipated. Souls who were blind report that now they can "see," and those who could not walk can now move around freely, often demonstrating skilled flying maneuvers. They want all their loved ones to know that they are once again whole and want to be remembered that way.

Choosing Parents and Conditions

It's important to emphasize that we do choose the situations and circumstances in each physical incarnation. We pick our parents, and know the exact conditions to which we are coming before we enter the body at birth. I've had some wonderful examples of this through reading prospective mothers and fathers, grandparents, and even aunt and uncles.

Occasionally I see souls who are hovering around the parents-to-be, getting acquainted with the family to whom they will be born, awaiting the perfect time for re-entry. Incoming souls also hover about their chosen adoptive parents before birth. I have several clients with adopted children, and several adopting mothers are in communication with the child, yet to be born, who will come to another mother for birth, but will eventually reach the "chosen" mother.

The first time I connected with a soul before re-entry, I said to the woman I was reading that she must be pregnant (at the time she was not "showing"), because I saw the energy or projection of the soul who would come in as her son. He projected to me the image of himself at the age of two. He was wearing an outfit he knew he would have at that age.

He said, telepathically, that he was glad she had just moved the crib in the room she was fixing up over to the wall with the blue wallpaper by the window, because he was going to like lots of light. He also said that he knew the one who would be his grandmother; she'd been his mother in another life experience, and that he was going to "want some of that saltwater taffy."

The woman later verified that, indeed, she was pregnant, that amniocentesis had confirmed it would be a boy, that she had just moved the crib over to the wall with the blue wallpaper, and that her mother was famous for giving out saltwater taffy to little children. I guess he was going to want some, too! Of course, he was coming into this dimension for more important things as well, but this message certainly conveyed his awareness of the circumstances to which he was coming.

Another soul projected herself around her prospective mother, saying, "I'm glad you put red in my room."

I said, "You put *red* in the baby's room?"

She said yes, she had, and hadn't felt that good about doing so. In addition to knowing what we're coming to, we also influence and help set up certain conditions. It's not all up to the parents.

I have also found that we generally come into the physical body at the moment of birth. If we are quite drawn to

the physical dimension and have tended to define ourselves by our physicalness, then we might visit the fetus
frequently before birth. (I picture the body-builders
working out at gyms: "Can't *wait* to get in that body!")
Others of us have a harder time in this dimension and
have to be (I visualize) shoved in at the moment of birth.
We tend to walk into walls and remember our astral trips.
We also have to remember to stay "grounded" and take
care of these bodies.

When I assure people that we choose what we come
to and even pick our parents, they often respond, "Then
why would I ever have come to that!" I offer this explanation to help them not identify with the role of a victim
in their childhoods. If we came to the paradise we keep
wishing this were, here in the physical plane, we wouldn't
be apt to ask the questions or pay attention to the lessons
that pull us back again. The old themes (that our consciousness automatically creates) push us to come to new
truths which will take us a step closer to Home, back to
our source, to God.

If this were a "paradise," we might get pretty lazy and
forget there is a place where we need to get! So we set
up circumstances that will hit us over the head and make
us pay attention to those beliefs and emotions that keep
separating us from the "oneness," from Home.

Sometimes we choose a parent who will mirror back
to us a self we have been but now have chosen to move
on from. A little girl might watch her mother being over-
powered and overruled by her father. She might grow

up thinking, "How could Mom take that from Dad; why couldn't she stand up to him?" Thereby she becomes conscious of giving away her own power in adult relationships, something she may have done in many life experiences.

Another soul might have been afraid of the female aspects of self (intuitiveness, creativity, sensitivity, and so on), which need to be balanced by the male aspects (aggressiveness, assertiveness, intellect, and so on)—both of which we all carry—whether we've chosen a male or female body. That entity may choose to enter a male body, to a father who exaggerates that fear (of the female aspects)—a "macho" father who, in pushing his son to prove his maleness, actually serves as a catalyst for the feminine self, turning the boy away from insensitivity. This process dramatizes the soul's fears, thereby forcing him to trust and accept his own female aspects.

Sometimes we come to a parent who reflects our own light back to us, as my mother did for me, knowing that I had some gifts to give, *and* several lessons to learn.

We purposefully design events in life that will force us to take another view of fears or beliefs that have held us back. If we have an extraordinary fear of death and are ready to come to the realization that we don't die, that life is eternal, we may need to experience several losses to force us to ask the question that some inevitably ask, "If there is a God, how could he take this life?"

A soul might come to a couple, knowing that she'll be leaving at an early age, and that her passing will serve as a catalyst for the spiritual growth of those parents and family. We really don't tend to take another look at things, or from a new perspective, unless we're jolted by the dis-illusionment that life isn't what our little self thinks it should be.

The following is a quote from a December 1988 *Look* magazine article entitled, "The Meaning Of Life." Eleven-year-old Jason Gaes wrote:

Why are we born was a really hard paper to write. I think God made us each born for a different reason. If god gives you a great voice maybe he wants you to sing. Or else if God makes you 7 feet tall maybe he wants you to play for the Lakers or the Celtics. When my friend Kim died from her cansur I asked my Mom if God was going to make Kim die whan she was only 6 why did he make her born at all. But my mom said even thogh she was only 6 she changed people's lifes. What that means is like her brother or sister could be the siontist that discovers the cure for cansur and they dicided to do that because of Kim. And like me too. I used to wonder why did God pick on me and give me cansur. Maybe it was because he wanted me to be a dr. who takes care of kids with sancur so when they say "Dr Jason, I get so scared" or "you don't know how weird it is to be the only bald kid in your whole school" I can say "Oh yes I do. I had cansur and look at all my hair now.

It wasn't until I lost both of my parents within four years of each other that I started asking the questions that brought me to a new awareness that also tuned me into my psychic gifts. With the challenges come the gifts.

I know a woman who lost her mother, father, cousin, aunt, lover, and brother, all in about six years. When her brother was killed by a drunk driver, she finally asked, *"How* could his life end?' Her search for answers has gradually brought her to the awareness that life doesn't end; it continues on and on and on.

The woman, needing to move through the fear of death to contemplate eternal life, didn't create the passing of so many loved ones in her life; they, on their own paths, having chosen how and when they would pass from the physical dimension, intersected with her path for all that she needed to experience and gain from their passing.

Life is not an accidental, haphazard play of events. The interrelatedness of all our paths is quite perfect. Some of our greatest challenges are the ones that we were the most eager to come to experience and move through, freeing us to move on to higher levels of our evolution and awareness.

Anticipating Returns

Introducing re-entering souls to their prospective parents is an enjoyable aspect of my work. Many times these souls have connected in past, special ways with the ones they've now chosen to come to. The session becomes more of a re-union than an introduction.

One reading became a delightful three-way conversation with mother and child-to-be, and I was simply serving as interpreter. Connie was due to deliver her new son the following week. I sensed that soul who had chosen to come to her the moment I began her reading, so much so that I had to telepathically send (what would soon be a) him the thought that I had some other topics to cover with Connie before I identified his presence to her. Even though we're not in any time frame before we come into a body, I perceived that he would wait patiently for his turn.

I related scenes that I viewed about Connie's other two sons, ages seventeen and six, who each had different fathers. I could see that she was a competent mother, a single parent who worked as a nurse and teacher in a large hospital. I saw flashes of her at soccer games and school events. I also saw her looking very concerned at parent conferences about her oldest son.

Connie had become very realistic about what she could and could not expect from anyone else in life, particularly from a partner. The father of the child she was carrying had had a sudden change of heart about the pregnancy. The more the new baby developed in Connie's womb, the more the father distanced himself from her. She was determined to raise her new son alone, just as she had done with the other two boys.

When I presented the soul who was hovering around her, he identified himself as the one who had been her beloved grandfather. Connie had recently dreamed that he was talking to her, and the dream was reminiscent of the love and acceptance she had always felt from him. She was delighted that he was there, confirming to her that he was the soul who would enter as her new son.

The soul related his version of the birth, which would occur on the following Wednesday. He was pleased that she'd be using the midwife who was her friend, told her to "hang in there" (my interpretation of his thought projections) in the third to fourth hour, and then went on to convey his ideas about the relationships that he would experience.

He said that he had a special connection with Connie's oldest son, who would soon be his oldest brother. He smiled, saying that he'd be there to help, assisting the brother in taking himself a little less seriously, in having a little more fun in life. According to him, that brother would access new talents, would learn to trust his inner visions, and would explore creative endeavors.

Concerning his own path, he said that he would have a great determination to explore some things at a very young age and that she should trust her intuition about allowing him to do this, even when challenged by others. He showed me a future scene of him at three or four years old, trying to assemble a toy that looked very complicated, vehemently refusing her help. Then he smiled again, very lovingly, and said that he was also coming to be a comfort to her. The bond they had as grandfather-granddaughter still existed.

Then Connie's son-to-be said that he would have a few things to work out with his father. He said that the father, who was ambivalent about his birth, would be available as much as he, his son, would need him, in order to balance issues from past lives. The theme that pulled them together had something to do with respecting each other's paths.

I could see a life space around the time of the Civil War when one blamed himself or the other for making a choice that cost one or the other his life. I suspected involvements in other life spaces, for I have found that unresolved intersecting paths often develop from more than one little karmic vignette.

I often view the patterning of interrelated paths that will involve a soul when it joins the physical body developing in the prospective mother or that will be cared for by the adoptive parents. At the time that a soul anticipates its return, there seems to be surprising clarity about the conditions and challenges that will come into play in his upcoming incarnation, and sometimes that clarity remains after birth.

One woman, who adopted a little girl after having a hysterectomy, relates that when her daughter was very little, she told her mother, "I tried to come to you, but there was no room. So I picked a mommy who would know where to find you!" As mass consciousness expands in these times, souls coming in will be *remembering* more and more—forgetting less and less.

When I hear from incoming souls anticipating their new birth, I usually sense a lack of emotion regarding upcoming challenges. There seems to be anticipation for the opportunity to "have another go at it," but it's definitely more a matter-of-fact acceptance than a fearful dreading or angry anticipation of all that lies ahead to experience.

A pregnant client was also informed by her deceased grandfather that he had chosen to come to her as a son. He conveyed that he looked forward to incorporating past talents of organizing (sometimes controlling) people with a balance of spiritual awareness. My client responded, "Grand-Dad organized the unions before he died."

Most certainly, it is *after* we gain a physical vehicle to experience life in this dimension that we once again begin to relate to all the perceptions and emotions that keep us returning here in the first place. We don't hold these perceptions and emotions when we're disengaged from the physical plane, but they do get reactivated by the gravitational pulls of unfinished business upon our returns.

I find it amusing that when we re-enter, we remember to forget all that we know about the "bigger picture," then we spend the rest of our lives trying to remember what we forgot. It's only in the remembering of deeper truths, those that go beyond the illusion of the physical manifestations in our lives, that we begin to make some true progress in our evolution.

Conditions of an "Almost Child"

A client called me recently to ask for my help. She wanted to know how to respond to her daughter's recent disclosure that she'd had an abortion a few years ago while still in high school. The abusive and condemning accusations that antagonists screamed at her daughter when she had entered the abortion clinic had traumatized her way beyond any after-effects from the abortion.

Her daughter had not been able to pursue new healthy relationships with other boys because of the guilt she was unable to release. She felt that her daughter's guilt had bound her in a negative way to the boy, the father, who had accompanied her that day.

The horror she confronted that day also led to a subsequent bulimia problem, and her mother had arranged counseling for her to overcome the eating disorder. She told her mother that it was through the intensive therapy that she discovered she had become obsessed with keeping her body very thin so as never to approximate the size it was in her former pregnant condition the day she visited the clinic. Therapy helped her resolve much of the eating disorder, but she still had the nightmares which replayed the scenes of angry people screaming, "Murderer!"

I reminded my client of what I always maintain about abortion. We're no dummies. We're not going to sign up for a body that's not going to make it. We might visit the fetus as it develops through pregnancy, as we travel in and out in our etheric body, but we generally join with the physical vehicle at birth.

A soul is never killed. A soul is energy that is part of God. Energy can be transformed, but not killed. Coming to a body that's in line for an abortion is not the most expedient way to begin a life's journey. But if there is the karmic need for a soul to experience abortion in a fetus, that choice will be made.

Fear of death and remnant beliefs in a vengeful God are often projected onto a woman who makes the choice to have an abortion. Most often, when I view that there has been an almost child in a woman's past, the memory, often buried, lingers in the dark shadows of her consciousness.

The scorn and judgments that she has absorbed have gone to where other misperceptions exist, combining to create the negative thoughts which separate her from her true identity as part of God, and from God. Convinced of her malevolence, she believes that she will have to be punished.

Those beliefs can draw circumstances into her life to punish herself or by which to confirm the negative aspects that she carries from her combined earthly adventures. Those beliefs haunt her, dim her light, and divert her from the path towards Home.

In the readings wherein I try to pull the memory of an abortion out into the light, I sometimes find very interesting scenes that help explain why that experience might have come into a client's life. These insights come when I view past-life overlays that take me to relevant deathbed scenes.

For example, I might view a past scene that shows the woman dying in childbirth, having brought many children into the world which were not conceived in love and respect for human life, and having experienced great sacrifice, pain, and unhappiness to care for them all. Sometimes that woman, about to leave the body that lies on the bed, feels tremendous guilt, believing that she should have done better, that she failed as a mother, and that she is dying because God is punishing her. Those beliefs go with her to create future experiences that encourage her to explore issues of self-trust.

Most often, however, I see the woman asking, in her last dying breath, why she couldn't have had some choice about all that her body had had to bear. The present-life abortion experience was actually the opportunity that she chose, the very one she had prayed for. Unfortunately, the answer to her prayer can become the fuel for more self-scorn.

The woman who receives the blame and judgments from fearful antagonists will have to eventually illuminate the darkness within herself. Those who condemn her will also have to balance the effects that their choices have had on others. Neither one will be any closer to Home until this is done.

Chapter Six

Replaying Old Themes: Choosing New Outcomes

Some Day My Prince

When I was married, my husband, two children, and I used to stay at the grand old Ahwahnee Hotel in California's Yosemite National Park. I fantasized about living in an old hotel, graced with the details of old elegance and occupied by interesting people who would texturize my life.

One day, I was coming up the elevator in my wonderful old apartment building in Oakland, staring down at the vintage carpet, thinking about its durability—hearty enough to withstand moving van trackings, Christmas tree needles, and Styrofoam packing overflow. Suddenly I remembered the fantasy I had conjured up at the Ahwahnee Hotel. I realized that I had succeeded in creating both: I lived in what resembled an old hotel, and colorful characters resided on floors above and below me. But in Oakland!

I thought, that's often the way: Prayers are ultimately answered—successful, manifested, created feats, disguised in different wrappers. I used to tell my classes how important it is to identify those triumphs in present life that might be existing, unrecognized. The answers always appear in a different guise than our personality-self would anticipate. Future speculations are only projections from past experiences and learned expectations, which rarely approximate how new situations actually come into our lives. It's good to identify these triumphs, to remind the subconscious that this soul, working through this particular "persona," *happens* to be a successful and powerful manifestor/creator.

The elevator stopped at my floor, the wrought-iron gate automatically slid to the side, and I stepped out into the long hallway, turning towards my apartment at the far end. Finding the right key, opening two locks—one for security, the other just in case, I heard a voice coming in over my answering machine. I didn't rush to catch it.

I like the idea of respecting another's time (and one's own rhythm), rather than the implied availability people feel they must make of themselves to the world at large. And sometimes the calls come from around the country—desperate people asking for help in finding lost jewelry, car keys, children, and rejecting lovers—not the kinds of requests to which my work is relevant.

I unloaded my purse and mail pouch, and sat down on my bed beside the answering machine. I replayed the call that I had just missed. "Louise! It's Joanne in Michigan! You're *wun*derful! I love you! You were right! *I found my prince!* Just as you said! In May, just last week, in Tucson! I'm so thrilled, I'm sending you a bottle of champagne!" The machine rambled on with more messages, and I groaned, staring down at my feet.

I usually don't remember the information that comes for people in their readings, but sometimes when I hear their voices, I can recall some scenes which I viewed while reading them. I tried to remember Joanne's reading. I know that she, like ninety percent of my clients, had asked when she would meet her prince ("Mr. Wonderful," or in the case of the fellow from New York, "Ms. Rightchki").

I knew that I had given her my frequent spiel about soulmate hunts. I had said that Walt Disney lied. No prince would arrive to make her more whole or complete. Many of us had already lived that one out in other incarnations and paid too high a price—the loss of our integrity and power. *Present challenges were tempting us to re-play an old theme.*

Past deathbed scenes in readings often reveal a past self, dying with disillusionment and a longing to get off the manor/ship/island/plantation or out of the hut/cottage/fortress/cabin, to act out a new script with the "lords and masters" whom we believed to have held our truth. I've seen that those who dominated and controlled others *also* died in bewilderment from an external sense of power that misled them to believe in their false identity (an understanding of self—"that which I am, by that which I possess or control").

I had quoted John Bradshaw to Joanne and other searching female clients. Author of *Healing the Shame That Binds You,* and *Bradshaw On: The Family,* Bradshaw once wrote in *Lear's* magazine that many women grew up with Snow White, whose mother talked to herself in the mirror, whose best friends were little men in the forest, and who attracted a man who preferred lifeless women.

I had recounted what I emphasize in my Introductory Tape, an orientation that I request new clients to hear before scheduling a reading, that:

> It's only by living fully in the moment, as if you alone are all that there will ever be, that you will evolve most completely and eventually start to project out a new "collage of self." By that time, you will have begun to access and trust new aspects in yourself that will then allow you to attract new, healthier, and fuller relationships with partners who will thereby recognize and relate to that new combination of you. *Those* relationships facilitate your expansion into sovereignty and self-realization.

I had also emphasized that we have to be doing for ourselves whatever we would anticipate or yearn for another to do for us. If we can't give it to ourselves, there's no way in the world that anyone else can.

Healthy future relationships that I view in readings always have the same qualities about them: two whole individuals, standing side by side, facing outward in the same direction. This implies relationships where each partner stands alone, with potentials more realized and true identity more recognized by the coming together of the two. Both facing outward indicates having no issues of trust—not having to turn to check on each other—and having acceptance, recognition and respect for the wholeness of each partner within the relationship.

I started to remember that in Joanne's reading a connection had been made with her father, who had passed over a few years before, when he projected himself from the Other Side into her reading. He came to help release her from her pattern of attracting emotionally unavailable men who felt familiar, like Dad, and from her obsession of trying to obtain from these men all that she'd been unable to receive from him.

I recalled an emotional moment when, with the help of his teachers or guides, he lovingly made amends for the emotional abuse she'd experienced from him as his daughter. Sometimes, lifetimes of resolution are accomplished in a single, loving moment of connecting.

I also remembered telling her that I could see her compulsion for perfection—coming from the belief that she needed to be perfect in order to be loved—would be easing in her. In the next few months, she would begin to see the outer manifestation of these inner shifts that had been evolving. I related a few examples of how this would be evidenced in her professional and private life. And yes, I did view and cautiously relate the fulfilling relationship that was already existing in a future space, but I *would* have relayed it with all the proper caveats outlined above.

The machine had reported its last message and clicked off. People do hear only what they want to hear. I could only hope that what I had related to her in her reading a few months earlier had helped to open her up to the new possibilities, rather than to have caused her to jump with impatience at the first semblance of what seemed to hook up with the scenes I had described to her. Whatever experiences she was choosing in her life, however, I knew would provide exactly what was needed for her growth.

The Stockbrokers

From my experiences reading a wide cross-section of people I find that every individual comes from his/her own direction, perceptions, and lessons. It's very difficult to judge another's lessons. A success for one might be the opposite for another. It might be a triumph for one person to learn to achieve success in the material world in an honest, responsible fashion; for another, who may have defined himself by money and success, it would be more of a triumph to amass a great fortune and lose it, in order to learn that he is far greater than his possessions. That would be the challenge, and the true success, for the spiritual warrior.

Once I read three stockbrokers in the same week. They all came on different days, wearing similar three-piece suits, designer watches, and driving big black Mercedes cars. It would have been very easy to "put them in a box" and categorize them as Newport Beach Stockbrokers. However, as I tuned into them during their readings, I saw (from my point of view) that they all had very different lessons, challenged by old themes with regard to abundance.

The first fellow seemed to be coming from lifetimes (or a dominating belief) that one cannot have money and be spiritual. I saw a past life around him, a very nomadic one, wandering the desert, dressed in robes, and judging harshly those with gold coins. Strong judgments go with us and separate us from Home, the God-force, and inevitably have to be balanced. As I've mentioned, sometimes that neutralizing is accomplished by experiencing exactly what we have judged. I often say, "Watch what you're judging—you may be *just* about to experience it!" So, in this instance, the fellow found himself quite financially successful, attempting to balance wealth with his spirituality.

The second stockbroker appeared to have attached quite readily to his wealth in other life experiences and had become miserly, even to the point of having caused hardships to others. I said to him that from my point of view, it looked as if he were back to learn to share his wealth with others who had been good to him and with those who had suffered from his power and wealth, to learn that there is more than enough for everyone. He commented that he had just about had it with friends asking for money, and had decided that he might as well loosen up and be more generous about it.

To the third, I described a scene that I viewed around him of his black car coming up suddenly to another car, then quickly taking off. He squirmed a bit, and asked if we could move on to something else. Apparently I was viewing a scene of a hit-and-run that he had committed the previous week.

I emphasized that this wasn't a judgmental approach; this vignette simply showed me, symbolically, a belief or fear that he carried that was making life pretty tough for him: that in order to have what he needed in life, he had to "get in and get out quick," even at another's expense. I posed the idea that he might be back to learn that the Universe, through his God-Self, can provide more than he would ever need, if he could open up to it, believe it, and begin living in a higher way.

So the appearance of the similar props or trappings in one's play do not necessarily relate to the same lessons or developmental needs of different souls. One can sign up for fame in his or her life's plan for many different effects and results. Shirley MacLaine has written about her realization that while she used to think her purpose in life was to be successful in show business, she may have actually

needed that experience to help her become less self-con-
sciousness about "going out on a limb," courageously
presenting metaphysical views to the Western world.
Again, "You never know what's for what!"

The Power of Old Themes

Much that we respond to in our daily lives has little to do
with what we understand on a conscious level. Our soul
carries an accumulation of beliefs and emotions from
many lifetimes of adventures here on earth's physical
playground, influencing what we refer to as our reality.

Just because all of those notions get stuffed into our
suitcases for future excursions doesn't mean that they
hold any truth. In fact, the lack of truth and light of these
leftover conclusions from these many incarnations keeps
us coming back. We repeat the old themes like robots,
mechanically responding to the misbeliefs that eventually become patterns that control us.

These old patterns influence our relationships and
our ability to make new choices, preventing us from
succeeding in new ways. They also block the flow of
creative energy through which the God-force expresses
itself. That divine energy cannot flow through one who
is not wholly present. When we live on automatic pilot,
reacting reflexively within these old patterns, we are not
present.

This unconscious repetition of old patterns reminds
me of the patients I used to work with in state hospitals,

who would sit all day on vinyl covered chairs, consumed by their perseverating behaviors. Perseveration is the uncontrollable repetition of a word, phrase, or gesture. I can still picture these men, women, and children rocking back and forth with a frenetic intensity, often heavily drugged on Thorazine or Stelazine.

Sometimes their perseverations included staring at their flicking fingers as they rocked, or repeating nonsense such as, "Is black as white and white as black? Black is white? True or false, true or false?. . ." Sometimes they would laugh inappropriately or would fixate on something in the room and look away, then back at the object, over and over again. Their days and lives were filled with these controlling impulses.

We perseverate as we are pulled back into this physical plane over and over, unconsciously repeating old patterns, reacting to the residue from all that we have erroneously deduced from lifetimes of experiences. The misbeliefs and negative emotions that we are afraid to confront get shoved into dark corners.

Everything that accumulates in the dark corners of our consciousness becomes the nature of our demons. The more we run from the demons, the bigger and more monstrous they get. The irony is that our avoidance keeps us from those feelings and ends up controlling us, preventing us from living as free agents and as creators of our own reality.

We drug ourselves, and fill empty spaces in our lives with obsessive and compulsive behaviors, effectively numbing and suppressing the feelings from those dark corners. When seepage occurs, we feel twinges of shame, guilt, betrayal, abandonment, unworthiness, and self-scorn. We feel incredible fear that what lurks in the shadows will pounce out at us to consume and control us forever.

We overcompensate for qualities in ourselves which we fear, if discovered, will reveal us to be unworthy or unlovable. So we live defensively to cover all of our bases, to appear to be okay, without error. We become compelled towards unattainable perfection.

Sometimes we give up trying to cover up and give in to negative beliefs about ourselves, dedicated to proving how unworthy and undeserving we are. I call it "perverted joy"—living our entire lives creating situations which will validate those beliefs, so that on our deathbeds we can feel that we won, that we were right: "See? I never got *anything* in life. See? I proved it. I'm not worthy."

I remember a dramatic example of how we unconsciously replay old themes. I was working with a group of about ten women, had given a special presentation, and was concluding with short individual readings to make the information relevant to each of their lives. I sometimes give such a presentation on a Friday evening and schedule these sessions throughout the rest of the weekend.

I was reading Sally, a woman who worked in a law enforcement agency, as did the hostess of the group. She seemed to be a strong and determined person but had learned to bury her feelings in order to survive many challenges.

I responded to issues in her present circumstances that challenged her to trust herself in dealing with responsibilities involving the maintenance of a large ranch, left to her with the passing of her husband two years before. As I started to address her need to believe in herself, Sally's deceased husband and grandfather came forward on my right. They projected themselves with "hats in hand," literally, with their heads lowered.

I first addressed the grandfather, seeing a scene that had taken place in Sally's childhood, near a barn surrounded with bales of hay. Sally was quick to respond, "That was where my grandfather sexually molested me." Then I turned to Sally's husband, and tried to describe the next scene that appeared.

I saw her husband standing in a doorway, looking into a room where cowboy boots lay beside a bed. Again, Sally responded without hesitation, "That was when my husband had a friend of his rape me, while he stood in the doorway to watch."

Both the husband and grandfather had come forward in an attempt to help heal the wounds that resulted from choices they had made and that had deeply affected both Sally's life and her sense of self-worth and trust. They told her their behavior came more from their own fears and inability to confront their own issues than from her deserving of such demeaning abuse. The session progressed with an emotional dialogue between Sally and the men who had been responsible for such degradation.

The moment came, in which I'm always grateful to play a part, when I experience the break of a karmic link, and when forgiveness and understanding allow light and love to flow in. The release of pent up emotion floods through the client and I can sense a definite shift in the person coming from the resulting healing.

I nodded, listening to Sally's reaction to the meaningful reunion that had just taken place, when I had to interrupt to relay a past-life overlay that began to appear to my left. I saw Sally allowing herself to be raped to divert soldiers who were coming into her village to overtake her family and friends.

She and a few other women had placed themselves outside the gates of their village as human bait for invading marauders, distracting them from the villagers who were attempting to escape on paths leading from the back of the town into the hills.

I told her that it was important to go back to scenes such as these, to replay them and to create new outcomes. The most important thing for her to realize was that she was continuing to react in the present to an old pattern created from retaining an erroneous belief. She equated being a giving, loving soul with self-sacrifice, even to the extent of self-abuse.

Sally could now begin to empower herself by becoming conscious and awakened to her misperceptions about herself and her worth, which pulled abusive situations to her and elicited these automatic, reflexive, and demeaning responses.

I have another vivid memory of reading a woman named Donna, around whom I also saw a revealing past-life overlay. In another concurrent life space, I watched her in the sixteenth century, having just been thrown to the ground by several men. She was looking up at them, feeling accustomed to this kind of treatment.

I tried to capture and present to her what it was that she believed about the incident, what she retained and brought forward with her into this incarnation. I moved into her consciousness as she lay on the hard, stone floor, and caught her thoughts: "If I weren't a woman, this wouldn't be happening to me!"

Donna had come into this life experience to a strict father, a high-ranking officer in the military. All her life, her passive mother mentioned the longing her father had for a son. She spent most of her life trying to be the best "son" a father could want.

Her self-definition came from her success or failure in her attempts to fit into a male framework, owning the projections of men who were scared of their own female potentials—intuition, sensitivity, and ability to nurture, to name a few. Over the years, Donna had continued to attract dominating men. These repeated patterns reflected her own hesitation about her femaleness and kept her from the exploration and development of that kind of power.

Most people are completely unaware of why certain situations arise in their lives. There certainly must be more than meets the eye. We have the opportunity, in this lifetime, to become conscious of these controlling patterns and to stop responding to them as automatons.

When a boulder is rolled away from a cave and the light filters in, it's as though there had never been any darkness. The same is true when we shine a light in the dark corners of our inner lives. Once I attempted to show the people in one of my classes how much they had accumulated and added to their dark corners already in this life experience and to which they were responding automatically. I helped them get into a relaxed state and asked that they be shown a scene from the past of which they were embarrassed or ashamed. Many had blocked or tucked away (into the corners) the scenes which they viewed.

One woman saw herself standing in the parking lot at her previous job, seven years before, on the day she was fired. She had completely "forgotten" about it. Another saw herself feigning illness for a couple of weeks in junior high school. These are the kind of experiences we learn to take as confirmation that we are rejectable or irresponsible. The thought patterns lurk in the shadows and follow us.

Once you start to awaken to all that you have accumulated, what do you do with all that clutter? Instead of encouraging people to forgive themselves, I ask people to send love to that self back there in the past. To me, forgiveness implies a righteous standard. Holding oneself to such a standard only promotes more self-scorn, which is how we started accumulating the stuff in the first place!

I encourage clients to go back to some of those scenes, picturing themselves clearly that day with as many details as possible, seeing lots of light around them, and feeling love for that person who had the courage to be out there experiencing and taking risks from which to learn!

I always have to practice what I preach, so I had occasion to view a day a few years before, spent with a person on whom I'd had a "crush" since grade school. I had wanted to forget about that day, because I felt like I'd made a fool of myself, baring my soul about my life and the feelings I'd always had about him.

I saw myself that day, in my purple cotton dress, and tried to feel compassion and love for myself, for that person who was trying so hard and had the courage to at least "put it out there," risking rejection or embarrassment. A week later I received a letter from the fellow, asking why he hadn't heard from me for so long, that he missed communicating with me.

When you heal something within yourself, it also heals the universe. We're all part of the whole and we all affect it, positively and negatively. When I healed that past scene, the other person felt it; something shifted, and there was a little more light in this world.

So it's important to ask to be shown that which you have denied or shoved into your dark corners. You won't have to view every scenario that ever grabbed you, but you will be shown scenes that will symbolize basic themes that you're back to deal with and that you keep repeating. It's well worth the effort for such an attainable triumph, to disengage and free yourself from the power of these old themes.

Chapter Seven

Meeting Ourselves

Captain of the Ship

During our returns to this dimension, we replay old themes with new variations and from new directions. We change the script enough to stimulate new perceptions. Sometimes, however, we symbolically retain similar characters, circumstances, and even props, in our repeating dramas. The next two cases are entertaining examples of clients catching up with old "selves," which exist in other life spaces. They discover that the script writer—their Higher Self—has made use of repeated, familiar elements in their play. *It's as if the soul puns with lifetimes, the way our subconscious does in our dreams!*

The first was a reading with Don, a kind, good-looking young man who owned a successful ship-building company in the beach town where I lived. He was in his thirties, well-tanned, in excellent physical shape, and carried himself in a confident manner. He'd had a few sessions with me through the years and I had seen that he'd achieved tremendous and early success with his business. Although he enjoyed his work, he was proud of himself for resisting the constant temptation to sail away, to leave his wife, two young children, and all responsibilities back on the shore, behind.

In one of his early readings I had seen that the temptation plaguing him was the soul memory of a choice he had made in another life space, a maritime adventure. In that experience he had given in to wanderlust, which can sometimes be interpreted as fear of commitment. He had sailed off from wife and family, leaving them behind in a small seaport village to fend for themselves, struggling against starvation and humiliation.

Don's business was now experiencing a sharp decline. His sleep was restless, disturbed by fears about his employees and their families, who would suffer from the threatening failure of his business. The reading had begun with my identification of this troubling situation. Sensing how deeply he cared for all of his workers, I could see that his loss of sleep was affecting his performance and better judgment, and inevitably, his business. A very clear and alive past-life overlay appeared to my left and captured my attention.

It was the same life space that we had discussed months before, that validated his passion and familiarity with ships and the sea, and that revealed that his impulse to sail away wasn't a new one. But this time there was more to the scene, a new segment to the filmstrip. I'm always given information that is relevant but no more than the client is ready to absorb and process at the time.

"I'm seeing you on that ship again, in that life space where you're sailing off," I began.

"Oh yes!" he responded, his eyes brightening several watts. "What do you see?"

"Well, for one thing, you're the captain of the ship!" I described all the details of the ship that were visible to me.

"Oh!" he beamed, eyes still bright, back now straight. "What else?"

"Well, you're running around the ship, looking pretty agitated and worried," I continued.

"Why?" he asked.

"Because the ship is sinking, hull first," I replied, gently, "and . . ."

"What?" he interrupted, eyes dimming.

"Yes," I went on, "and everyone aboard is going down with the ship."

I told him that the significance of this scene would come from his understanding that many of the souls who drowned on that ship were back again as actors in his present-life play. Don, the shipbuilder, had been the ship's *captain.* Many of his present *employees* had been "victims" who had drowned on his ship!

By this time, Don looked quite deflated. His proud-captain demeanor had quickly shifted to one of disappointment, shame, and guilt. He again felt the weight of all the responsibility he carried for his employees.

"Don," I began, "this may come as a surprise to you, but meeting your life's challenges isn't necessarily dependent upon the success of your business."

"No? Well, I've worked hard enough for it, and a lot of people are depending on me!" he exclaimed.

"I understand that. That's the point," I continued.

I went on to explain that indeed, his attentiveness to his business had been an important piece of the puzzle which comprises his life and its challenges. But the focus of the challenge in his current dilemma was not the success of his business. Rather, the potential learning would come from a more realistic respect for the free will of his employees in the face of the failure of his business.

The ship was sinking again. Don had the opportunity to release the souls for whom he still cared to their own paths and to absolve himself from responsibility for their lives. This would free him to explore deeper levels of his true identity and make inroads towards greater self-realization. It would also empower his employees to grow from this opportunity—to make new choices and trust new undiscovered aspects in themselves.

We so want to do and be the best we can be, expanding from all the "stretching" that comes from doing so. But sometimes our ambition for success and (unattainable) perfection takes us on a detour from our own path and carries us too far onto others' paths.

We begin to take responsibility for others' lives without respect for their own choices and directions. That sense of responsibility for others gives us a false self-worth and identification. We begin to believe that we are significant and loved because we are so desperately needed.

I have mentioned that I view many deathbed scenes wherein the soul reflects back on his/her life with regrets, that he/she may have misled those who followed and obeyed him/her, believing (as he/she led them to) that he/she held their truths. That belief rendered followers helpless and powerless to trust their own instincts, choices, and sense of direction in life.

I concluded the reading by describing another scene of a concurrent probable future wherein Don learned a valuable lesson-of-lifetimes from the failure of his business: that his employees had chosen to work for him and to face losing their jobs—their paths intersecting with Don's—for their own individual reasons and challenges. Their paths intersected his by choice.

In the possible future, he no longer took responsibility for their paths and for the choices they made. In this future moment he continued to act in a compassionate and caring way, but he had more energy and clearer focus to attend to his own personal challenges, including his fears of intimacy and commitment.

In Don's case, the enlightenment gained from clearing away unnecessary guilt and shame allowed more light to enter into his life. This rendered him a greater receptor for the flow of creative energy. The result became inspiration for the development of a new, more exciting and successful business venture—the result of lessons learned from a failed business.

Ronald was another client who was struggling with his job. He worked as a stockbroker and had tried several times, in vain, to find other work that would be more financially and spiritually rewarding. When I began his reading, he asked about Steve, a client who had recently passed over.

"We conducted business over the phone," Ronald explained. "I never met him in person, but I just loved the guy. The last time we talked, I expressed that to him, just before we hung up. I felt very odd about telling him."

"Yes," I responded, "Steve's here. He's wanting you to know that you both came together again to balance some past issues. The passageway to another job will open up by embracing the issues challenging you with your present one."

Then I viewed a past-life scene of Ronald and Steve, working together (again), as politicians in Rome. I described the scene to Ronald, adding, "I have to say that you and Steve considered yourselves to be a bit above it all and took advantage of those whom you thought were beneath you. You stole silver from the coffers—from the treasury."

Fitting the pieces together, Ronald leaned back, exhaling slowly.

"We *traded* in silver this time! Does Steve know that I wasn't always completely honest with him?"

Steve signaled me, and I related to Ronald, "What makes you think that he was always honest with *you?*"

"Ah hah!" exclaimed Ronald, "I *thought* that he might have used another broker!"

It became clear to Ronald that the way out of "breaking stock," a job that had proven to be unrewarding, as well as unfulfilling, was by staying long enough to face the challenges and balance old unfinished business, by operating in a higher way, with honesty and integrity—making a difference right where he finds himself.

That accomplished, I viewed future possibilities, where Ronald was speaking to large groups, guiding them in stimulating, spiritually inspiring ways. His new work was fulfilling as well as monetarily rewarding.

In both cases, Don and Ronald "met themselves" where they had played similar roles, even utilizing similar "props" in their plays. Even more important was the realization that they could trust the design of their life's plan—they were both right where they needed to be.

The Minister

At times I observe a client witnessing the evidence of a past self catching up with the present self to resolve unfinished business. To my amazement, I occasionally find that I've played a part in the client's past drama.

I was already aware of Linda before she came for the few readings that I did for her, having heard her preach at one of the local metaphysical churches. She was a dynamic, charismatic speaker who used humor and keen perceptions to teach and enlighten. She would look directly at (if not through) people with her penetrating deep blue eyes. When I watched her, I had a curious ambivalent feeling which pulled me towards her but pushed me away at the same time.

Many other people were aware of Linda, as she had become very well-known for her endeavors in developing effective self-realization programs in the area. Clear thinking, aggressive, and dedicated, she'd developed and earned a large following. She was also a concerned and devoted mother, active in the community.

The first time I read Linda, I felt that same push and pull, quite drawn to her, but cautious. Fortunately, I am able to set aside personal impressions when I disengage to go deeper for readings. Moving from one level to another involves two very distinctly different levels of consciousness.

Pleased with her first reading, Linda responded by giving me a big bear hug. Saying that she felt a strong connection between us, she invited me to walk and talk on the beach together one day. When she left, I felt overwhelmed by her intense energy.

It was in the last reading I did for Linda, shortly before my move north, that she expressed frustration and bewilderment, asking me about the women she continued to attract who sought her guidance. She said that she doesn't hesitate to lend whatever wisdom or guidance she can offer, but that too often these friendships ended in misunderstanding. I was well aware of Linda's inclination to draw women in, not only from what I had personally experienced, but from other sources as well.

Jan, a neighbor and friend, had approached me out of concern for her friend, Nancy, whom she said was feeling quite confused about her growing friendship with Linda. Nancy had received flowers from her, was becoming increasingly disturbed about the friendship, and was taking more and more time from her family to be with Linda.

Another woman I knew had experienced the same pattern of "seduction" and resulting confusion with Linda. She had also received flowers. Without disclosing that Linda was a client, I responded to Jan that I was aware that Linda presented herself as a powerful, charismatic person, thinking to myself that the pattern sounded familiar.

I began Linda's reading, deepening myself in order to view the situation from a new perspective. It was then that I viewed a hologram coming forward, over to my left, in the overlay of a past life experience that helped explain it all.

Linda was a minister (again), a large, stout man who delivered a "hell-fire and damnation" sermon from the pulpit, elevated high above his congregation. I could see unpainted planks that were the walls of his small church, which had been raised by the people of the town. He spat out his words, delivering his message loud and clear. He punctuated his diatribe with abrupt, long silences.

During those silences he would look out at the congregation—and specifically, into the eyes of some of the women who sat in the pews before him. They were captivated by him. They were mesmerized.

Then I realized that I wasn't observing this holographic scene from where I sat in my chair, in the present, nor from the congregation in that little church. I was watching him from the wings, to the side of the pulpit, over by the organ. I was his wife!

I felt angry and hurt, watching him look out at the young women. I knew that my husband was seducing many of them in the congregation. Something didn't feel right about that. But he was our interpreter of God's word. He translated the scriptures to tell us how we should live our lives. Everyone followed and trusted him to lead us to salvation. He had a way of looking right into people's souls.

I knew that many of the young women had fantasies about him, but he had chosen me. No one knew him better than I—sometimes, I thought, even better than he knew himself. I was the one to care for him, the one who truly understood him. This made me feel very special, anointed.

Unfortunately, there were no "co-dependent" awareness groups to support women in trusting and taking care of themselves first and tending to others next in puritanical early America. But now I understood the connection with the present. "Uh, well," I began, pulling myself back out of the hologram that had absorbed me and turning back towards Linda. "It seems this isn't the first time you've wrestled with the challenges in the use of power." I went on to relay all that I had viewed; when I finished, Linda and I stared at each other for a few long moments.

She left, giving me another bear hug. As I watched her go down the front steps, I surrounded her (and myself) with white light, and blessed and released her/him, asking in that moment that we be done with whatever we had come together to resolve.

A few years later, Linda scheduled a phone consultation. When she called, I proceeded with her reading, addressing her present situations, challenges, and probable futures. We joked, shared a few ideas at the end of the reading, and hung up. I figured that "she/he" had forgotten our past and long ago encounters. I assumed that we were "done."

Months later, I received a letter from Linda, expressing feelings of disillusionment. She had run into Jan's friend, who related that she had been cautioned about getting involved with Linda. She was hurt that I would have cautioned anyone about her.

I considered a response to Linda's letter for about a week, searching my soul to uncover anything that I might have missed in the replay of our past drama. I tried to remember all the details, now so remote, about the role I'd played with her.

Finally, I wrote to her and explained my interpretation of our interactions, and the reason for my reflexive, intuitive reactions to her, identifying ours as a karmic vignette, without which I doubted that we both would have felt such strong emotions about each other. You don't feel such push and pull with someone with whom you've never "rehearsed" before.

I apologized if I had caused her any grief. I closed with my wishes that whatever remained between us now be resolved, trusting that she, like myself, was committed to traveling a well-lit spiritual path and, I assumed, had no desire for more reruns of past drama. I haven't heard from her/him since.

When you've done everything you can in a karmic replay with another—played it out in a higher way, allowing emotions to move around and out—then it's time to release it all from your heart and soul. Turn it over to your Higher Self, or visualize tossing the matter up into God's hands. Keep doing it, until you feel it leaving you.

I tell clients to see themselves putting issues or people they need to release into the basket of a big, beautiful hot air balloon. I send the folks up with a nice picnic lunch, then watch the balloon rising higher and higher into the blue sky, seeking a higher resolution—out of my hands, out of my limited little self's consciousness.

Whether or not you get confirmation from the other that all is resolved (and people's need for it varies, depending on their own level of self-trust), it's when you no longer feel that karmic pull that you can know you're done. You'll no longer feel a tug in the heart, or a heavy sensation in the solar plexus. The emotions—the thoughts and feelings—will feel clean, dissolved. Sometimes we start up new karma that will need to be balanced in other incarnations if we stay too long, seeking that confirmation.

Mother Superior on my Couch

I recall one other time when I found myself a participant in the scene of a client "meeting herself." The reading involved a very unhappy woman who was a school administrator. Betty's abrupt manner and tough exterior no longer protected her from very deep feelings and vulnerabilities. Her demeanor struck me as quite military. In spite of all her defenses, I instantly felt very warmly towards her, but again, instinctively cautious at the same time.

In Betty's reading we recreated some childhood scenes in which she was humiliated and treated harshly, receiving little affection or sense of self-worth from her parents. She learned that she had to be tougher than those who raised her. She also learned to avoid emotional intimacy as a safeguard against further potential pain in life. Her rather had modeled for her his stoic, emotionally unavailable, and abusive behavior, and her mother never interceded.

Betty, now in her early sixties and "co-existing" with her passive husband, wondered if she hadn't missed something along the way. She had a good job with many respectful employees but felt unfulfilled. She looked at me with sad eyes and said, "I feel so alone. I've done it all by the book, the way I was taught. Being in charge isn't gratifying anymore. I guess I had to prove something to myself. As long I controlled everyone, I couldn't be harmed or hurt. It worked—I don't feel the pain, but I don't feel the joy either."

I felt a lot of love for Betty in her moments of surrender. I knew that it took a lot for her to unbutton the heavy exterior that she had cloaked around herself for years. Then I had the most peculiar feeling that I had longed for her to step out of that old protective coat before. In the next moment, I experienced time collapsing, a sensation that has become increasingly familiar to me.

When it happens, no perceivable time exists between a past, a present, or sometimes, a future event. Once it occurred when I saw a client step off a dusty wooden sidewalk in the 1700s, to seat herself on my couch in this life space. It happened again when my son, as my father in old England, dying in my arms, rolled over onto his bed in the present where I was tucking him in for the night.

Rather than viewing the holograms that come alive to my left (the past) or right (the future) as usually occurs, in this case a past moment catches up with and blends with the present space that I am occupying. And so it happened with Betty. Suddenly I recognized her as my Mother Superior, from one of those convent (we've all had 'em) lifetimes.

I was ducking into a dark corner, leaning against a stone wall with a large cornice overhead. I recognized a few of the girls with whom I was hiding. They are present clients with whom I like to joke, saying, "Nice to finally see you out of the convent!" Then I suddenly understood what prompted me to say that. Watch what you joke about!

The other girls and I were whispering about Mother Superior, who was coming down the hall. We teased and played with her a lot, but I could feel that because of our deep dependency on her for spiritual, emotional, and physical sustenance, we were cautious not to jeopardize our connection to her. We'd been with her since we were very young, and she was our lifeline.

I think that our teasing was more our way of coaxing her over the line that separated her from sharing love with us and with the rest of the world. We also had a strong intuitive sense of her boundaries, and we were careful not to loosen the tie that did exist between us, cold and unfeeling as it often felt. Now, after I'd watched her walk down the long stone corridor, she sat down before me on my couch, finally ready to open up to love.

A wave of emotion swept over me, as the realization became clear. I tried my best to relate what had just transpired. She must have seen it or sensed it in some way. She simply nodded, with tears now softening her stern face. We hugged and said very little. The experience went far beyond words. The potential for growth, completion, and resolution in this dimension is limitless. It does often leave one speechless.

Return to the Slave Plantation

Betty had made a decision to move to South Carolina with her man-friend, Harold. She had scheduled phone consultations with me in the past, but this time she had some very specific questions about the move. Her choice to move so suddenly, almost impulsively, left her baffled, unsure that such a change in lifestyle was practical. Yet she remained determined to follow through and buy the farmhouse on the land to which she had been very drawn.

As I deepened myself and started to view the scenes in Betty's reading, I felt the presence of a soul on the Other Side, but decided to attend to it a little later on. I began with a description of the house that I could see on the land that Betty was planning to purchase. I saw the house as it now existed, as well as an overlay of how it and other structures had stood in the time period of the pre-Civil War, the Old South. I described the scene, adding, "A stream runs by an old building that housed many people. Several were buried in a nearby forest. There's a significant connection here, between you and this piece of land."

"Yes," Betty replied, "I believe that must be true. When we were first shown the property, it felt very familiar to me. I'm compelled to return for some reason, as if I'll be completing something by moving there. I was told that it was a slave plantation. I was greatly disturbed to learn that over one hundred slaves were buried in the forest you've just described."

At that point, I tuned in to the visitor I had sensed earlier who, for now, was existing between physical life spaces. "We have a soul here," I said, making introductions, "whom you knew when you both lived on the plantation. He's showing me a scene of you tending to him when he was very ill. I see that he lived in that house by the stream. He was a slave who died from a fever. Many others also perished from it.

"Apparently you were very concerned about the treatment of the slaves. Your path has intersected with this soul in several incarnations. The love you showed him has not been forgotten. You put yourself at great risk to care for him as well as many others who caught the fever.

"Now I see the owner of the plantation, a man you loved but were unable to marry. You came to live with relatives on the plantation after he'd already promised himself to another. I believe the man is Harold."

"That's curious," Betty interjected, "Harold and I plan to be married there, on that property, once we're settled."

"I'm sure that you *will* be completing something," I said, "perhaps a new ending to a story of unrequited love, I'd imagine.

"There's more here," I continued, "that might be helpful to you regarding some of the challenges you're facing, concerning your move back to the 'plantation.'

I'm now seeing a scene of your mother. I sense that she has issues about you moving there. She also plays a part in the past scenario.

"I believe that she was the 'lady of the house,' possibly Harold's mother in that life space, and she greatly resented your boldness and determination to rectify the attitudes towards the slaves. You didn't question your heartfelt beliefs concerning your connection to all people.

"Trusting your truth and having the courage to act accordingly, sometimes quite aggressively, was very disarming to the one who is now your mother. It challenged her to look at her own beliefs, which supported a false identity perception that she was significant and unique because others were not. I don't think that she was able to resolve any beliefs to the contrary."

"And she *still* hasn't!" Betty chimed in. "She has always been very prejudiced—no, I'd have to say bigoted. She has a real blind spot when it comes to people of other races. I remember her getting very angry at me when I had friends who were other than Caucasian in high school. I went to a dance with a black friend once, and she called me, er, an expression that demonstrates her narrow views."

Betty went on with more details, relating how resentful her aged mother was about her plans to move to South Carolina. She said that her mother had been in satisfactory health, but since Betty announced her plans to move, several new maladies had occurred. Her protestations that Betty was abandoning her, that she was selfish and irresponsible to make such a move, made Betty feel very guilty.

I reminded Betty about the resources and strengths that had carried over from that past life experience. Those resources were still a part of her, and now she was being challenged to use them. I pointed out that she had successfully created the circumstances in this life space that would allow her to override any hesitations she still carries about trusting her truth. The strong pull that she now felt was effectively guiding her to do that.

I suggested she surround her mother with loving light and release her to her own path. To respond to her out of guilt or a sense of duty would cause her to betray herself and her own mission. Releasing her mother to confront her own dark shadows would also nudge her mother towards healing and self-realization. That, in turn, would promote a little less bigotry and a little more love and acceptance of others in this world.

Replay in Spain

I find that, in these times, the courtroom or lawyer's office becomes the setting into which many men and women are pulled by karmic ties in order to balance past misgivings and loosen the unyielding emotional grip that two individuals have had on each other. The arena of divorce is also one in which many women and men are learning to sink (cave in to feelings of helplessness) or swim (hold their ground, appraise and trust their worth, and respond with action).

Lack of acknowledgment and respect for another's individuality and the need to heal wounds left from unreasonable expectations of one another have slowed our evolution towards wholeness and a recognition of our true identities. Courtroom drama also magnifies tendencies to make another "wronger" to make ourselves "righter." This takes us all the farther from personal responsibility, an important step in our awakening process. The resulting absence of self-love, respect, and trust in ourselves masks our true nature as part of God— having the capacity of unconditional love. This is also what leads to our intolerance of others.

Ellen is a client who was a participant in that kind of legal drama. During that time, she called for her first reading. It was a phone consultation that led to insights about repeating patterns within which she would often "meet herself."

When we began, she said that she had a specific question in mind that she hesitated to ask until I'd given all that I initially picked up on. I told her that it looked like she was meeting up with quite a few past dominating husbands. This time around she was being challenged to find her power in the midst of marriages with and divorces from these powerful and influential men.

Ellen responded to what I'd just reported, saying that she wasn't surprised that her marriages and relationships have involved many past, powerful husbands. "I seem to attract them right and left," she sighed. She was currently divorcing an heir to one of the wealthiest family fortunes in the country. The husband before him had been a renowned physician. The one before that was from a wealthy European family.

Ellen is extremely intuitive, and she had seen some spontaneous past-life scenarios by herself. In fact, that is why she had scheduled the reading. However, she wanted me to finish before she stated her mission.

I saw a European lifetime with scenes of a royal court. People wore stiff, ruffled collars, such as those worn by conquistadors. It looked like Spain. I saw Ellen as very effective behind the scenes in the lives of many men, particularly her husband's. He was one of her present ex-husbands.

I saw that this man was (and is again) very influential, wielding his power over others' lives, while she tried to short-stop the effects of his misuse of power. She left that incarnation carrying the determination that he should have done things differently, rather than focusing on her own self-realization.

The times didn't allow Ellen to credit herself or be credited for all of her leadership abilities and intuitive gifts. I also saw that she was talented in handling large amounts of money. In spite of all her skills, she learned to respond to her needs in passive, sometimes beguiling, and often manipulative ways—that has been the way for many women, throughout many incarnations.

Moving this viewing to her deathbed scene, I saw Ellen in despair, sad that she never got a clear view of herself except through the perceptions and projections of men. She never really got to know herself.

Ellen's present life had become so entwined with that past husband that it was difficult to discern personal boundaries—where she ended and he began. I could see the challenges in recreating this conglomerate of past scenarios in the present life: she had to come together with him to eventually pull apart in order to gain a clearer definition of herself, rather than to change him or force him to see the error of his ways. The grief she experienced with these current-life marriages resulted from the actual opportunities she had prayed for. The desired outcome was the salvaging and regaining her own power. Making new choices promised her tremendous freedom and new avenues in which to release unlimited creative energy, no longer blocked by past patterns.

Several scenes then followed at once, difficult to sort out, like flashbacks into incarnations where she continued to play out this similar theme. A tall tower appeared in one of the scenes, and a solemn procession in the center of a seaport village appeared in another.

Ellen then confirmed much of what I presented to her. She said that twice she has been given the job of handling money. In fact, she had developed a foundation for one of her husbands. However, rather than receiving satisfaction from contributing to her husbands' affairs, her greatest fulfillment had come from her artwork—painting and sculpting.

She said that she had had four husbands in all, each one wealthy and powerful, and she went into some detail about them. Ellen added that she doesn't remember ever wanting to get married, but each time she felt a strong pull to accept their proposals. She was amazed that these men kept choosing her.

She wanted to give me some background information before she asked her specific question. She began by saying that when she was married to one of her former husbands, he took her to Europe to meet his family. They had no intention of ending up in Tarragona, Spain, but through peculiar circumstances, that's where they found themselves, and where I had first viewed her.

She related that Tarragona is a medieval town, with a distinctive cathedral that was closed when Ellen and her husband went to visit it. A man appeared in sixteenth century garb and asked if they would like to see the treasures inside. They responded enthusiastically, and he took them through. This personal tour was offered even though the church was closed to visitors that day.

The man showed them incredible treasures. When Ellen touched them, she felt as though her head were spinning. At the end of the tour, he guided them through the last door, which brought them up to the altar. As she walked across it, she suddenly felt very ill, as if her body was getting smaller, with excruciating pain moving throughout. She looked through the existing wall, as though it wasn't there, and saw a coastline.

Ellen knew she was experiencing herself in another time but through all of her present physical senses. She was walking beside a man along the docks, urging him to maintain a blockade that was preventing enemy ships from storming the city. She was frustrated that she wasn't getting his support.

She reached the end of the altar, collapsed, and fell against the existing wall. As she fell, she reached toward a large tomb that lay against it. Suddenly she felt compelled to lift herself up in order to kiss the face of the stone sculpture, a representation of the person entombed within it. Her lips touched the face; then she backed away, gasping, having seen the face of her present husband on the sculpture. At that point she fainted.

When Ellen opened her eyes, she felt nauseated. She looked over at her husband, seeing the look of horror on his colorless face. He had also seen the face on the sarcophagus as his own.

Ellen and her husband returned to the hotel, both feeling quite ill. The next day, on their way out of the town, they again went to the church. They asked about the wall and were told that it had been built in recent times and that the coastline did at one time come up to the dock outside the church.

They experienced other such episodes, one occurring inside a tower of a castle in Antwerp, Belgium. When they climbed the stairs to the tower room, Ellen again lost control and attempted to jump out of the window from the landing, fearful of entering the room. Her husband's uncle grabbed her and led her through the room, since it was the shortest way out.

As he pulled her into the room, Ellen felt like she was being tortured, although there was no evidence of this having been a room of torture. She felt a tightness around her neck and pain in her limbs. The uncle seemed also to sense something and sympathized with Ellen's anguish. Her husband was embarrassed and indignant about her behavior, particularly in front of his family. On their way out, they learned that the room had been used for torturing uncooperative relatives and subjects.

The husband started to fear the relationship, the strange occurrences they kept attracting, and Ellen's reactions to them. They eventually divorced.

Ellen said that something similar had happened with one of her other husbands, the physician. He insisted on taking Ellen and his daughter to an exhibit featuring artifacts from a primitive Scythian civilization. When she entered the room, her eyes caught sight of the display case across the room that housed remnants from the ancient culture.

She again experienced intense physical pain, her husband and his daughter catching her as she started to swoon. They helped her outside for some fresh air, although she insisted on returning. As they re-entered, she told them that she could describe the contents in each of the cases without reading the identification cards attached to the case fronts. This she did, with remarkable detail.

Then Ellen asked her question. She asked me how to handle the violent physical reactions of her body in these situations, when she finds herself meeting up with past "selves" and events. She planned to return to Tarragona and other places that mesmerized and magnetized her, to explore the history and details of some of her other life experiences. She was expectant that such a journey would help her piece together the themes that she is tired of replaying. But she feared the recurrence of such ill effects.

I told her that she was meeting herself in parallel realities, a bit like bumping into holograms of herself. Her etheric energy, expressing itself through her present, temporary body, was connecting with the energy, or vapor trail of sorts, of a past self that pulled from the energy of her present physical self. In a sense, she would leave her body to experience and express her energy through the self that still exists in another concurrent reality. As her energy went from the present physical self to the other self, she was bound to experience some very odd physical sensations.

I suggested that in future explorations, when finding herself in such situations and starting to feel these sensations, she breathe deeply, pull her energy up to her crown chakra, then let it filter back down, directing it with thoughts that it would infuse throughout her present self, allowing her to be an observer of the other self in a healthy, safe way.

I also reminded Ellen to surround herself with white light and to ask that she be guided to receive the information and insights that are for her highest good to receive and those which will help illuminate the path that will lead her out of old themes and into greater self-discovery.

I've never met anyone so pulled by past scenarios, experiencing so vividly their dynamics, as Ellen. Once she recognizes all these past segments as being a part of her present integrated and whole self, she will be more in control of her future choices.

Meeting a Guru

One day, on a Monday, something disappointing happened. Hopes of future anticipated plans were dashed when a friend had to back out of a collaborative venture. Later that day, an old friend, an enlightened one, consoled me by reminding me that every event and situation in life provides the opportunity to meet a guru. So often, it's the guru within *oneself* that opportunities introduce you to. In this case, I found the guru—self-trust within myself—which became evident as I allowed myself to play out the opportunity.

On Tuesday I was invited to a gala event whose promise of elegance and activity distracted me from Monday's news. From Tuesday to Friday, I was obsessed with thoughts about Saturday's International Croquet Tournament, an annual charity affair given at an exclusive winery in the lush hills of the wine country in northern California. I was told that everyone wore white.

I went back and forth between two outfits. I thought the white cotton one with stylish shoulder pads, long skirt, and a modern design accidently-on-purpose spilled over the shoulders and down the front might do, but didn't lend to the Victorian elegance that I envisioned for such a traditional event. Maybe the Laura Ashley-looking flowered dress, with the little white crocheted collar, teasing with imposing and proper modesty, and seducing with the v-shaped neckline, the bodice narrowing into a tucked and fitted waistline. But it wasn't white.

Finally, Friday evening, David on the sixth floor settled it for me—the flowered one, and definitely with the wide white straw sun hat. Who would notice that the dress wasn't white? The important thing was that I would look elegant. The next morning I woke up early enough to get my things together—anything that I hadn't laid out the night before. I carefully carried the flowered dress on a hanger, the white hat dangling from its thin elastic cord, down to the underground garage. I passed David who was waiting for a load in the laundry room. He commented that my makeup looked just right, and to remember that it was *I* who carried the elegance, not the dress.

I arrived at the event, meeting my hostess between the cars parked in casual lines over the rolling hills surrounding the winery. I had known Claudia in southern California, before I transplanted myself to the Bay Area three years before.

I scanned the large crowd, all looking like bobbing white marshmallows, filing in and around the smooth, green terraced croquet lawn and huge tents erected in case of rain. There were white linen skirts and blouses, white culottes and trousers, white L.L. Bean sweaters, white silk blazers, white heels, flats, and oxfords, and straw hats, sun hats, golf hats, and berets. We filed in also, names checked on a list, auction paddles issued, and directions given to our table.

Claudia had purchased one of the best tables at which to gather her friends, on the upper level overlooking the lawns and the less expensive seating arrangements. She was annoyed at the young up-and-further-to-come couple who had been bumped from the adjoining table, apparently not yet claimed by their hosts, and who sought refuge at her table. Others of her friends shifted around the table until she was satisfied with the positioning of her entourage.

She placed the good-looking lawyer from Sacramento between us, and I gathered that this was one of the two men she had mentioned to me who would be there—the ones she still hadn't decided whether to retain as "potentials." I decided not to get too involved in any in-depth conversation with him, respecting the importance of Claudia's quest.

I gathered that the other potential was seated at the neighboring table, which he had bought for a collection of women modeling designer whites. He and Claudia would pop in at each other's table, back and forth, greeting each other's friends with such enthusiasm that I couldn't figure out if it was because they all hadn't seen each other for such a long time or because they were so eager to meet for the first time and see what it would lead to.

We all involved ourselves with lunch, filling our plates with nouvelle cuisine from tables on a back lower tier of lawn: wonderful delights such as rolled chicken stuffed with herbs and hazelnuts and topped with sun-dried tomato chutney (a great temptation to vegetarians such as myself), potato salad doused with hazelnut oil and vinegar instead of mayonnaise, and pre-season, fresh strawberries. Hot fudge sundaes, chocolate and cinna-mon-laced, were passed around later to nearly a thousand guests.

Bottles of excellent Chardonnays from the hosting vintner were placed and replaced unobtrusively as if replenishing water glasses. A strong wind came up, blow-ing over huge striped umbrellas at the tables down below, over the heads of those seated under them, who didn't seem to notice, even as the stewards scrambled across the lawn after them. I mused at how it was that they didn't blow over at the more costly tables.

The auction proceeded, raising over $50,000 for a convent that cared for babies with AIDS. A priest in charge spoke, noting the contrast of the day's event with what was before him at the other end of his trip to Romania in a few hours to tend to the unfortunate chil-dren who had been discovered in the unveiling of that country. The auctioneer announced the recipients of fine wines donated by neighboring wineries, getting much mileage out of announcing, "and this bottle goes to the lady in white," each time reminding me that I wasn't.

Wines were chosen from the glossy catalog by a few guests seated at my table, but auction paddles came down much faster than they went up. Two magnums of a Petite Sirah found a home with the man on my left, who had gone in together with the young displaced couple across the table. Plans were made as to how they would split it, and how large an occasion would warrant the use of such huge bottles. The young couple eventually resolved the dilemma by designating such fine wine as tantamount to a nice piece of furniture, like a lamp, to be simply left in the middle of one's living room.

My seat came right up to the short slate wall, half a foot high, separating our upper tier from the croquet lawn. I was grateful, when conversation waned, to be able to shift around and rest my feet up on the wall, focusing my attention on a very complicated version of croquet that I had never seen before. It looked more like billiards with a mallet—yellow ball through the corner wicket— and I observed that they could only hit one ball by hitting another. I remembered playing a very different version on the lawn in front of the house where I grew up and the satisfying sound of placing my foot on my ball, and knocking the one of an opponent (usually one of my brothers) cleanly into the bushes.

At some point, I turned back around and noticed that everyone at the table had shifted again, most trotting off to renew acquaintances or start up new ones. Claudia had left the one prospect on my left, who seemed to be becoming less of one, as she floated over to the other table, sitting by the other prospect, meeting all of his lady friends. Meanwhile, a pleasant but anxious-looking woman came to sit by the remaining male, introducing herself with, "Oh, I'm sure whoever's sitting here won't mind if I drink her wine."

She appeared to have already tasted her share. She wore a white silky blouse with white see-through pull-on cocktail pants. When she stood up, she kept pulling the top down over her rear, probably a great deal more hesitant about the statement she wanted to make here at the event than as I imagined her trying it on for admiring salespeople in a Union Street boutique.

Claudia looked back at the woman in her place, shrugged, and waved me over to meet her new friends. They were in the middle of a discussion on reincarnation.

I usually have no problem in feeling the rhythm of a group and can take my cue for the proper time to jump in. But the uneasiness I felt from Claudia, wondering what to do with me, combined with often-heard comments in these types of discussions, such as "Well, I'm afraid to believe in reincarnation because then I might come back as a dog," prompted me to excuse myself to walk the beautiful grounds.

It seemed as though everyone who wasn't carefully surrounded with a pre-planned assortment of friends with which to gather was married or hooked up with someone, except maybe the woman in the see-through pants. I love meeting interesting couples, but I'd gotten glares from the women on the arms of the two men who stopped me to comment on my great hat, and that "even though my dress was flowered and not white, that's how people should look at these things."

I really didn't have the inclination to raise my enthusiasm level to approach any more folks whom I didn't know and was unlikely to see again. Besides, I'd sampled more wine than I'd consumed in several months. It was now about the time of day that my body's system was used to meditating, so I strolled out to my car and crawled into the back seat for a twenty-minute meditation.

Refreshed and with a better attitude, I put the hat back on, adjusting it in the reflection of the car window, and marched back up the grassy hill to return to the white figures, now moving over to the patio on the same level far to the right of our table for wine tasting, fresh oysters, delectable appetizers, and a Dixieland band.

I passed Claudia on her way out, arm in arm with the fellow whom I thought had been left out of the running.

"Oh, there you are, Louise! Where have you be-en?" was her high-pitched greeting. I replied that I'd been meditating. "Oh! What did you *ge-et!*" The fellow who held her arm smiled and turned to her gently, answering,

"That's the point, Claudia. You're not *supposed* to get *anything.*"

Claudia disappeared for over an hour, and I again planted myself, leaning against the far end of the slate stone wall that supported the patio and looked back down to the lower tier, where guests were paying to take their turns hitting balls through hoops. Carefully setting a bottle of mineral water and a napkin holding three stuffed grape leaves between the uneven stones, I breathed in the beautiful bucolic setting and reflected on the day.

I was grateful for my ability to reframe situations in which I sometimes find myself that give me the distinct feeling of being "twanged." Disengaging and viewing a situation from a different perspective often changes a scenario entirely for me. I find this ability to be very useful and am pleased that with practice it's becoming easier to do so, even amidst the "twanging" circumstances. I remembered when I used to be able to take a more objective look only in retrospect.

In how many lifetimes had I been seduced by the illusion that glitter is gold, that more is better, that elegance can be assured to contain depth, and then came to the same disillusioned conclusion? Pretty people, excellent food, beautiful surroundings, and the setting certainly fed a hunger for nature, but I did long to return to my wonderful old apartment overlooking Lake Merritt in Oakland where I had fantasized about this day.

My thoughts were interrupted by a man who came up to the wall on my right, trying to balance camera equipment on the stones. He was good looking, medium height, said that his name was Cooper and that he was a professional international photographer and a personal friend of the owner of the winery. I smiled, thinking that he looked like Jackie Cooper.

He had agreed to take pictures of the day, and he wanted to take one of me with my hat. As he focused his camera, he talked about how he is always challenged to capture scenes from unusual angles to give his work unique and different emphasis.

He related the example of an assignment in the past, where he was to take pictures at a new war veterans' monument. Many photographers were grouped together, all aiming to shoot at the monument. He stepped away and took shots of the photographers taking shots of the monument. It changed the story completely.

He asked me for my phone number. I started to write it on a napkin, just as Claudia stepped up to us, asking loudly if I was ready to go. I introduced her to Cooper, and she glanced, bewildered, from me, to Cooper, and back to me again, finally looking as though she thought that she understood what she had interrupted. She excused herself, asking me to let her know when I would be leaving.

I drove back to Oakland that night feeling peaceful, appreciating all that's tried and true in my life. Like the photographer, by refraining the situation in which I found myself, I had changed the day. The picture I carried away with me—different from the one I had anticipated—left me with a gift. I had met another Guru, in the awareness of all that I could trust within myself. The event had pushed me a step closer to enlightenment.

Chapter Eight

Meeting Old Friends

Returning a Favor

I've viewed overlays of souls playing out past roles as Minutemen, horsemen, guardsmen, footmen, troopers, stormtroopers and paratroopers, in cavalries, legions, battalions, armies, brigades and militia, sometimes with a steadfast determination and other times with great resistance. And many times I've watched the final scenes of those life spaces, souls experiencing "deathbed hesitations" about the sacrifices made in war, and have viewed subsequent life plans involving pacifist endeavors.

Sometimes other emotions concerning war are being balanced. Naomi is a client I met over a computer communications program, whose son was sent to Iraq. He'd had an avid curiosity about war since he was two and amassed a prized collection of war paraphernalia over the years. I remember the day that she urgently wrote to a few of us who had regrouped over electronic mail, having been censored on another system for discussing spiritual interests on the bulletin boards. Her son, dubbed "Michael Marine," had just called home to say that he'd been issued the last chemical warfare gear and was being shipped out.

She asked me why he had chosen this path. I saw an overlay of him reluctantly having to stay home from the Civil War, feeling sad, bitter, and incomplete the rest of that lifetime, fantasizing and idealizing about the adventure of war. It was likely that there have been many other war experiences in his repertoire of adventures during his evolution on earth, considering the eons of time we keep repeating this physical experience of man at war, but this was certainly a dominant theme he was working out.

I told her, from my point of view, that he needed only to touch upon the experience for a realistic appraisal, rather than to fulfill some vow or bring some closure to a karmic debt through death on the battlefield. As his Marine division hit the sand, she received information that he would be on the front lines. Then she learned that he had been assigned to a bunker in the rear, where he was to analyze air samples for chemical content. He came home from the war, satisfied and whole, with ambitions to become a high school teacher.

Ranae's reading was another one that involved the themes of war and peace. When I began her session, I could see immediately that she had been a peace-marcher in the sixties, a theme that's viewed every so often in readings. I then watched an overlay of another life space where she was a nurse on a battlefield in France, cursing God and the heavens for allowing the carnage of war. I see this almost as a stimulus-response karmic effect, the present lifetime scenario existing in reaction to a past experience.

In this case, as in scenes of other vehement peace marchers, souls are presented with opportunities to expand through an awareness of the difference between loving peace and hating war. Vindictiveness and bitterness going with them into future life experiences, these souls carried the same anger into their motivation for peace. The soul was seeking to balance those deep emotions through contrasting experiences.

I told Ranae that it seemed she had some need to reappraise peace through love, rather than by hating war. I said, "I see that once again you have come to the experience of nursing in this life space, and that you were called upon to nurse one with whom there exists a bond of love and gratitude." I described one particular day, when she was leaving the hospital where she tended to an older man.

I could see her pausing on her way to the parking lot, soaking in the gorgeous, pink sunset that evening. I told her I could see that later that night, in her sleep, she had had a vivid astral experience, wherein she had left her body to help that patient make the transition from his physical body.

Ranae began slowly, relating what she had remembered to be a very peculiar chain of events that had occurred a few years before. She verified that yes, she had marched for peace in the sixties, had been trained and worked a few years as a nurse, but at some point had quit that profession, feeling overwhelmed at the task of nursing others.

She had moved to Santa Barbara, north of her previous residence, and was searching for her next job. One day she received a call from a hospital requesting her to special-duty a particular patient. She declined, replying that she no longer had either a uniform or her nursing license. The party who had reached her obtained both for her in only two days.

She remembered the specific day, and the beautiful pink sunset she enjoyed at the end of that long day tending to the old man. She also remembered a vivid astral experience in her sleep that night. When she returned to the hospital the following morning, the man had passed over.

A few days later, Ranae was told that the man she had nursed, in this, his present life space, had single-handedly been responsible for the escape of 20,000 Jews from Nazi Germany. Ranae knew now that she had been one of them. She looked at me, then told me about the nightmares that tormented her as a young child, running from angry men and seeing dead bodies all around her.

In a moment of realization, Ranae smiled at how perfectly the script was written. She was still trying to piece things together in her mind, but her heart could feel the love and recognition for one who had saved her in an adventure existing in what had been a present life space for him, and a past one for her. She expressed her gratitude for having been pulled into events that allowed her to return a favor.

"Please Help Me Die"

At times we connect with a person with whom we feel immediate rapport or towards whom we feel a definite pull. We try to define these meetings or relationships in terms of the ones we already have, but these people come into our lives in a category of their own. They are old friends or acquaintances with whom, in another or many other incarnations, we have formed a bond of love. With that heart-felt emotion, the evolving soul carries with it a desire to give back and acknowledge the love and gratitude. I recall a situation that pulled me in as I've described, and which helped me trust the circumstances that bring me into such adventures.

Helen was close to six feet tall. The first time I saw her, we were both at a volunteer meeting for a local repertory theater. She walked like Kathryn Hepburn, long legs moving her forward in definitive, aimed strides. She was wearing the long camel coat which I would see often in the following months, draped around her angular shoulders. Her hair was grey to white, and she looked to be about in her middle sixties. Later on, I learned that Helen was close to eighty.

When I first glanced over at her across the foyer of the theater where the meeting was being held, our eyes connected immediately. It took her only two or three long strides to reach me. "Hi there!" she greeted me, extending one of her demonstrative hands. "It seems like I should know you!"

Helen had been a screen star in the 30s. She told me about dropping in on a friend one time who was watching a movie. As she glanced over her friend's shoulder to see what she was watching, she exclaimed "Wait a sec!—That's me!—I guess I was in that movie!" Helen didn't live in the past, but rather as though she couldn't get enough of the present and of everyone in it. But every once in a while, she would hint at memories of a lost love, a broken heart, and exciting adventures. Unfortunately, her thoughts would usually skip onto other subjects before she would divulge deeper emotions or endings to her stories.

Very early in our acquaintance, Helen showed loving concern for me, correctly perceiving me to be unhappy in my marriage. She always knew the right time to call. The phone rang early one evening as I was getting ready to go out with my non-communicative husband. "Hiya!" she announced, when I answered. "Wanna come over and mess around?"

Helen made me laugh with such "get down" expressions tumbling out of one whose physical demeanor projected such a dignified, stately presence. "I'll show you some of those old Hollywood pictures I told you about!" I told her, sighing, that I was going to the theater with my husband. "Well!" she concluded, "then just put on a smile and enjoy it!" For me, Helen was a wonderful mother-figure, buddy, and sister spiritual warrior all rolled into one very engaging persona.

One day I picked up Helen to take her to lunch. She had mentioned in the previous weeks that she'd been wrestling with an intestinal flu. As we drove to the restaurant which she'd heard about—"The best soup and salad deal in town!"—I suddenly detected a less light-hearted dismissal of her symptoms.

Helen looked over at me from the passenger's seat and whispered, attempting to hide her concern, "I think that I might have terminal cancer. We've talked about what you do in your work, and you know that I'm certainly no skeptic. Louise, would you help me die?"

In the previous weeks, I had encouraged Helen to see a doctor and intuitively asked if she'd had her annual check-up, both suggestions she had impatiently waved off. But now I could see that she knew it was serious and maybe too late. Despite the realization of what was becoming clear to Helen, I told her that she might be jumping to conclusions. The next couple of days proved that she wasn't.

Helen was in the advanced stages of ovarian cancer. Looking back, there seem to have been so few days between her diagnosis and her last days in the hospital. I visited her daily, taking her through guided meditations, encouraging her to imagine the drips from her IV to be raindrops from tall pines in a lush green forest. I've heard that people die as they have lived. Well, it was certainly true in Helen's case. She kept everyone in stitches, often giving outrageous commentaries of her ongoing TV "soaps" and talking without hesitation about how she was feeling, as her life was slipping away.

A few weeks after I first met Helen, I went into a meditation with the question about our connection. "How or why is it that we have connected as we have?" were my thoughts, before "transcending." I immediately went to another life space, where I was being sequestered in a large building against my will. I must have been in my teens.

I knew that Helen was in the building, and that she was bringing me food and helping me plan an escape. I could feel her coming down the hall and felt overwhelming love and gratitude for her. Then I knew that with the love I had carried for her I also had carried a desire to give back in some way and that deep emotion had gone with me, pulling her into my life in the way that souls' paths interweave so miraculously.

One night, very close to morning, about three weeks after Helen's hospitalization, I had a very vivid experience in my sleep. It wasn't a dream from the subconscious, nor was it a lucid dream, where one is conscious of being the dreamer, dreaming the dream. It was most definitely an adventure I experienced through my astral body, the sensation of standing on a diving board with Helen. I was holding her hand, helping her to jump. We were doing the "one-two-three-jump!—no—now!—no—now!" that was so familiar from childhood.

At the point when we should have jumped together, I yelled out "Helen!" I stuck my toe into whatever it was that we were diving into, and she went on ahead. I felt indescribable peace, light, acceptance, and perfection. I woke up and saw that I was clutching my husband's wrist. He had awakened when I called out Helen's name, and was staring at me, his forearm firmly in my grasp. These kinds of experiences no longer surprised him.

Moments later I received the call that Helen had just passed over. Then I understood. She had been there for me in a past drama, assisting me with an escape and giving love. I was to be there for her, assisting in *her* escape.

Tending the Gardens

"Mom! I'm home!" Oh great, I thought, what's Dylan doing home at this hour, and with me running late for my first reading. "The bus didn't show! A bunch of us missed it, so we're going to the mall." "Whaaaat?" I yelled down the stairs, not trying too hard to maintain my composure. "Do you think that no bus means no school?" Motherly instinct told me that this was one of those drop-every-thing-to-show-you-mean-business moments. My son was trying to put one of the greater ones over on me. I had to act fast.

I shifted into that super-woman gear that's meant to astonish (but often ends up impressing only me), flew down the stairs, and landed in the front doorway, announcing, *"out"* and nodded towards the car. My son crawled into the back seat, and as I started the car on this cold winter morning, I noticed yet another obstacle to overcome with my already botched morning schedule. A green light and flashing hyphens on the dashboard reminded me that I'd forgotten to get gas. I had barely enough left in the tank to get him to school and on to the gas station that took the right credit card.

I dropped Dylan off at the front of his school, maintaining my "no funny business" posture, and drove faster to the gas station than I'd ever admit. No time to fool with self-serve, I reasoned, considering (a) the likelihood of arriving back home late for the scheduled reading, (b) no time to fool with the gas cap, and (c) a degree of self-appreciation for my think-fast efforts so far this morning; my situation warranted a splurge. I'd just let the attendant handle it. Besides, by this time I had really locked into my Huffy Hassled Lady mode. Pumping my own gas would ruin the image.

The old man moved very slowly out from the station office. He took several small steps which eventually delivered him to the front of my car. He turned, faced me, and waved "Good morning!" through the windshield. Terrific, I thought. This is all I need. A real slow one. Then he took several more very calculated steps, bringing him around to my side of the car. He motioned for me to put down the window.

"Super unleaded, please!" I barked, but he waved me off. He leaned in the window, oblivious to my Huffy Hassled Lady performance, and asked,

"So, do you have kids?" He enunciated unbearably clearly and slowly.

"Yes, yes," I nodded, motioning him to please get on with the gas dispensing.

"Well," he continued, "you ought to take them to that mall over there next Saturday." That was two too many mentions of that darned mall already this morning.

"I'm sorry!" I interrupted. "I'm really in a hurry. Could you please get me my gas so that I can run on?"

I took a deep breath, and let it out slowly. Again, oblivious to my deliberate attempts, he continued, announcing,

"'Cause I'm going to be the Santa!" Suddenly I stopped and looked at him, his head stuck halfway through the driver's window. He looked directly at me, and smiled, his eyes twinkling. The moment that our eyes connected, Huffy Hassled Lady remembered the illusion of it all. His smiling eyes shifted something in me.

Suddenly I had been ejected out of the pretense that imposing my will on this day was all that mattered. I felt no rush, and remembered the perfect timing, the perfect flow of life that has its own rhythm, when I get out of its way. He filled the tank, I drove home at an easy pace, and arrived just as my morning client was coming up the steps.

I'd come upon other old soul gas station atten-
dants, seeming to attract them at the most unexpected
times. There was the one who had also stuck his head
in my window around the time I was going through
divorce. He'd asked, "How's it going?" catching me
in a vulnerable moment. Feeling an instant trust with
him, I let him know. Weeks later I pulled into the same
gas station, this time with my daughter in the passenger seat. He waved me over to the right pump, leaned
in towards me, and said, "Things going better now?"
My daughter looked over at me and asked, "You know
him?"

I also find old souls in the guise of public servants,
although not often enough at the DMV or in post offices.
One most memorable old soul turned out to be a very old
friend whom I had not forgotten deep in my soul, nor will
I ever forget. His name was Sam, and he worked for the
City Water Department.

This happened before I moved north, when I was
living in a beach town filled with many wonderful restau-
rants and cafe hangouts. I loved to drop in at the Jolly
Roger at the end of the main street on Balboa Island for
coffee, tea, or breakfast on my way back from driving car-
pool across town.

One day, I sat snuggled in a booth arranging my datebook, when I signaled my waitress for more hot water
for my tea. A man in an adjoining booth, separated from
mine by a short divider, looked up at the approaching
waitress and said, "She'd like some more hot water for her

tea." Then he looked over at me and remarked, "How did I know that?"

He was sitting with two other men who looked like part of his crew, all with the same blue shirts, names written in cursive over the chest pockets. His monogram indicated that he was Sam. He looked to be in his early sixties, with thick grey hair, matching mustache, and sun-baked laugh lines around his eyes.

We started talking, introductions seeming super-fluous, and somehow found ourselves in the middle of a discussion about reincarnation. He said he knew that it must exist, judging from his experience years ago touring Hearst Castle. He said that he knew what was in each room before he reached it. I commented that he would have had to "re-enter" another life space pretty fast for him to have known the layout of the castle from a past life.

It seemed more likely that he had already explored the territory in his astral body, as if having sent out the etheric scout before the physical body arrived to expe-rience it. I often find that to be the case with what we sometimes call "deja vu."

As we talked, I started to see an overlay of another existing reality where I had known Sam in a different way, in another life space. These overlays, sometimes distract-ing, slip in now and then when I'm in the middle of one of these spontaneous reunions with very old friends. I saw myself in twelfth or thirteenth-century England, and I was riding in a carriage coming around a corner which bordered a large field on a road leading out of a wooded area into a clearing.

The carriage had stopped alongside the field, and I was talking to a man who was gathering dried grass into bundles of hay. I'd come to know this man, having traveled this road regularly, and apparently was accustomed to stopping in passing to say hello. I asked him how he was doing with his ambition to save enough money to leave England. I knew that he hated damp fog and longed for southern climates. He would report to me all that he had saved towards the venture.

Sam was watching me now, as I shook off the distracting images. I felt compelled to ask him, "Sam, how do you feel about England?" "I hate it!" he replied without hesitation. "Don't know why, never even been there, but I have no desire to go there!" In the next moment, still a bit stuck on that level of consciousness that I access when I do readings, I said to him, "I think that there is someone named Beth who needs you."

He laughed, not pausing to question my declaration, which I would have thought to have come out of left field if I'd been in his heavy-duty shoes. "Oh, you're picking up on Beth, the dispatch operator who's just radioed my truck that we have to get back to work!" He pointed to one of his crew, who had just returned from outside, sliding back into the booth, whispering something across the table to him.

In the following months Sam and I would run into each other, and we chatted often over morning coffee at this cozy village gathering place, talking about many things. We shared thoughts that we trusted deep in our souls, that defied intellectual understanding.

Sam had been a professional ice skater, maintenance man, and race car driver, just a few of many jobs. He had learned much about life from his grandfather, an elderly native American, and considered anything that he happened to be doing in life an adventure—even working for the water department.

We found that we had this uncanny ability for one to think a thought about the other, and that same day running into each other on odd streets, often while I was doing "around town" errands. When we'd see each other's vehicle, he'd pull his truck over to the side, get out, and hop into my passenger seat for a friendly, brief chat. His crew had become accustomed to this, knowing what to expect whenever they'd spot my black Peugeot, and they never questioned Sam about the quick visits he'd make with me. They knew that Sam had been happily married for many years, and they didn't even try to understand our connection.

After about a year, I no longer saw Sam at our shared hangout. I asked the waitress if she knew what had become of him, and she said that a very unhappy town citizen had sent a letter to the water department complaining that Sam and his crew were wasting taxpayers' money. He had actually clocked the time Sam took one morning, standing out on the sidewalk to chat with one of the town merchants before getting into his truck.

Without a second thought, I yanked a sheet of paper from the back of my datebook and started writing a short letter. I only paused for a quick moment, second-guessing myself, that it must be that time of the month when I tended to act on things, sometimes impulsively, but most often intuitively.

I proceeded to write a letter, to whom it may concern, that I felt it was such a shame that present day pressures and overbooked time demands were forcing the extinction of a lovely old custom, that of townspeople gathering together over morning coffee: lawyer visiting with schoolteacher visiting with public servant visiting with public official. I concluded that I believed Sam to be a very responsible leader of his crew, and that to my knowledge he always completed the day's tasks even if it meant putting in more time at the end of the day.

The water department happened to be several streets behind where I lived. I dropped the note off on my way home, asking that it be delivered to Sam's boss. I didn't think much about it, or about Sam, until several months later. I was driving on my errand route, and heard a honk behind me. I checked the rear-view mirror and saw Sam's truck. By the time I pulled over, he was already standing on the curb with a big smile.

Sam slid into the passenger seat, and began slowly, "A funny thing happened. Seems that an unhappy citizen complained about how I spend my time. Someone else wrote a letter; I have no idea whom it could be. Seems that it went all the way to City Hall. If you should run into that person, would you please thank her for me?"

Sam looked at me with a very warm, loving smile, then jumped out of my car and back into his truck. I never saw Sam again, but felt satisfied that two old friends had met again, and might another time, in some other life space.

I often quoted a favorite line to my classes, an excerpt from the book *Messages from Michael*:

"There are many old souls tending the gardens on the estates of some very young souls."

I am always grateful for those old souls who come onto my path, cloaked in the most interesting disguises.

Chapter Nine

Intersecting and Repeating Paths

The Woman in the Shop

Events in my life continually confirm the ways that each of our paths intersect meaningfully with those of others. People with whom we connect in that way are often from another "tribe," ones we might otherwise not be knowing.

There was a time when I needed a break from doing readings, being a bit on "overload," so I drove up to a mountain lake resort about an hour from where I lived. The change of scenery and the mountain air was refreshing, and I wandered into a little shop with handmade goods from South America.

I was trying on a beautiful belt when the owner of the shop came over and happened to ask about my occupation. I usually steer away from discussions on that subject; it often tends to monopolize a good segment of time. But I felt that I should tell this woman. When I told her, she replied, "Oh, do you think that you could help me? I have some urgent questions!"

I told her that I was a spiritual counselor and not a fortune teller, that it was my profession, that I charge for it, and that I was there taking a break from it. She said, "Why don't I just give you that belt you're trying on, if you'll just give me a few minutes of your time?" Again I felt another "nudge" and agreed to sit outside with her for twenty minutes.

We walked outside the shop and seated ourselves on a bench to the side of the front door. I took a deep breath, looking at the trees surrounding the newly-developed shopping area. It used to be a little Swiss village with a cozy restaurant built of stone called the Chalet. Now the village was a town, paved with cement, featuring a crowded McDonald's restaurant and another around the lake—a grill with a smoky, noisy bar.

My thoughts came back to the woman beside me on the bench, who sat patiently in anticipation. I took another deep breath, relaxed myself, and went to that place in my consciousness where I can merge my awareness into another's energy field. I began by telling the shopkeeper that from my point of view, she needed to trust her feelings about her dilemma and that the move about which she was ambivalent would be stimulating for her.

I continued, telling her that her husband—I got the name "Bernie"—who had passed over several years ago was around her. He wanted to remind her that she knew from the time seven years ago, when she went through this with "the boy," that it didn't work out. He also related a private joke from the past. Then I also saw her—a glimpse into a probable future—walking over a significant hill in arid terrain, in very practical shoes.

She nodded, looking both relieved and sad, and said that the night before she had prayed that God would send her someone with an answer to her problem—whether to let her son come back and live with her, as she had allowed him to do seven years before, or to do what she really yearned to do—to move to the desert by the "hill" she loves and open another shop.

Her husband was still the same evolving soul, sharing his point of view, as was I, also lending another point of view. We were both simply confirming that she should trust her heart.

We never know the part we're playing in another's drama, often backing into another's path in a very significant way. Even without our awareness, all the pieces fit perfectly into each other's puzzles. Always.

The woman thanked me, and stepped back into her shop. I remained seated on the bench, thinking about how I used to come up here when I was growing up. My family had been invited here for several Fourth of July weekends by a family whose father was a dentist and accomplished violinist. My mother used to accompany him on the piano.

The family was Mormon and very religious. I was raised a mild Presbyterian. My father entrusted the spiritual development of my three brothers and me to my mother, saying to her, "You take care of their spirits; I'll take care of their physical needs." He lived his life with an open heart and stressed the importance of living with honesty, integrity, and dignity. But it was confusing to me to have to go to church with my mother, the church organist, while my father played golf. Why was it important for me to go but not important for my father?

I always felt a special, personal closeness to Christ and my own understanding of what I believe He came to teach. I could not relate to what I was supposed to be learning in Sunday school and I guess that Lane, my twin brother, must have had a similar problem with religious dogma.

He and I used to ditch classes to spend our collection money at the Foster's "Frosty Freeze," only two long blocks from the church. We'd return in plenty of time to meet Mother, mingling among the exiting congregation. I guess that's probably one of the most deceptive deeds I can remember committing in my respectable childhood.

Compared to the mild Presbyterian dogma which failed to engage me, the ways of other religions seemed mysterious and even ominous to me. Whenever I think about how we people on this earth group ourselves by races, religions, and any possible ways that emphasize "them and us"—that anyone different from ourselves is strange, even weird or wrong—I see us all as tribes. We move around in bunches, adopt the customs of those who have settled nearby, and are suspicious and condemning of those who live on the other side of the hill, who might differ from us in any way.

The night that John F. Kennedy was elected, my mother and father sat in silence. A Catholic president. Judging from their speechless reaction, I could only estimate that this meant disastrous ramifications. I interrupted the historical moment by asking if this meant that now all Americans would have to become Catholic, cross themselves when they prayed, and eat fish on Fridays.

The ways of the Mormon family who used to invite us to their second home in that beautiful mountain resort were no less mysterious and strange to me. Parents have a way of letting out just enough information about things in life, leaving the child to arrive at her own outrageous conclusions.

Mother had mentioned something that I understood to be that a Mormon woman has to wear some kind of tee shirt at all times in order to get to heaven to be reunited with her husband. I tried to figure out how our lovely hostess would take a shower or wear a bathing suit, forever wearing that special tee shirt.

I looked forward to sneaking peeks of her in her suit when we would go water skiing, but she never came with us. Years later, her husband ran off with another woman, and I wondered if his ex-wife still had to wear the camisole to be reunited with the man who had left her.

It is the true way of our soul to connect us with all of our fellow beings, knowing no boundaries or differences. Evidence of intersecting paths is just one more way that emphasizes our inter-connectedness.

Train in China

Kim was very wealthy, having invented, developed, and marketed a successful car product. She was proud of her success, but less so about her life. Long ago, she made a vow that she never forgot. It became the focus of her life, her motivation, and her obsession. The success from her invention bought her a slick and glittery lifestyle. It afforded her all the cocaine she could use and more unhappiness than she ever could have dreamed.

In reality, the depth of the fulfillment that she received from her success was very shallow. The vow she'd made gave her great determination, but it came from her pain and hurt, not from having set forth higher intentions from the soul.

I viewed a new beginning for Kim in her reading—a move, a new relationship, a new way of operating in her life. This time her victories wouldn't be the results of her old determination; they would be because Kim had given up. The momentum that she'd gained from the vow she made years ago had ceased.

Before Kim moved to California, she lived in the east. By her early twenties, she was in a relationship with Jim, the one she believed to be her true love. They "recognized" each other instantly, thought each other's thoughts, dreamed the same dreams, and eventually agreed to spend the rest of their lives together.

Jim was from a very old and moneyed family, and Kim from one with more modest aspirations and income. That was the staging for the circumstances played out by Kim and her true love, which read like those in an epic novel, or the Sunday Night Movie.

When Jim and Kim decided to make plans for marriage, Jim's mother secretly took Kim aside to tell her that she wanted her to leave her son's life. She didn't feel that Kim matched the quality of Jim's character, the greatness of his vision, or the sophistication of the lifestyle in which he'd been raised. She assured Kim that she would make her life miserable if she married her son, and offered her a large sum of money to simply disappear from her precious son's life.

Kim was well aware of the strong ties binding Jim to his family. In spite of her love for him, she was not enthused about signing up for a future with such a vindictive, venomous mother-in-law. She took the payoff money and disappeared to the west coast. But she vowed (I picture Scarlett O'Hara's last scene) that she would one day show that woman that she would more than survive her rejection. She would achieve money and success in her own right. And that she did, along with all that it bought her.

During the time of the Nixon administration when US relations were being restored with China, Kim was invited to join a group that was among the first to be allowed to travel by train through that country. It was on that trip that she experienced how purposefully one's path intersects with another's.

Kim was staring out the window by her seat on the train, shocked at the reality of the people in the streets, the violence and the disorder. Suddenly she heard a loud laugh at the back of the train. She knew immediately to whom that unmistakable laugh belonged. Kim remembered hearing stories about Jim's sister, the disconcerting non-conformist of the family. And she recognized the laugh as identical to that of her brother Jim.

Kim made her way down the crowded aisle to the seats at the rear of the train, and introduced herself to the woman whose laugh had called to her. They talked, and at the end of their conversation, Jim's sister said that there was something she thought that Kim should know. She said that Jim never got over losing her. He eventually married a woman who had gained their mother's blessing, the sister related, rolling her eyes. And she said the name Jim chose for his first daughter was Kim.

Kim smiled and said, "Please do one thing for me. Tell your mother that you and I met here, on this train in

China. Maybe she'll realize there's a greater play than one she could ever direct."

Another confirming tale about intersecting paths involves a woman whom I met years ago in a hotel. My husband and I had sailed down the coast to the Ritz Carlton, a lovely new hotel a few hours (by water) from where we lived.

My husband was in one of his silent, depressed moods, so I decided to entertain myself by joining in the afternoon tea that had just been laid out in the alcove at one end of our floor. There I met Rita, her husband, daughter, and son-in-law. Rita was in her eighties, but looked to be in her early sixties.

Very intuitive, she looked over at me and noticed the absence of my husband. She began talking about how she had long ago learned to do what she needed to, in order to take care of herself within her marriage. She nodded over towards her husband, dressed in tennis shorts, chatting enthusiastically with his daughter and son-in-law about that afternoon's match.

She said that she loved cruises, but he liked to fly. So when they traveled, she'd go by boat and he'd leave after her, traveling by air. Then they'd meet at their destination. She loved sunsets; he couldn't care less, but he'd be the first to point out a beautiful one to her, for her enjoyment.

Rita said that there was a period in her life when she became immobilized by agoraphobia, unable to drive anywhere and fearful of venturing out. One day in the market, suddenly overcome with anxiety and on the verge of passing out, she made a conscious choice to conquer her fears, rather than allowing them to paralyze her.

In the next months she took small steps towards healing her fears, and gradually brought herself to the point of driving on the freeway, up one on-ramp, and off the next exit, up more on-ramps, off more exits. As she attempted driving greater distances, she continued to assure herself that she could always go right back off the freeway at the next exit.

At one point in our conversation, she looked down, reflecting a little sadly. She said that her present marriage was comfortable, and that she had put a lot of effort into making it work. But, she said, her husband wasn't her true love.

She continued, telling me that years ago she had been a clothing designer in New York. The one she loved, a man named Jack Pernod, became consumed—incurably, she believed—with alcohol. After much grief, she decided to move out to California to start a new life.

Rita eventually married her present husband, and together they raised their daughter. There came a day when her daughter phoned to say that she had met an interesting man. She thought that she might invite him to join them at their next outing to the Hollywood Bowl.

"Wonderful!" Rita replied to her daughter's suggestion. "What's his name?"

"Bill," answered her daughter. "Bill Pernod."

"Oh. That's interesting. Would you ask him, please, if he has any relatives named Jack?" Rita inquired.

Rita's daughter eventually married Bill, who turned out to be the son of Rita's past love. She learned that Bill's father had died of alcoholism. And now his son was her son-in-law.

Trusting the interweaving of our paths and the sometimes karmic directions in which they lead us, we can know there is a much greater road map beyond our limited, linear perceptions. It will connect us up with those whom we've invited back into our play, without fail.

Soulmates and the Holographic Partner

I wish there were more ways to convey to a client how real a future partner is, one who already exists in his/her future. But then again, the frustration, loneliness, and emptiness from yearning for a soulmate can eventually create the impetus to give up the hunt and to focus on and live in the present, striving towards sovereignty.

Sheryl did everything she could think of to take care of herself in her personal and professional life. She tried hard not to live with the yearning for a soulmate, challenged to maintain a healthy balance in being a strong independent woman, while allowing herself to remain open, vulnerable, and receptive. Sheryl was in her mid-thirties, and the energy she put into her career helped divert anxieties concerning biological clocks.

In one of her very first readings, I told her that there was a soul who had chosen her, to come to her as a daughter. (The soul is the one I mentioned earlier, who was hovering around the prospective mother, saying, "And I'm going to want some of that saltwater taffy!") Sheryl was comforted to know that although she saw no prospective husband in sight that she would one day have the family she had desired since she was very young.

Some women feel guilty in having no longing for a husband and/or a child. I have a friend, my daughter's "Fairy Godmother," who has never felt compelled to be a mother, but was invaluable to me, helping ease me into motherhood. "Huh? Punky-Poo?" I repeated slowly, echoing her cooing to my first-born. She has a gift with children, and I've seen many of her own "etheric children" around her, from past life spaces. Her soul had no need to pull her towards her own mothering experience this time.

Sheryl came months later for a reading, wanting guidance about some choices concerning her job. We covered that and other issues in her life, and then I moved into a scene of a man standing by a small stream. I said to Sheryl, "There is one who stands overlooking water, wondering when he will know you. This is the one you will marry."

Time passed, and Sheryl did meet Dick. Early into their relationship, Dick took Sheryl to meet his mother in the east. He took her to the grassy bank by the stream, where he used to go to think alone, wondering when he'd meet his love.

Sheryl and Dick had grown individually from the challenges in their separate lives, until the perfect timing for their paths to intersect brought them together to extend that growth within a relationship. A year after their marriage, the little girl was born.

Certain special relationships seem to be predetermined intersections (or "strong future events") in people's paths. Clients yearn for these mates, sometimes because they have an intuitive sense that there *will* be a special person in their future. The challenge lies in trusting the right timing of these connections, which the impatient little self usually perceives most inaccurately.

Scenes in readings that reveal clients' future relationships occasionally appear to me as very alive holograms. The holographic image of the person who exists in the client's future moves into my vision and relates to the client in her present.

The first time this happened, I was visiting Cynthia, a friend who had assisted me for years with my classes. We were sitting on the sun porch in the house where she was staying. In social interactions, I'm usually not at the same level of consciousness at which I do readings, but when I'm with Cynthia, our combined energies make it difficult to avoid extra-sensory perceptions.

I suddenly saw the image of a man I had been seeing in her readings for several years. I viewed the same details from past future glimpses, but this time he was walking out onto the sun porch to join us! It was as if he thought we were in *his* present, taking time out from watching something on the television to come chat with us. "What are you girls up to?" was his greeting.

He was talking about people that he and Cynthia knew, so I telepathically started asking him some questions about his work, his hobbies, and his life in general. He answered, but didn't seem to notice the fact that we were in his past.

Cynthia could feel him, saying that he felt quite familiar, although they hadn't yet met in her present. She said that she could easily have said to him, "Don't forget to pick up the cleaning tomorrow on your way home!" Sometimes that strong sense of familiarity can be attributed to past life space connections, and sometimes we're already communing with another on the astral plane before connecting in the physical.

It was very comforting to Cynthia, even as she continues to focus on her personal growth and independence as if she alone is all that there will be. But in weak moments, she remembers the visit from one whom she will know, when both have accomplished what they first came to do apart.

The Girl with the Cane

I opened the door to my morning client, a beautiful, red-headed girl in her early thirties. She smiled, introduced herself as Kate, and walked in very slowly, steadying herself with a cane. The girl's mother, whom I had read a few months before, followed closely behind, reintroducing herself. As I escorted them to my living room, I tried to remember what had come in her mother's reading concerning a daughter, although it's usually very difficult to pull up information from past readings. But it seemed that I would have remembered picking up on a child with a disability.

The mother checked to make sure the daughter was comfortable, helping her onto my couch. She started to leave, hesitantly, saying that she'd be back in an hour. I chatted with the girl for a few minutes before giving the invocation and tuning in. Having listened to the Intro Tape, she said that she agreed with the information and was accustomed to living in accordance with much of it. She added that it put into words many subtle thoughts that she had carried for years, something that I hear often from clients.

I'm told that the Intro Tape gets passed around quite a bit. One client was referred by his favorite waitress, who had given him the tape. Another called from the east, saying that her chiropractor had given it to her. A couple in Iowa were listening to it as they took a drive on a trip through mountains. The husband said that he became so engrossed by it that he accidentally hit a deer. Maybe I should put a warning sticker on the Intro Tape: Do not listen to this tape while operating heavy machinery.

No one can imagine what I went through to record that tape. I think that my subconscious fought me all the way, stirring up old soul memories and fears about what communicating my truth has cost me in other times. Of course any persecution, on some level, has to have been reflecting back some of my own hesitation.

When I was ready to record the Intro Tape, I (accidentally) spilled a glass of water all over the recorder. Then, while rearranging logs in the fireplace, I burned my hand (the one used for operating the tape recorder). I finally finished the first complete version, having monitored the volume and recording quality as I went along, but when I finished, I could barely hear my voice on the tape.

My inevitable solution was to rent the back room of the local video shop, where I sat on a stool for six hours. I had to stop the owner's equipment every time a customer came toward the back of the shop to survey the "adults only" video selections. In spite of my subconscious efforts to sabotage the project, I finally did complete it.

I wasn't very far into Kate's reading when I stopped, opened my eyes, and said to her, "I just have to tell you that this disease is simply not a part of you! You're really not attached to it! You've only hooked up with it temporarily for it to symbolically connect you to a plea from another time, which went out and was heard. It's come around now, through this disease, the opportunity for you to experience that which will set you free—from what you have prayed to be released!"

When I picked up on her in her mother's reading, I didn't see her physically handicapped in any way. Now, as she sat before me, I was not seeing her affliction as part of her. Some people actually become their disease, just as people can become their fears. Both can get interwoven into our identities, especially when holding on to them serves a purpose. We can use physical illness as a challenge to lead us deeper into our beliefs and fears, or it can provide a justification to give up. Either option is a choice, a preference.

I closed my eyes again and let myself go to a deeper level, to see more that would explain what I had just sensed about Kate. I turned all the way to my left, further to the left than where I view clients' childhoods, as opposed to the future scenes which I see to my right. It's amusing to me that although I view scenes that exist in a non-linear dimension, I seem to watch them lined up, linearly, around the client.

Far to my left I watched a concurrent past life space, wherein Kate still existed as a very old woman. I moved closer into the scene, and described what I was observing. She was huddled over a gnarled cane, walking out of town to a place where the death of that physical self would take place. It's usually important to view the deathbed scene, to see the challenges or unfinished business with which the soul is about to exit, and this little vignette seemed no less revealing.

I moved into the consciousness of the old woman and felt anger, bitterness, and a strong sense of betrayal. Even more, I felt feelings of deep regret that she had allowed vindictiveness to eat away at her, and eventually at her withered, stooped old body.

She was thinking about a man who lived in a large estate up the mountain behind the town, overlooking a large valley. She had carried anger for the man most of that adult life. In her late teens, he had taken advantage of her, impregnating her, and never came forward to identify himself as the father or to give her son his name.

Even more, to cloak his embarrassment, he had publicly scorned and condemned her as an evil woman, causing her to be ostracized by neighbors and family. She lived that life in loneliness, and in absorbing the beliefs and fears of those around her, their condemnation became her own self-scorn.

It's fascinating to me when I view a concurrent past scene that connects so clearly and directly to what the person is acting out in the present life space. I've mentioned the client I viewed with the parasol in the 1700s—having thoughts about her possessive husband—step off a wooden sidewalk into the street and onto my couch. She was presently in a quandary about freeing herself from the rigid expectations of her current spouse.

The old woman, as I watched her in Kate's reading, hobbling out of town to the end of her life, connected with no time or space existing between her and the young woman who sat before me. I went on, relating that she had picked up that thread in this life experience, recreating a variation of the same theme in order to free herself from the crippling anger she carried about the man who lived on the mountain.

Then I saw what I see much too often in readings. When I view a wandering hand coming toward a client in their past, it usually means sexual abuse. A fast hand and arm taking a swipe at the client usually signifies physical abuse.

I said, "I can see that a stepfather, your mother's second husband, molested you when you were young."

She said, "Yes, that's true."

I continued, "And I can see that your stepfather had many issues to resolve with your stepbrother, the son he had with your mother."

"Yes, they have their problems," she answered.

Then I went on to say that it seemed that her step-father had played the past role of the man who lived on the hill, by whom she had conceived that illegitimate child, and her stepbrother had been that son. They had all jumped in together again, with a strong pull to sort it all out.

Now Kate had the opportunity to allow, feel, identify, and release those negative emotions, to vindicate herself and reaffirm her true, whole identity. In releasing all that still lingered within her, all that her physical body was now presenting, she had the potential to move on, freer, healed, and empowered.

We talked about ways that she might think about validating herself after the humiliation from the sexual abuse. Kate was concerned about her mother's defensive reaction whenever she attempted to discuss the repeated molestation by her mother's ex-husband. Confrontation only stirred up her mother's guilt about being a good mother.

I recommended family counseling and added that I was impressed with the abilities of many very intuitive therapists I've met. I find that they are especially capable of facilitating the healing of clients who have been involved in such situations. Many of these therapists have a growing intention to respond to the whole individual, helping to integrate an awareness of the timeless soul of the client.

I reminded Kate that all paths intersect, that each player in her drama is playing something out that has a potential for healing and growth, and that no one can resolve another's challenges.

Finally, I viewed a probable future around Kate where she sat on a stool by a counter in her house. She was running her own business, and doing some very creative and meaningful writing, stimulated by her experiences. I looked everywhere into that (future) room, and could not find the cane.

Suicides

Those who perceive life from a metaphysical point of view often hold a belief about suicide that when one makes the choice to end his life, he risks returning back to this dimension too quickly, doomed to repeat similar challenges. The cycle brings him right back to where he ended his life.

In other words, there are no short cuts, no matter how intolerable one's life appears. The unfinished business tempting one to "check out" stays with the soul and continues to keep it booked on return trips until resolution and balance is achieved. I envision souls leaving the physical dimension after suicide, going to the light, then looking back, thinking, "Shoot! I forgot how long it took me to get that body in which to work through those challenges." Then the soul rushes right back in to repeat it all again.

When I become aware of an individual who has chosen suicide, I encourage the friends and family to send that soul thoughts—telepathically or in their prayers—to encourage him to take the time he needs to reflect back and learn about the alternative choices that are available in life.

Seth (who channeled through Jane Roberts) mentions that when souls who have chosen suicide arrive on the other side, a state of amnesia is created to allow the soul to reflect back without the memory of how the life was ended. This lets the soul consider other options that might have been chosen, those which would have allowed it to move through and out of the difficult challenge forever.

That information becomes part of the soul's awareness and an influencing factor toward making other choices in the next experience. Apparently this reflecting process, considering new paths that would have resulted from making different choices, adds to the soul's growth almost as effectively as having experienced them in the physical.

Keeping this metaphysical caveat in mind regarding suicide, I also believe that one simply cannot judge a soul for making that choice. Two contrasting examples demonstrate this.

Netta had been very concerned about her husband Bill for over a year. His business had failed, and he had become increasingly depressed, showing less and less motivation or energy to do more than sit on the couch each day. Bill had been very proud of the financial success he had previously attained for his wife and two small children, having strived ambitiously since his move from a small eastern town to the west coast.

He had focused on making business-wise moves, often referring to all that's required to achieve "success in the fast lane." He at one time owned several properties and was proud of his material acquisitions. Netta had often suggested to Bill that they dismantle their financially demanding life and move back home to a simpler, less stressful lifestyle. She'd also encouraged him to seek counseling, which he did for a short time.

One night Netta's neighbor called to ask for my help. That evening remains a vivid memory. The neighbor told me that earlier in the day, the hospital had notified Netta that Bill had been brought in DOA. Bill had shot himself. The neighbor said that Netta asked that I stay for the night, when she would have to tell the children that their father had died.

I took the time to explain my departure to my children, then drove over to Netta's house. We cried together as Netta recounted the startling events of the day. Then we composed ourselves, hearing Netta's son come in through the front door.

I stood by while Netta explained to Brad, her seven-year-old son, what had happened to his father. His younger sister was still playing at a friend's house. "He did it because he loved us," Netta told Brad.

"He wasn't able to provide for us any more, and wanted to leave us the insurance money."

"Didn't he know that we'd rather have *him* than the money?!" protested Brad.

All during that emotional evening, I continued to feel Bill's presence. I mentioned to Netta that he was there, and to send thoughts to him, guiding him to the light and encouraging him to take his time in reflecting back and learning from the life he'd just left. For years, Netta had heard me relate about my metaphysical adventures, and I felt she was never quite sure of what to make of them. But she seemed to understand what I was saying to her.

I felt Bill's presence again at bedtime that night, and saw a life space around him that revealed a "karmic debt" that may have been repaid. I watched him as a very ambitious landowner who mercilessly taxed the peasants who leased and worked his land. Then I saw a family with several children who lived in a very small cottage on that land. The father was a tenant, struggling and despairing, unable to pay the high taxes. The last scene showed me that the man eventually hanged himself.

Life challenges created from karmic issues involve circumstances that pull and influence a soul towards experiencing a particular outcome. The experiences often involve playing out the other end of past scenarios. I call that "literal karma."

A person always has free will choices, but unless the soul has awakened, he or she will more or less be pulled along the karmic conveyor belt. Becoming conscious in life allows the soul to jump off the conveyor belt and come to new realizations, free to make new choices. In Bill's case, it seems that even the decision to commit suicide may have come within the parameters of a choice-less karmic drama enactment. The act itself is what he returned to and was pushed to experience.

Another experience involved Dan, a down-to-earth, pragmatic psychiatrist and family friend. He had a very different way of looking at suicide when his son, Randy, made that choice. Randy was a troubled young adult who had struggled with drug abuse for quite some time. He was on a group outing one day from the rehabilitation facility where he had been staying.

The group was driving home on a busy freeway in a small pick-up truck, after spending all day at the beach. Randy had jumped into the back of the truck with a few of the others. He took off his watch and jacket and handed them to one of the other boys. He then jumped from the truck out onto the freeway, where he was killed instantly.

Dan gave a beautiful eulogy at his son's memorial service, saying that although he grieved deeply for the loss of his son, he thought that he understood. He felt that for the first time, Randy had made a courageous, definitive choice about his life, even though it was to end it.

Dan wasn't advocating suicide, but he knew his son and knew that Randy was tired of all the failed attempts to redirect his life; that he was unable to access in himself the tools to do so. Dan understood what Randy had done, perhaps choosing to "go back to the drawing board" for a new game plan.

Some might hesitate to view a suicide in such a light. It may be helpful to recognize that there are many less definitive ways that people end their lives by the choices they make concerning their health, relationships, jobs, and lifestyles. There are many forms of suicide.

Another situation demonstrates the fast return and repetition that can result from suicide choices. A client and friend, Lois, had a cousin, Nan, who had a difficult childhood, living back and forth between her natural father, and her mother and stepfather. Eventually she chose to live with her mother, stepfather, half-sister, and half-brother. Nan became an extremely difficult teenager, disrupting the family with her uncontrollable behavior.

Nan's mother finally sent her back to live with her father, feeling helpless and unwilling to let Nan pull the family apart. Nan tried to reach her mother for several years, but her calls were rejected and letters returned. By the time Nan was a young adult, she had also been turned away by her father, her behavior having become too much for him to handle.

Nan eventually became a nurse and joined a branch of the military service. She sought psychiatric help for herself, but eventually committed suicide through carbon monoxide poisoning.

One cannot judge the choices of another, for one cannot understand the limits of another's tolerance or point of "overload." Nan's mother was on a journey that challenged her to make choices that would enable her to take care of herself, sometimes by setting clear boundaries. Both mother and daughter had very difficult challenges, magnified by the intersecting of their paths.

I used to feel Nan around at times and sensed that she would soon be returning. Then Nan's half-brother and his wife had the family's first grandchild, a little girl. I felt strongly that Nan was back to try it again, this time as her mother's granddaughter, returning as the first child of her brother. My hope is that the new positioning of this soul will allow her and her family to move through the difficult challenges that tempted her exit when my client knew her as her cousin Nan.

Lois remembered her grandmother hinting to her that something was bothering her. It was after the first visit from that great-granddaughter, who was now three or four years old. The little girl had gone into her grand-mother's kitchen and asked if she had any "doughnut holes." They had been Nan's favorite treat, and she always asked her grandmother for them whenever she visited.

Free will allows us to make choices in our lives. As we awaken, we expand, and that expansion makes us conscious of many additional alternatives from which we can choose. We still feel despair and pain, but that expanded, higher vantage point helps us detach and observe ourselves within the context of the bigger picture. The ability to do that then helps us consider alternatives to suicide. Again, at any point in one's evolution, a soul can step off that karmic conveyor belt, come to new realizations, and make new choices.

Divine plan is carried out when we operate the best we can within the scope of our knowledge, intuition, and higher intentions in each present moment. That is when we can trust the choices that we make.

PART TWO

The Other Side—
What They Communicate

Chapter Ten
Not So Far Away

When souls who have passed over—having gone to the light—project themselves from "the Other Side" into a reading, they're not coming from some "place." They project themselves from the non-physical dimension that exists *within* our more visible, physical dimension.

Discarnate souls are only a thought away. It's like bringing forward a plate or hologram that reflects their essence with all its thoughts and memories. Realities exist within realities, and some people are more sensitive to sensing, hearing, or seeing beyond this most obvious, dense physical one.

There are people who sample other realities, when deep in meditation, and describe having traveled up a helix similar to the structure of a DNA molecule. Stuart Wilde in his delightful book, *Affirmations,* writes about many trips up such a tunnel and believes that it is the same one through which people report they have traveled in near-death experiences.

Years ago I gave a reading that was one of the most futuristic ones I have experienced. I viewed glimpses of times ahead when we will have dislodged enough sludge from our collective consciousness to again be the light receivers of gifts and abilities that were once inherent in us. This was before we became as heavy and dense as this dimension in which we came to play. I viewed people working in centers, able to communicate telepathically and literally able to open doors with their focused thoughts. Beautiful gardens grew outdoors, healthy and lush, without chemicals. There was a pervading feeling of oneness among everyone, except for a few souls on the perimeter (of what, I'm not sure—larger than centers but smaller than cities) who still held on to thoughts of separateness, of "them and us"—beliefs that kept them held in the bondage of negative emotions and fears.

The message that came through as I viewed these scenes was that we were approaching times of "boundarilessness"—no boundaries between people and no more illusion about the boundaries between the physical and non-physical dimension. People will also be conscious of their own abilities to travel back and forth between dimensions, in and out of the body, many even *with* the body.

Death will not be feared, but will be recognized as an illusion, the shedding of the physical vehicle. People will have come to trust their awareness and memories of "going to the light" and will communicate easily with souls on either side.

Shifts in mass consciousness now taking place will have helped us to trust the unseen and non-rational awareness without fear or ridicule. We will have indeed progressed from five-sensory to multi-sensory beings.

Unaccustomed to perceiving life beyond the physical illusion, some people have a hard time believing that we don't "die," or that we live many life experiences. At the same time, they may have no doubts that they can feel the presence of a deceased family member. They've just never thought to doubt it. When a client wants to know how to tell if a loved one is making a quick visit, I tell them that if they are thinking about something else and suddenly get thoughts about Grandma Mae, she's probably there.

I have several clients who have experienced seeing a loved one or friend make an appearance at the foot of their bed on their way to passing over, as the friend left the physical body. Some even preplan the communication with some sort of sign that the passing spouse will signal back (upon his or her arrival), confirming their aliveness, wellness, and continued existence.

On several occasions a loved one has been referred for a reading in an "amazing way" (but not really) so that the "departed" one can deliver the message. A woman once called from Los Angeles, saying that the night before she dreamed that her deceased mother was telling her to call. In the dream she found herself in a phone booth, frantically searching through a phone book.

"But I don't know the *number!*" she remembered calling out.

"Here it is," her mother replied, and she gave her daughter my business phone number. The woman awakened the next morning with the information still clear in her mind, and decided to call the number.

"What is it that you *do?*" she asked, when I answered her call.

"Are you sitting down?" I answered, and proceeded to tell her.

Some people attribute way too much wisdom to the projections of discarnate souls, simply because they're no longer in the physical body. When we're out of the body, we are still the same evolving souls—the same energy with the same thoughts, emotions, and lessons to learn. Some feel that since loved ones are no longer stuck here, that they must know a whole lot more than we do. When souls join us in readings, it's truly like coming to join us for coffee. How much power would you give the input from your next door neighbor, or your past employer?

Souls often come to join in on the theme I am about to present in a reading, to add their impression. They often give examples of memories to demonstrate that the love is never lost. Or they come to lend another point of view, to relate positive messages, or to help resolve unfinished business. (It's never too late, but best to resolve issues while still in this space!)

Interpreting and relaying communications from these souls is sometimes challenging for me, because (a) the communication is done telepathically and (b) their thoughts aren't restricted by sequential time. Therefore, they will often know the thoughts I am gathering to present to the client. While I'm still trying to formulate a way to communicate them in an orderly fashion, they will add their two cents worth. Or two or three souls might arrive at the same time, all projecting at once. (Whoopie Goldberg's character in the movie *Ghost* wasn't that far off!) So I often have to telepathically ask them to stand in line until I'm ready to speak their thoughts.

If I am about to present a theme concerning a woman's repeated pattern of attracting unhealthy relationships, time after time attracting what feels familiar—for example, what she knew with her father—the deceased father might pop in to add that he's now learning new tools about opening the heart, the release of emotions, and is looking forward to giving it another try back here in the physical. A father who was abusive to a son might come to give some insights about behavior patterns that had continued to pass from one generation to another, cheering on the son, encouraging him to break from the old ways.

Interspersed with these messages are details of memories which are fresh to the discarnate soul but which take more time for the client to remember. Sometimes they transmit private jokes or unforgotten, memorable scenes. Some of the messages are very touching and intricate in their meaning. They help people release old grudges, to see past situations in a new light, and, most importantly, confirm that life doesn't end.

When the souls communicate these messages, they project themselves in ways that will be easily recognizable, in certain outfits with certain physical characteristics emphasized. A deceased spouse might project herself in the pink wedding suit, fluffing up her ever-permed hair with dainty hands, and half-closing one eye as she laughed. (This also indicates to me, how strong a sense or thought-form the entity still carries of the "past" physical self.)

I once read a recently retired man who hadn't listened to my Intro Tape. Unaware of this, I presented all that I was viewing, rapidly and in a matter-of-fact manner. I was dealing with some of his past themes when I felt his deceased brother arrive.

"And Vito is here, projecting a scene of where you both went fishing years ago, on a beautiful river that flowed by steep canyon walls. That's where he finds himself, and to where he will help you over, when it's time for your transition."

"Vito?" he exclaimed? *"Vito, here? Vito's dead!"*

I opened my eyes and looked at my client, thinking of how to backtrack, and to gently fill him in about the fact that we don't die. I did the best I could, and he then responded, a little more informed, "Then Vito's not still mad at me?" I was pleased to be able to assure him that the energy he had known as Vito was taking another look at things and learning a lot.

I was even more pleased to respond to his last question, that no, he would not be going to hell. Even more, I was able to confirm to him that he and his very intuitive wife weren't that far off from manifesting their wish—to stage their eventual "lift of?" in close proximity to each other, within the natural flow of their life together.

Sometimes it feels like the visiting soul is being counseled to come forward and communicate the new insights that he is learning from his teachers as he reflects back on his life.

The revelations that souls convey, resulting from viewing their lives from new angles or from a greater vista, bring about important shifts for them, just as new insights do for us while we're still in the body. The messages are usually very loving, positive, and reflective about the ongoing growth of the soul that continues beyond this dimension—most of the time.

I relay messages the best I can, but can draw only from my own repertoire of experiences to interpret them. I told one client, David, that Fred, an old friend of his, was present, joking about a Vicky, and making motions that looked like a vaudeville act of someone losing his toupee as it was pulled off by a string by someone behind a curtain.

David said that they had worked together and, until Fred's dying day, they had mistakenly called a co-worker

Vicky when her name was really Becky. David found out the mistake after Fred's passing. Fred wanted to let David know that he knew. David added that Fred had committed suicide and had shot off the top of his head.

I could tell that Fred hadn't paid much attention to his lessons while here, on his "tour of duty," and still seemed distracted from what he needed to be learning from where he now found himself. I sent him the thoughts that it would be a good idea for him to turn back around and pay attention to his teachers, lest he rush back in—as those who have exited from suicides tend to do—often repeating the same choices.

A space occurs between lives where we rest, reflect, and regroup, so to speak. I often took my classes back to that space, where they were able to grasp much about their journeys—the roles they have played out and for what purposes. Many therapists have learned a lot from patients who, under hypnosis, have gone to those between-life spaces. Dr. Brian Weiss, author of *Many Lives, Many Masters,* discusses how enlightening this has been for him. Helen Wambach documented countless regressions in her book, *Life Before Life,* of people who detailed their experiences in that enlightening space.

When we leave our physical bodies behind, we aren't flown or swept away to some place and we aren't lowered or banished to purgatory. Our energy is simply transformed, no longer pulled by the lower vibrations of the physical plane. We continue on to meet with loved ones and teachers and to reflect back on the experiences we leave behind but which remain a cumulative part of ourselves. The good is never lost, but the negativity, bitterness, vindictiveness, and fears that go with us will continue to influence our future realities.

The less unfinished business we leave behind, the less debris exists to pull us back here. We're then free to move to higher vibrations, to explore many more dimensions and realities.

Chapter Eleven
Gratitude

Thank You for Victoria Street

I experience many readings which demonstrate that feelings of love and gratitude go with us beyond what is too often understood as life's end. The soul records and retains the essence and gifts from all our earthly experiences. Souls often take the opportunity to come forward in a reading to convey this.

One particular soul who had gone to the light did this, presenting himself into Clara's reading with a projection of the male body he had inhabited before his passing. His thoughts were very clear and lucid, and he seemed very pleased to be able to join us. Apparently his thoughts had been quite foggy during his convalescence at the end of his life. But he wanted Clara to know that he had been aware of everything that had gone on, and he showed me the scene where she had tended to him, sitting at his bedside.

"Thank you for Victoria Street," were his thoughts of gratitude, which I related to Clara.

"That's where my father stayed until he died, in a nursing home on Victoria Street!" exclaimed Clara, smiling, as she made the connection. "He had Alzheimer's Disease and required complete custodial care by then. He seemed 'out of touch,' but I continued to talk to him as if he were aware. I had to trust that he could understand me."

Friends and relatives who have left the physical dimension often present themselves in readings to confirm that they had complete awareness of all that transpired before their passing, despite the condition of their bodies at that time.

I recall another reading wherein I viewed a present scene of a client's mother. I saw her lying in a bed beside a window with Venetian blinds drawn, having been in a coma for several months. There were many loving souls who waited for her on the other side for the time of her passing. My client asked if I could see what kept her mother from leaving her body, which was now barely functioning.

Sometimes a coma provides a soul with needed time to pause, to go into neutral before either returning to consciousness or making the transition out of the physical body. I've also seen people who have become immobilized by a stroke when they needed to slow things down, to pay more attention to life. The effects of the stroke can force a person to watch and experience life in slow motion.

In this case, I moved into Clara's mother's consciousness and sensed that it was fear and worry that kept her clinging to her body and the physical plane. Then I sensed that her fear was for the beloved cat that she would have to leave behind.

I suggested to my client that when she went to visit her mother later that day, she talk to her, assuring her that the cat would be well cared for, that she need not worry. My client called a few days later, leaving a message that she had given her mother those assurances. She was grateful to report that her mother had passed over peacefully the next day.

We are most definitely able to retain awareness of all that's transpiring around us, even when the mind isn't functioning properly. We travel in our astral body, learning and experiencing outside of the physical body, and our consciousness goes with our thought projections beyond time and space. It's not surprising to me when souls who have made their transition come forward to report back that they had known and heard all that was occurring around them before passing, despite the condition of their bodies at the time.

We need the body, a vehicle, in which to function and experience this dimension, but the ability for us to sense our world (and others in it) goes way beyond its physical limitations.

Another time, it was my impression that an entity who appeared in a reading to convey his gratitude was well-oriented and resituated in his non-physical space "on the Other Side." He thanked my client for having been there to keep him company earlier in his life, and for comforting him at its end.

My client couldn't place him until I related the scene he gave me, one of him working on a farm. I said, "He's saying that he was the man who called the pigs!"

"Oh yes!" replied my client, finally making the connection. "He worked on my grandfather's farm. I loved spending time with him. He was never in a hurry, and he always took time to be with me. He never let me feel that I was being a nuisance. But he hasn't died! In fact, I'm on my way to the hospital, to go visit with him. He is very close to dying. I'm glad I can be with him now, knowing where he's headed!"

It's quite common for us to travel in our etheric body, going in and out of the physical body as we prepare to leave it. We meet with those who wait for us on the Other Side. And, as stated earlier, on our way out, we sometimes visit the friends who will remain behind.

One client reported that while taking a shower, she saw her mother pass by. The mother, living in England, had been very ill. My client then stepped out of the shower to answer the phone. It was a long-distance call, her brother calling to notify her that their mother had just passed over.

Messages such as these confirm the continuum of life and the loving bonds that connect us to each other. The love felt by a soul is never lost, nor is the gratitude, even after moving out of this dimension.

The Scientist and the FBI Agent

A touching expression of gratitude came through in one of Beverly's readings, which were always fascinating. They often contained flashes of action-packed suspense. Those scenes were quite a contrast from the calm "so-what-else-is-new" demeanor that she projected. I remember her first reading, as I tried to make sense of the scenes that were difficult for me to interpret, since they related to aspects of life which weren't in my repertoire of experiences.

Beverly never went into detail nor did she explain what it was that I was interpreting, but would simply nod and smile, confirming the information I received. At the end of that first reading, similar to a game show when the big clue is revealed, she informed me that she was an FBI agent. "Ah yes, that explains it," I thought, replaying some of the scenes in my head.

"And what a good one she must be," I mused, thinking about the contrasting dramatic scenes, which showed her on the job—the competent, capable, intuitive, aggressive agent—and the way that I always perceived her in her peaceful, personal life: gentle, feminine, spiritual, loving wife and mother. She seemed to keep both lives well separated.

One reading included a scene of intrigue that she felt comfortable explaining to me. I was relating other information to her, pertaining to her personal life, when a discarnate soul popped in, right into the middle of the reading, into the middle of the room. I digressed, attempting to interpret for this entity.

"He has a beard, shows himself wearing a blue shirt, and wants to thank you for your assistance in directing him towards the light! He's also saying that what you were looking for was in the cockpit." I opened one eye. Beverly smiled broadly and simply nodded. She seemed to know what this was all about.

It certainly made no sense to me. But, so as not to invade the confidentiality involved with Beverly's profession, I didn't ask her for an explanation. The visit from this soul seemed so purposeful though, that at the end of the reading, as I again opened my eyes, recalling the scene with, the visitor, I said, "Well! That was interesting!" allowing her to either drop the ball or "run with it." I guess that this case had gained clearance, and Beverly was comfortable in offering me an explanation for all that I had relayed to her.

"Do you remember the plane crash in San Luis Obispo, a few years ago?" she began.

"Yes," I answered, recalling something about a shooting on board a plane, and several people killed.

Beverly proceeded to piece together the confusing bits of information that I'd received from the man in the blue shirt. "It involved a disgruntled airline employee," she continued, "who went berserk and shot himself and others while the plane was in the air. The minute I heard about it on the news, I knew that I'd be called to investigate. Sure enough, I was paged soon thereafter and drove right to the scene of the crash.

"Several other agents and I had to sort through all the rubble and debris from the crash, searching for passenger identification. One of the most crucial aspects of the search was in finding the 'black box' which was stored in the cockpit. It held the recording of the radio transmissions—all the evidence of what transpired just before the crash.

"It was particularly difficult with this crash, because the plane nose-dived straight into the ground, embedding itself into a huge hole. We had to dig way down into the earth to reach the cockpit. The box was severely damaged, and the entire surrounding area was covered with fuel. But we found the recorder intact. I guess that this visitor was participating in our investigative efforts!"

Beverly, reflecting back on that day, said that there were some moments when she was thinking about all the souls from the crash who would be going to the light at that time. She sensed many of them around her, several feeling lost and confused.

She remembered learning that when souls experience sudden, violent death, they often go into a state of "wondering" for a while, which lets them collect their sense of being. It allows all of the events that led up to their demise to catch up with them, so to speak. So she said that she intuitively felt the need to send them all lots of light, to help them on their way.

Then she started thinking about one particular passenger whom she knew had been on board. That man was a German scientist, returning with several of his graduate students from a visit to a research facility in southern California. They had been instrumental in some research that had also involved some investigation on Beverly's part.

It had to do with the Russian and American combined interest in the atmospheric effects of Halley's Comet relative to the time of the Phobos Mission, a (not successful) Soviet project with which Americans assisted. "That's probably the connection with me that prompted him to come forward today," Beverly concluded, quite accepting that he had done so.

I would think that with all that has come into clients' readings for so many years, with all the revelations and learning material that is presented for their growth as well as mine, nothing would astonish me anymore. But when Beverly casually gave me the whole picture of what all this meant, I sat quietly, thinking about how it all fits together.

Beverly's loving thoughts, extended to the souls who had been violently catapulted out of their physical bodies in the plane crash, had been well received. That one soul in particular, only a thought away, came forward to thank her, to acknowledge and validate the intuitive thoughts she'd carried about him and others on that day. These are the kinds of realizations and confirmations that keep me doing what I do.

Chapter Twelve

Awareness

The Body I Left Behind

Doris's mother stepped into her reading near its end, just as I was summarizing all that we had covered. She had passed over a year ago, and Doris confirmed many of the memories her mother projected. Doris then became very determined with her questions.

"So what does my mother think?" Doris began, certain that her mother would know what she was talking about.

"About what?" I answered, still tuned in to her mother's thoughts.

"About what I *did!*" Doris exclaimed, sounding impatient that her mother and I weren't smarter contestants in whatever contest this was that she was trying desperately to lead us through.

"Well, I see that your mother carries memories of many things that you and she did together. What specifically do you have in mind?" I asked patiently, trying for clarification.

"The *urn!* About what I did with the *urn!*" Doris nearly shrieked, then smiled, sitting back on the couch, arms folded, looking very satisfied with whatever it was that she had done.

Silence. I couldn't pick up on what Doris was looking for, or what she wanted me to relay on behalf of her mother. So I telepathically asked her mother to comment. The mother then showed me a scene of a cemetery with headstones covered with flowers. Then I caught her thoughts and related them to Doris.

"Your mother is talking about a cemetery, and . . ."

"Yes!" Doris interrupted, "I *wanted* Mother to be buried there, for her to be placed in a beautiful coffin at the cemetery! But my sister fought me about it, and went ahead and had her cremated without my consent!"

"Your mother wants you to know that she's not there," I tried to respond, but again she interrupted.

"Not *where?* So what does she think about what I *did?"* Doris insisted.

I paused a moment, trying to let Doris's questions and her mother's thoughts fall into some comprehensible order.

"Doris," I began gently, "your mother wants you to know that she is not in that body anymore. It doesn't matter to her what you did with the body. She doesn't need it anymore."

Then Doris' mother projected another scene, that of a large dining room table with some sort of decorative arrangement in the center. I described it to Doris, and she straightened herself, now inching forward, saying, *"Yes! That's what I did! I really showed my sister! I took moth-er's ashes from the vault and put them into a centerpiece, marched right over to her house, and said, 'There! You wanted mother in ashes, you can have her, right in the middle of your table to remember her by!'"* Doris again pushed herself back on the couch, again looking very pleased with herself.

"Doris," I began again, "your mother is no longer attached to the body she left behind. It was only a vehicle that allowed her to function and move through her life here. Souls who come forward from the other side often comment on the lovely service that was given in remembrance of them, sometimes sending me the scent of the carnations or roses that filled the church. They want loved ones to know that they were also in attendance.

"After going to the light and experiencing a rest period, if needed, they are usually more involved with reflecting back on all that they learned and experienced in this life, and with their "counseling" concerning all that yet has to be experienced and balanced. Drama resulting from making final arrangements, how things are or aren't worked out, is really more engaging for the living."

I finished, then looked at Doris, who now sat on the edge of the couch with her head bowed. She was muttering to herself, "I still think that I did the right thing. My sister shouldn't have done that."

Such drama can keep a loved one busy during the grieving process until passage of time assists in the healing of the painful feelings of loss, or it can keep them from the feelings as long as they choose. Unresolved grief often transforms into anger, and family is the handiest on which to project it. As long as people stay engrossed in the resulting drama, they can effectively keep themselves from feeling the emotions that can move them through their grief. Or it can delay the healing of those emotions until the person finally becomes receptive.

I guessed that Doris was still too frightened to let herself feel the hurt from losing her mother. It didn't matter that she now had assurances that her mother still existed. She was still fixated on the drama with her sister. Fighting battles involving decisions about her mother's remains let her feel dutiful and devoted to her mother and kept her too busy to feel her own sadness.

I hoped that she would allow the feelings to move through her when she was ready, so that the unresolved emotions, held in her body, wouldn't be forced to turn inward and create illness for Doris. Then, again, each in one's own way, according to one's own, individual choices.

Mountain Man

I watched Richard drive into my courtyard, his big old Cadillac lumbering and maneuvering around the curve down into the parking area, then back around into a parking slot, gears shifting from forward to reverse, back and forth, until the car was placed perfectly between the two white lines. He seemed to be taking his time getting from his car, and I watched him reach over into the passenger's seat and then turn back to open his door, pointing an imposing walking cane affirmatively to the pavement before lifting himself out to make a slow but deliberate trip to my front stoop.

My first impulse was to run down the steps to greet him and take his arm to help him up safely. But I quickly stopped myself. There was something about the way he carried himself, with a proud dignity, rather than moving as though he would have preferred to have left his encumbered body behind in the car. He seemed to carry it with reverence and high regard. So I stood at the top of the stairs and waited, probably feeling far more uncomfortable about whatever it was that inconvenienced him than he did.

Reaching the curb, he smiled a greeting and introduced himself, then looked back down, sizing up the climb ahead. Showing intense concentration, he slowly made his way up the stairs, grasping the handrail with his free hand with each hoist of his body. He was of medium height, very muscular and tanned, and looked to be maybe in his early sixties. I figured that his disability had to have been recent, or at least minimal, for his body to be in such excellent shape, with no visible loss of muscle from a long illness or convalescence.

I had left the front door open, and he took this as an invitation to go on past me, nodding and smiling again as he made his way into the house. I indicated the way up another short flight of steps and back to the left of the mirrored wall, into the family room off the kitchen. I saw him catch a quick glimpse of himself in the mirror as he walked by it, straightening his body and tilting back his head proudly, a momentary self-satisfied pose.

Finally, he settled himself down at the near end of my L-shaped couch, resting both hands on the bulbous gold knob on the one end of his carved wooden cane, now secured between his bent knees. He gave me a broad smile, his big brown eyes twinkling, and was now ready to begin. When Richard started to speak, his voice cracked, sounding as if he were about to cry. We renewed our introductions, and he then announced why he had made the appointment. His daughter had come some months before for a reading, and had recommended that he try a session with me.

Richard explained that he had Lou Gehrig's Disease, a rare muscle-wasting affliction, which had already affected his larynx. The disease, he explained, had forced him to open his heart, make amends for past abuses with his children, and point him towards a few self-realization programs, where he'd learned about the power of the mind over the body.

He looked directly at me with his warm, now moist brown eyes, and asked when God would take away the disease. He pleaded, "I've learned from my disease. Now when will God take it back?" I answered him gently that he would have it as long as he needed to learn from it. Richard did not seem to be stuck in a victim mode, and his question told me that he had already taken responsibility for his disease, but now was impatient to be done with it.

I offered to place a pillow behind his back for support and encouraged him to relax as I seated myself in a straight-backed chair, a comfortable distance in front of him. I took a few cleansing breaths, began to relax into my invocation, and then went deeper, starting to view all the scenes around him.

It's as if the information I view and understand through pictures, clairvoyantly, all exists in a dot. It's all there: strategic scenes from the past, present challenges, and future glimpses; plus an occasional discarnate friend or loved one, or a soul in preparation for "re-entry" may transmit in on my higher vibrational frequency to pay a visit. It's challenging to retain all that I'm viewing in this first stage of a reading, then attempt to spread it all out to relate in linear form, while trying to include all the nuances and significant themes that are known to me the instant that I view the scenes.

I immediately saw an overlay of a past-life around Richard, a very alive, still-existing life experience. When I view a past life in a client's reading, it's usually a concurrent life space that relates in a specific way to what the person is acting out in his present life, at the time of the reading. In this particular overlay Richard was a robust peace officer in the Pacific Northwest in the early 1800s, looking like a burly mountain man. I watched a side view of him stepping up and into the doorway of a building, set among several others on either side.

When I view this kind of scene, I'm tuning into a part or frequency of the client's consciousness that is operating through another co-existing physical form in a concurrent but different time period. I can telepathically connect with the thoughts of the person, operating through that "past" persona, then direct their thoughts back to me, to communicate with me about what's occurring with him in that particular scene. Sometimes past selves turn around and face me, as if to have a chat, much like the way souls communicate who project themselves from between life spaces, or from future glimpses.

I started to describe the scene to Richard, and added, "I have to say, Richard, you strike me as a pretty 'macho' guy back there!" I hadn't intended this as a compliment, but he took it as such and, throwing his chest out, answered, "I know!" He himself had seen what I was describing, in some of his own meditations. I went on to view other overlays that dramatized a theme Richard continued to repeat, that of defining himself and his worth in terms of his physical brawn. I saw that in this life space he had excelled in athletics, as a welterweight in boxing and a black belt in the martial arts. I also viewed some past glimpses of him physically beating his children when they were young.

It seemed as if, in his own words, God was taking away that which he had made his god—his muscle—to which he had become extremely attached. When he could dominate or win over others using his physical strength, he held himself in high esteem. When he was defeated in strength, he felt less purposeful, less validated.

Richard had long ago divorced and had since married a woman whose weight had increased to obesity. He made no attempt to hide his disgust at what she had allowed her body to become.

In the following sessions, held over the next few months, I worked with Richard through meditations and astral projection exercises, to help give him a sense of his essence, the existence of his total being, beyond his understanding of his physical body. At times I would feel we were really making progress. He seemed to radiate with joy at the realization that he was far greater than the physical body that, having served him so responsively, only temporarily housed his enduring and continuing spirit. Then, at other times, it was as if none of our work together had made any difference at all.

At the end of one particularly (I felt) successful session, he pulled himself up from the couch and readied himself for the walk down to his car. He turned to me,

leaning on his cane, with a big grin. I mistakenly anticipated some sort of spontaneous testimonial. "Don't think
I told you," he began, "about the other day on the freeway! Cut in front of this guy, and he edges me off onto
the shoulder. . . . I get out, and he starts to come at me,
looks at my cane, and figures me an easy mark. Man," he
beamed, "I knocked him flat."

The significant part about Richard's story came a
year later. I hadn't seen him after that last session, and
months later I received a call from his daughter, inform-
ing me that her dad had passed over. She said that she
thought she believed that we don't "die," and that her
dad still existed somehow, somewhere, but her faith had
failed her. Hesitantly, she wondered if she might come for
a reading.

Richard had no problem projecting himself into his
daughter's reading. His big, beautiful smile and twinkling
eyes made me smile. He transmitted several messages, as
I relayed them to his visibly moved, loving daughter. He
applauded her for figuring out where important forms
had been left in his desk, was glad that she had found his
wallet under the living room chair—misplaced during
his final days in bed at home, and allowed me to move
into his consciousness to experience the sensations that
were his, as he was passing from this dimension.

He had complete awareness of all that took place in
the house and around his bedside (as well as of those
who waited for him on the Other Side), even when he
appeared to be losing consciousness. He knew that the

lettuce in the refrigerator was wilting, and he had a keen understanding of who did or didn't understand what he was experiencing. "John knew," he added. His daughter said that John was the mailman, who happened to drop in one day and stand by his bed. Richard conveyed to me that there was an almost telepathic communication or understanding with him and anyone else who was intuitively receptive, while Richard's life force was slipping away.

Finally, he turned to me, beaming, and announced, "*Now* I get it!" I knew from his thoughts, exactly what he was trying to say. Now he finally understood that he was more than the physical body that he had left behind. It was in the *passing* from the physical plane that he finally understood the lesson that he tried in vain to comprehend while fighting for his strength, trapped in his failing body.

Proof of the Continuum

Over the years, I've read many people who come for proof that a loved one didn't die. Sometimes they come with an obsessive intensity, like the woman who came to ask about her deceased husband, Harry. I later found that this woman had experienced personal interviews with many notable people in fields specializing in the understanding and acceptance of death and the dying process.

Among them, she had met with Elizabeth Kubler-Ross, noted psychiatrist and pioneer of valuable work with the terminally ill, and the developer of hospices. Those facilities provide an environment where the dying are fully supported in experiencing their last days as a fulfilling, enriching episode of life. They're encouraged to share and value that time without shame or denial.

My client estimated that she had allowed herself to go through the grieving process. It became clear, however, that she had yet to find any peace or acceptance about the loss of her husband.

As I tuned into her, Harry showed up immediately. He tried to project every possible memory he could come up with, to prove to her that it was indeed the energy she had known as "Harry." Memories are very alive and present when we're out of the body, because our perceptions aren't limited by the illusion of time being linear or sequential. He showed me a scene of how they used to watch TV and eat popcorn, tossing it in the air and trying to catch it in their mouths.

Harry transmitted a scene of the blue floral picture they had purchased, early in their marriage. He showed me the imitation gold necklace he'd given her, which, he added—with all that he was learning in reviewing back on that life about fears of lack—if he had it to do again, would be a necklace of real gold! It felt like Harry was performing a three-ring circus over to my right, trying to help his dear wife from whom he'd departed accept that he, his energy, wasn't dead and buried in the ground.

None of Harry's feats seemed to convince her. At the end of the session, I understood why. "Well!" she started, as she watched me return to normal consciousness. Sometimes when I come out of it, my eyes are a little crossed; both my twin brother and I had eye operations for strabismus when we were young. Being in such a relaxed state and not fully operational in the body during readings, my eyes are sometimes out of focus when I "return." A bit unsettling to my clients, I imagine, as I open my eyes, looking at them cross-eyed.

"Well?" I answered.

"Well," she repeated, "the Christmas after *my* friend *Dorothy's* husband *died,* er, passed over, *he* blinked the Christmas tree lights on *her* tree, at the *exact* time that *he* had *died!*" Suddenly it was clear to me that she was seeking the same kind of dramatic display of "proof" that her friend had experienced.

I asked her if she'd known Harry to have had a flair for the dramatic in life. *"Oh, no!"* she replied, "he was the most unassuming, unpretentious man!"

"Then why do you think he would present himself other than how you had known him?" I finally asked. The essence of Harry, as she had known him in this dimension, simply continued on, whether or not Dorothy was able to accept it.

Chapter Thirteen

Resolution

Never Too Late

Trusting the perfect timing of events in the lives of my clients as well as my own, I'm not surprised when they are nudged to call for readings at significant turning points in their lives, though they may be unaware of it at the time. Clients often call when they have undergone major inner shifts in their growth, and are pulling themselves up onto a new plateau. New events and situations are just about to become manifest in their physical lives.

At those times, clients often call out of frustration. They feel that something has shifted, but their lives appear to be unchanging. So I'm able to preview for them and alert them to many of the changes ahead. It doesn't spoil any surprises; rather, it gives them patience as well as confirmation of the upcoming outward reflection of their diligent efforts as travelers along their spiritual paths.

One of the most healing aspects of readings comes from the fact that the client is in a seeking, receptive mode. That particular vibration attracts discarnate souls who present themselves to resolve and heal old issues that remain unbalanced even after that soul passed from the physical. It usually takes two to maintain dissonance and discord.

The meeting between a client and a soul in process of reviewing life, able to see from a broader perspective than when in the physical, can bring about resonance and harmony, and can heal deep wounds and mis-understandings. The "reunion" can make possible one moment of resolution that has a balancing effect, potentially releasing two souls from future dramatic enactments forever.

Additionally, just as clients' growth is facilitated by the re-framing effect of a reading, the progress of discarnate souls is also furthered by my interpretation of the thoughts that they come to transmit. (Maybe they're issued a "grounds pass" to come drop in on a reading!)

One client who experienced this type of resolution was a woman who had a phone reading from Chicago, who called to ask why she wasn't attracting more positive relationships. She was promptly greeted by her father who, she confirmed, had passed over several years before. He came with love and understanding for the purpose of validating his daughter, whom he had emotionally and physically abused.

The daughter had evolved just to the point of receptivity, ready to leave behind the blame and perceptions about men that she'd learned as a little girl. The father was ready to apply all his learning about the effect that one's own self-scorn has on others. She wept and he embraced her with love; in one brief moment, there was a shift. Love healed and transformed dissonance into resonance.

During another reading, an elderly woman was met by her mother who had passed over years before. The mother arrived for the purpose of freeing the daughter to live the rest of her life in peace, joy, and freedom from guilt. My client had lived with and cared for her invalid mother for years before her mother slowly, ever so slowly, made her transition to the other side.

The mother, while ill, berated her daughter for not being more attentive to her needs; she gave her many tedious tasks to perform and shamed her into an exclusive relationship with her. The daughter was left alone with no life of her own, feeling that she deserved little else, having failed so miserably in her mother's eyes. As is often the case, the two had "tangled" before, but now came an opportunity to break the unhealthy interweaving of their two paths.

The mother conveyed all that she was learning about love and self-worth, wishing she'd been able to pass her insights on to her daughter while she was still in the body. She encouraged her daughter to hold her head high and assured her that the mirror she had been to her was not an accurate reflection of her daughter's true identity. She now released her to her own path and self-discovery.

In another instance, a successful, hard-driving, corporate executive was met by his father, who had been an even harder-driving military man and who had died from the effects of alcoholism. He came forward to give his son the message, "At ease." It seemed to be an attempt to pass on, from father to son, a new way, before it was too late for the son.

"I can see all that I needed to prove about myself," the father transmitted to his son in the reading. "I believed that I was only loved for my achievements and hard work. That's how I defined myself. My compulsion for success kept me busy and distracted me sufficiently to keep me from looking deeper into myself. I was afraid of what I'd find. I wasn't ignoring you because you weren't worth the love. I was ignoring myself. Please take the time now in your life. Don't be afraid of the feelings that will surface. They will bring you back into life."

Sometimes I actually feel it's as though the souls who are learning on the Other Side, who have passed some level of Awareness and Higher Intentions Test, are presented with the opportunity to come forward into a reading. I see them being coached in applying all that they're in the process of learning to some unfinished business that they have left behind. I imagine that it furthers their growth and evolution tremendously.

Maybe that's why the receptive client gets the notion to call for a reading in the first place. Regardless of any suppositions about how this all happens, the one constant message that comes from these encounters is that it's never too late for resolution.

The other healing message in these reunions comes from relatives who want to encourage those who are left behind, asking loved ones to "keep the door open with love." They are currently viewing the bigger picture, now disengaged from the drama and ego needs of the personality that they had been playing out before their passing.

One discarnate soul encourages his sister to stay receptive on the day when her wayward son will want to re-present himself to his mother. Another helps strengthen her daughter's resolve to take responsibility for herself, heal her emotions, and thereby attract healthier men. At the same time that soul encourages her to receive the releasing effect that she will gain when the brother who molested her one day seeks her forgiveness.

Best to keep the door open. It's important to awaken to new perspectives and stay receptive to experiences that carry the potential for resolution while the parties are still in the physical. That is why we're here, after all; and again, it's never too late.

Your Sister Got the Pearls

There is a common theme that souls who have gone on to the light project. It reminds me of the joke, "You never see a hearse with a luggage rack!" We all know that "you can't take it with you."

Loved ones who are left behind, however, often cling to whatever they can, trying to hold on to the one who has passed over without them. They become quite attached to that person's possessions. Often times I observe much drama resulting from the sorting out and distribution of those possessions. It's as though the harder they fight for what one "would have wanted," the greater the statement of their love and devotion for the one they mourn.

An example of this is the grandmother who appeared to say that she was well aware of all that had come about with the settling of her estate. I interpreted her thoughts to the granddaughter as, "I know that your sister got the pearls."

Apparently the grandmother had told my client years ago, when she was a little girl, that one day she would leave her pearls to her. As it turned out, there had been much disagreement and discord among family members while attempting to sort out the grandmother's posses-sions. My client chose to step out of the conflict.

The grandmother said that all that she and her grand-daughter had felt and experienced together could never be challenged. She knew that her granddaughter recog-nized that in her heart. She added, "Those who need those things the most, get them. But you've been left with the greatest gift. No one can take that away from you."

These little vignettes, acted out in the wake of a loved one's passing, can become lifetime vendettas. Those dramas can extend into future and further life spaces. Healing takes place when one who is grieving a loss begins to trust the love and memories shared with the deceased. That promotes greater acceptance of whatever transpires in the aftermath. Then one is left with a sense of what really matters, that which can never be given or taken away.

Those who have difficulty trusting or knowing what is important can't help but cling desperately to whatever physical evidence they can find to hold and own. They have need for this proof that something significant existed between them and the loved one. Lack of trust that the Universe provides enough for everyone is another motivating factor for people's behavior in settling matters after the passing of a loved one.

Chapter Fourteen
Gifts to Give

Confirmation

Tony was on a downhill road towards self-destruction. An extremely artistic child from a traditional Italian family in New York, he always made unconventional choices which would allow him to express his creativity freely. He eventually became a successful clothing designer, living in a luxuriously-decorated apartment off Park Avenue, which had been featured in several magazines.

He had many friends—Mike, his devoted male partner, and many entertainment and fashion celebrities. Business opportunities were abundant. He had created an elegant life "in the fast lane" that buffered him from the pain he'd experienced from all the rejection for his lifestyle preferences.

Everything started to change around the time that Tony's landlord planned to do some building renovation. The landlord wanted to convert the apartment building into a co-op, and was required by law to offer a lower rate to the current tenants than to the general public. He attempted to evict Tony and Mike to circumvent the law. Months later, by the time they'd won in court, the apartment had been illegally sold and their prized collection of furnishings piled into storage, along with Tony's works in progress for a major international design house. This setback left Tony depressed and vulnerable to imprudent decisions.

On the New Year's Eve that fell during that period, Tony and Mike were about to go out with some friends, all having gathered at another's apartment. They were often accustomed to smoking marijuana before social events, but no one of the group had any available. So one of the men, a user of hard drugs, offered to share his supply.

In a moment's decision, they all agreed to join in. Tony had never before, nor since, used drugs intravenously. (Ironically, Tony's always had a terrible fear of needles. He thought that to be the saving grace which had kept him from using heroin). The generous friend used his own needle to inject "crystal meth" into all eight of the men, each one eager for the evening ahead. It was the evening that changed Tony's life and ended six of the others' lives, including Mike's.

The friend neglected to mention that he had tested positive for HIV. Everyone developed flu symptoms within the next few weeks, and all eventually also tested positive. The remaining participant, besides Tony, remains very ill today. The six years following that evening brought more and more darkness to Tony's world, often because of the less and less wise choices he was making. By the time Tony lost the apartment and the opportunity to create a fashion line for the major designer, he and Mike had become addicted to cocaine.

Tony was lying and stealing his way even further away from his family's respect or assistance. To his parent's embarrassment, he would go to their friends to ask for money, saying he was approaching them at his parents' suggestion.

He served several short jail sentences for petty theft and went through unsuccessful drug programs, while contending with rapidly failing health. His parents, as well as his brothers and sister, refused to bail him out any more and lost hopes for a successful drug recovery. Everyone who knew and cared about Tony felt extremely helpless and frustrated. Tony had lost all hope or vision for himself.

When Tony's sister, Jean (a friend and client), heard of his seriously declining health, she intuitively felt that now was the time to act. She could no longer do nothing. Although she lived on the west coast, within a matter of days she was able to track him down, after following a trail of angry, disillusioned friends, landlords, and employers.

Jean rounded up his medical records, long distance, and found her way through bureaucracy, making arrangements to admit Tony into a reputable drug rehabilitation facility, not too far from her home in California. She was looking forward to seeing her brother again, but was filled with apprehension because of Tony's past, and the effect that sending for him might have on the rest of her family. She was also hesitant because of her own lack of experience regarding the desperate and manipulative ways of drug addicts.

Within the few weeks that Tony was with Jean and her family, before entering the rehab facility, Tony put on weight and his previously precarious medical condition, aggravated by years of drug use, stabilized. He thrived from all the love he received from his sister and her family. They all loved Tony and were eagerly making plans for a family venture—beginning with designing handbags—when he finished his stay at the center.

Lazarus, a very informative and helpful discarnate teacher who "channels" through Jack Purcel, an embodied soul, has said that some who allow HIV into their reality need to know who loved them. Tony got to find out, before reaching the stage that most of his dying friends had.

Jean stayed up past midnight each night, talking in depth with Tony, wanting to know and understand the brother she had come so close to losing. She also hoped that keeping him up late would help him sleep more soundly, thereby helping him to avoid the temptation to go out and find drugs, before he entered the center where he would be monitored. During one of their talks, Jean learned that Mike had died in the previous year.

When I did a phone consultation for Tony, he was just about to enter his intensive rehabilitation program. He had heard the Intro Tape and was intrigued with this new way of looking at his life, without judgment, encouraging him to take responsibility for his past and present. He said that it seemed like a point of view that could give him hope for a future. It had nothing to do with fate, but rather with choices, the reality he could choose to create.

As I began his reading, I could see all the hurt and humiliation that Tony had experienced. I also viewed random scenes of the long trail of drama and deception he had left behind. I described scenes of gatherings in his past plush apartment and mentioned names of people with whom he had unfinished business.

I suggested that he round them all up into a meditation, invite them into his "garden" or see them back in his apartment, surround them all with white light, and have a chat with them. I encouraged him to communicate through his Higher Self to connect with theirs. He was relieved to be given a way to spiritually redo some past "transgressions."

I gave Tony other suggestions for changing some childhood scenes, to rewrite the script. By re-experiencing past scenes from a new perspective, he could heal his past and shift his present and future. Becoming aware of choices he might have made, and following and meditating on new resulting outcomes, would create an alternate reality that would eventually influence or "bleed through" into his present one.

Then Mike "arrived." Mike seemed very well-oriented for having "gone to the light" so recently. He wanted Tony to know that he was "alive and well," much more so than when Tony had last seen him. He laughed and related some private jokes to Tony, in clear detail. Then he said that he wanted Tony to know that even though he had died from the virus, Tony didn't have to.

Mike said that in another life space, in the complex but perfect way that our paths intersect with others, Tony had been the one to die out of a relationship. This time it was Mike's turn. He concluded that Tony's rehabilitation program would help both of them. Mike said that he had his own "classes," but would also watch over Tony's shoulder, learning from Tony's experience.

That brings to mind another of Lazarus' teachings: "If you don't love yourself enough to make wiser choices in your life, then find someone else you love enough to make them for that person." Mike wanted Tony to know that throughout his recovery, he would be doing it for both of them.

Jean told me that she recently listened to a tape from one of her readings that took place several years ago. On the tape, she said that I abruptly brought up her brother, incidentally mentioning that he had made a decision that would affect his life. Then she said that I then listed several names.

She informed me that she now knew those were the names of all the other fellows who died because of a choice they made, that one New Year's Eve. It must have all been part of Tony's path, a necessary experience to challenge him to go deeper into discovering his true spiritual identity. Mike was extending his love and support as Tony began that journey.

"She's Looking Beautiful"

Joyce thought about calling for a reading, but dismissed it because she was leaving on a trip in the morning. She didn't know how she could fit in a last-minute session, even if I would be able to see her. She decided against it, but something kept nagging her to call, so she finally gave in to the feeling and made the call.

She'd been given my name several months before by a well-known and well-loved yoga teacher in town, but hadn't gotten around to making an appointment until this most inconvenient time. She called, and I happened to have had a cancellation. I was able to schedule her the next morning, just before she and her husband were to fly back to an island on the east coast, where their family had lived before moving to southern California.

In her reading, I mentioned a Tom or Thomas who was in her life. It's often hard for clients to place the information which I sometimes relay very quickly, but if it's important that the connection be made, it will continue to surface in different ways, until the person can identify what has been said.

It seems the most difficult for analytical people—those who experience and understand much of their lives through their minds, with very concrete perceptions—to "place" much of what comes through in readings. Much too frequently, people cannot remember situations from their past because of abuse and demeaning events from which the psyche has protected them. But most often they are so involved in their life's adventures that standing back to identify details about their lives is difficult. For example, I remember reading a man when I worked at the magic club. I didn't recognize him to be a noted television travel commentator, and began his reading with, "Who is Phil, in the white Seville, who spends much of his life in airports?" He thought and he thought, trying to place whom this could be.

"No, I'm sorry, I can't figure out whom you're talking about."

His daughter who was sitting next to him finally exclaimed, *"Dad!* It's *you!"*

At first Joyce couldn't place a Tom, shelving it mentally until later in the reading. Finally, it came to her. She and her husband Karl knew a Tom from the east coast. They had been in a gourmet dinner group with Tom and his wife when they had lived there. She then remembered that he would be at the party she and Karl were to attend on their trip, celebrating the opening of a new office building.

When people are able to make these connections, doing so usually opens the door for me to go on with much more information, sometimes in the form of a message. That was the case in Joyce's reading.

I went on to relay there was someone present who had passed over around six months before, who somehow had a connection with Tom. She was saying, "My daughter who died was helped over by a young woman. I couldn't stop imagining her body after the accident and was so surprised to see my daughter whole. I was reminded in an instant that we don't die in the body." She concluded, "I have seen the one who went before, and she's beautiful!"

From what this soul projected of herself, the self that had known Tom in some way, I could tell that she had been a very organized person who liked to store things in little compartments. The characteristics that a soul projects are unique to each individual: the personality traits, facial expressions, mannerisms or habits still exist in that soul's memory.

The messages given to Joyce made little sense to her until the end of her visit to the east coast. When she returned, she called to tell me what had transpired, and the meaning of the messages.

She saw Tom at the party and asked to speak to him alone in a separate office, just as he and his wife were about to leave. Joyce described Tom as a very witty and gregarious man, well-liked, and entertaining. She also said that he was close to his family and had good rapport with his three siblings.

Joyce had taken her tape from the reading with her, to remind her of the details to deliver to Tom. She and her husband and Tom and his wife stepped into an empty office, and Joyce relayed all that the entity had transmitted in the reading. She said that Tom's face turned white, and that his reaction was further dramatized by his sudden, uncharacteristic silence. When he had collected himself and was headed toward the door, he asked if they could meet once more before Joyce and Karl returned to California. Joyce said that they were pressed for time, but would try to meet them at the airport before their departure.

When they met, Tom explained that his mother had died six months ago. She was known for being a very organized person, and had owned a gift shop filled with bins and many little compartments in which she delighted in organizing things.

She had lingered with an illness for several months before she passed and during that time had many long conversations with her family. She reminisced about the sixteen-year-old daughter whom she had lost in a tragic car accident twenty years before. Tom's sister's body had been horribly disfigured in the accident. His mother expressed her doubts about an after-life, but wondered wistfully if she would ever see her daughter again and what she would look like—if she *did* still exist—having been through such trauma.

It was through Joyce's reading that Tom's mother had been able to communicate to him that she had "seen the one who went before, and she's beautiful!" Tom said that receiving this information from his mother had had a profound effect on how he viewed life and had awakened him to explore his spiritual values. It had also given him and his siblings a great sense of peace.

Relief from Guilt: The Twin's Twin

I'm appreciative of the healing effect that comes in some readings, when clients have been carrying deep, tormenting guilt, secreted away into dark corners of their consciousness. The healing often results from a soul coming forward who played a part in the drama from which the client carries these intense, personal feelings.

I remember sensing a heavy blanket of blame being lifted in one particular reading involving a client who was a single parent. I could see, as I began her reading, that she had given birth to twin daughters. I viewed them both as toddlers in the past, but when I shifted to focus on the client's present, I could see only one daughter. Then I felt the arrival of a soul who was projecting herself as a little girl, but thinking more adult thoughts.

She showed me scenes of a little stuffed toy, a rabbit, and of a crib mobile. I related these scenes to my client, who started to weep. "It's my little girl," she responded softly. "She died last year. I had scolded her before bed, and then I took her twin sister into bed with me. The next morning she was gone. She'd just stopped breathing. I can't stop thinking that if I hadn't scolded her, if I'd taken *her* into bed with me too, that I wouldn't have lost her."

"Well," I began slowly, "she seems quite resolved about it all. In fact, that's one reason she's presenting herself here today. She wants you to know that it was truly part of her plan. She'd only signed up for a short "tour of duty!" It was an agreement among the three of you, that her early exit would serve as a catalyst, a stimulant for the spiritual growth of your other daughter and yourself.

"But it doesn't look like she's done here," I continued. "In fact, she's signaling me to tell you that she will be back, most likely as your granddaughter, the daughter of the one who was her twin sister. It's as if she hurried out to come back in to bring up the rear! She's laughing at my interpretation of all this.

"Most of all," I added, "she wants you to know that it wasn't your fault. As you heal your grief from your loss, you are also healing some beliefs that you brought with you into this life.

"It looks as though it has to do with carrying blame for the passing of a family member in another time, and again, it was not your fault. But even more, I think you and your daughters have set up this drama in order to dramatize that theme, thereby magnifying the truth that you can only take responsibility for your own path. Our children have their separate paths to travel."

Another reading disclosed the depths of a client's guilt, again brought on by the loss of a child. The scene came into the middle of the reading, projected from a soul who had passed over. I viewed the inside of a garage, and what looked like paint cans in the corner, sitting on newspapers. It was hard for me to connect the two, the soul who was present, with the garage scene.

I related this to the client, and waited for her response. She cleared her throat, then spoke very softly. It was difficult for me to hear her, so I asked her to speak louder. "It's my son who is here," she said. I could see that the memory was a painful one, so I encouraged her to take her time.

"My son drank the cleaning fluid that he found in that garage, and he died. He was two years old. I can't forgive myself, and I don't feel that I deserve happiness in my life." She confessed that it was even harder for her to live with the fact that she had never felt close to her little boy, the way that she believed a mother should naturally feel.

The woman was trying to maintain her life, having few expectations for a positive future. In this case, it looked like a karmic vignette, acted out by one soul, who had been the daughter (now, the mother), with another, who had been her father (recently, the son). Blame and self-scorn was again the theme, and it posed a challenging lesson.

I interpreted that there had been much discord between them in another life, and each had made choices that affected the other, choices made out of hurt and disappointment. They both had great expectations of each other, feeling that each one owed the other their happiness in life. In that past-life scenario, the daughter felt cheated, having lost her mother, and expected her father to make up for her loss. The widowed father felt frustrated that the daughter couldn't take the place of his deceased wife, and found it unbearable to face his personal loss.

In the father's despair, anger, and confusion, which related to his daughter's inability to ease his pain, he wandered off into the wilderness and died, more or less to spite her. She lived the remainder of that lifetime in deep depression and very much alone.

I surmised that it had been necessary for her to live through a replay of that soul's disappearance, this time as the son she lost, in order to bring herself to where she had left off, now presented with the challenge of arriving at a new conclusion: learning to take responsibility for her own pain, to find and use her strength and ability to respond to her own expectations of life.

The soul communicating from the other side acknowledged that their recent drama—and there had been several in other times in which their paths had crossed—had served to balance that which had kept them both from facing forward on their individual spiritual paths. Their interplay had repositioned them, thereby facilitating their journeys.

I assured my client that further resolution would result from her waking up to the potential that she had to create whatever she wished for herself in life. She was now free to do so. Sometimes the gift of a tragic loss is the awakening of the loved one who is left behind. I certainly hoped for my client that she was now ready to receive that gift.

You're Just as Smart as Billy

It used to grieve me deeply that neither of my parents stayed in their physical bodies long enough to know my children. When Adrianne, my first child, was born, I often felt my mother's presence, but I still missed her terribly. I kept thinking how she would have enjoyed and reacted to my little girl.

I felt that I had missed something ceremonious, to have been able to present my first born to my mother, to receive acknowledgment, as in, "Look what I have done!" It felt like a missing passageway into motherhood.

By the time my son Dylan was born, time had healed more of my grief and feelings of loss, but once again, I thought about how much my parents would have also loved this grandchild. At that time I was learning to trust my ability to sense and view the presence of discarnate souls, and to interpret their thought projections. I soon began including messages from these souls in readings.

Thus, it was handy and somewhat comforting for me to find that I was able to communicate with my mother. I mentioned earlier that Adrianne is also able to do so. She has had several lucid dreams in which she meets with her grandmother, and they communicate about when and whether she will return as her daughter some day, or remain as a guide.

I felt my father's presence at times. But after my children were born, I distinctly felt the absence of his etheric body around me. Shortly before that (I believe), he re-entered physical life as my middle brother's youngest son.

One day, when my children were about seven and nine years old, I found that I was still able to share my mother's humor. I had just brought them both home from piano lessons. Adrianne was upstairs in her room, and Dylan had just seated himself at the kitchen table to enjoy a peanut butter and jelly sandwich. I was washing dishes, standing a few feet away from him, when I suddenly felt Mother's presence. She said that she wanted Dylan to know, "He's just as smart as Billy!"

"Dylan, er, Grandma Ruth is here, and she wants me to tell you, er, who is Billy?"

Dylan always handled my "extra-sensing" very well and matter-of-factly. "Billy's the smartest kid in my room at school," he answered, with peanut butter stuck to the roof of his mouth, and jelly dripping down his chin.

"Well, I guess your Grandma knows all about that. She wants you to know that you're just as smart as Billy."

"Oh," Dylan remarked, smiling. He got up to get a napkin, located near where I was standing, and continued, "I was just thinking yesterday, that I'll never be as smart as Billy. I didn't do very well on my last spelling test," he said, looking down, wiping his mouth.

I started to give him a hug and confident assurances, when mother continued, "And Dylan is in store for a treat!" I relayed the second half of her message, while Dylan stood beside me, my arms around him. We both laughed, and tried to guess what the treat might be. Maybe someone's birthday invitation to Disneyland or something similar.

"Hmmm!" Dylan concluded, as he usually summarizes these metaphysical adventures. He returned to sit back down to his sandwich.

Just then, he exclaimed, "*Hey!* What's *this!*" He showed me a piece of candy that had just materialized on his plate. *"Whoa!"* we both exclaimed, looking wide-eyed at each other. We had recently seen the movie, "Ghostbusters," so we broke into our little rendition of the Twilight Zone theme, "Nu nu nu nu, nu nu nu nu!" But I really wanted to know how that candy landed on Dylan's plate! Like most people, I prefer reasonable, comprehensible explanations.

I then thought that I heard the front door shut. My searching thoughts concluded that Adrianne had just dashed out the door to go over to her friend Annie's house. I called over there, and Adrianne came to the phone. "Sweetheart, er, did you by any chance just drop a piece of candy on Dylan's plate, when you ran downstairs from your room to go over to Annie's?"

"Oh . . . yes!" She laughed. "I was taking one to Annie and, at the last minute, decided to toss one on Dylan's plate." I told Dylan, and we again stared at each other.

What a precious gift we'd received. Mother knew about Dylan putting himself down, thinking he wasn't very smart, and contributed in a very grandmotherly, loving way. She also knew, in her timeless space, that Adrianne had dropped the candy—the surprise treat that lay in store for him—on Dylan's plate, before Adrianne had even decided to do it.

Dylan was delighted. And so was his grandmother. I am always grateful for those special little gifts that I receive, reminders of the love, the humor, and the caring that my mother and I share, that never did, nor ever will, end.

Chapter Fifteen
From "Famous" Entities

Lord Mountbatten and Michael London

I recently sent letters to the widow of Michael Landon and to the nephew of Lord Mountbatten. I was finally going to trust the awkward position in which I often find myself when reached by "famous" entities who have passed over, who come through at times when I'm having wandering thoughts about them. I guess those thoughts must put up my antenna and I become a ready receiver.

There is no separate heaven for the famous. No different from lesser-known entities who are only a thought away, they also come to confirm things, to lend another point of view, or to resolve unfinished business that could take both parties lifetimes to balance. When it's possible, I willingly relay the messages, but sometimes it is seemingly impossible for me to respond.

I was "reached" one night (during a brief law school adventure) while reading a case history for a contracts class about a deceased grandfather who had left his general store to his granddaughter. The grandfather projected himself beside me, with a white beard and wearing a red plaid woolen shirt.

He wanted to clarify what really happened—to give his version. "Gads," I responded (telepathically, as I was sitting in the law school library), "I can't be receiving (much less relaying!) messages from deceased plaintiffs and defendants! *This* is *ridiculous!*" He showed up again in class the next morning when the case was being discussed. It was beyond me how to plead *his* case!

As I have mentioned, the non-physical dimension is not limited by time or space, but I often think that souls on "the other side" forget that *we* are! I'm often faced with the dilemma of how to relay these messages, particularly the unsolicited ones. In the physical plane we not only buy into the illusion of time and distance, but are limited by illusionary boundaries of fame and fortune.

Years ago, after the bombing of Lord Mountbatten's yacht by IRA terrorists, I was sitting over the morning paper that carried the headlines, thinking about the close relationship that he and his nephew, Prince Charles, had shared. I supposed or had read somewhere that Prince

Charles' beloved uncle had been a strong influence on his spiritual path, and (just a thought away!) Lord Mountbatten projected himself beside my breakfast table.

It felt as though he had much to say and to confirm. He projected an image from the past, a setting in which the two of them had talked. There was a red leather chair by an end table with a green-covered book on the table. It seemed to have been an important conversation, remarkable either in its depth, spiritual and emotional significance, or both. He was finding much that they had discussed about an after-life to be true, and he wanted Charles to know.

"Terrific!" I responded, telepathically. "So I should call up Prince Charles and give him the message? Sure."

I felt like Noah in the old Bill Cosby comedy routine, where he dramatized the practical aspects of Noah hearing God's message. "This is *who*? Uh huh, *right*. You want me to do *what*, God? Uh huh, *right*."

Years later I made my first visit to London. I felt a moral and professional responsibility to attempt to reach Prince Charles with a note. Feeling a bit foolish, estimating what any official would take me for, I'm afraid that I lost my courage when I came face to face with an official at Windsor Castle, who grinned in response to my query, "Could you please tell me how I could leave something for Prince Charles?" I thought no more about further attempts until, years later, I was prompted to write Cindy Landon, the widow of actor Michael Landon.

One night, a few weeks after Michael's passing, I was catching up on all the magazines on my night stand, and was thinking about the courageous appearance I had seen him make on *The Johnny Carson Show*. I thought about what an inspiring example he was to those who fear confronting and moving through their challenges in life.

And I thought of his wife Cindy, and the wonderful influence she had been for her husband, changing his diet, which eased the pain (for which physicians would only prescribe stronger pain killers), and nurturing him spiritually.

Well, no surprise, Michael popped in, and it felt like he had much to say and to confirm. There are many of us for whom it's no effort to reach that certain "radio frequency." I figured that Cindy may have been contacted by hundreds of "sensitives" by now. But having fallen short with Lord Mountbatten's request, I thought that this time I would not hesitate. I'd at least make the attempt to reach out.

Writing the one letter revived my intentions to also notify Prince Charles. I began both letters, "I trust that if my intuition is serving me well, which it does tend to do, then my letter will reach you in spite of the piles in which it might find itself." I included my Intro Tape and described the "grounded," responsible way in which I do my work.

The rest was up to their receptivity in being reached by those who still loved and cared about them. I felt satisfied that I had done my part, and liked the idea of transcending those illusionary social boundaries that separate us from each other. This was a good way to make a personal statement.

I've been asked if I think it might be more difficult for souls who leave a large following behind to make it to the "other side," as if weighted down by all of that energy "hanging on their coattails." I know that grieving thoughts are necessary and healthy for the healing of a loss. But continuing thoughts of deep despair can distract or hold a soul back from its transition.

Loving, positive thoughts and prayers that celebrate the release of the physical body most certainly help propel that soul forward. Ruth Montgomery's guides informed her that John F. Kennedy barely lost consciousness when he passed over after his assassination. I had the same feeling about Michael Landon when he came to visit that evening.

I received a charming typewritten note from The Assistant to The Equerry to H.R.H. The Prince of Wales, which read:

"Thank you for your letter and enclosures. I shall seek an opportunity to lay these before The Prince of Wales, who, I am sure, would wish me to thank you for taking the trouble to write."

Months later, I also received word from Cindy Landon, indicating that the messages and Intro Tape had been received, with appreciation. Where there is truth, love, and authenticity, the thoughts and messages *will* get through, to wherever they need to go.

Amelia

I looked out of the small plane as it veered to the right, tilting towards a clearer view of the northern coast of Africa. We were flying so low that I was able to enjoy the contrast of the solid green density of coastline trees with the blue-green sparkle of the Atlantic Ocean. I was aware of a small out-of-the-way supply station used for refueling, housed in an old wooden shack.

Then I knew that there were kites. They were being let out from the plane. "What's with all these *kites?*" I asked. I found myself in a timeless space that happened to be right in the center of Amelia Earhart's consciousness, as I was in the middle of a reading.

My client was Dick Freeman, whose wife Jane had given him a reading for his birthday. She had warned me, "Watch out. He has this special interest!"

And indeed, once we began his reading, he started to ask about a passion in his life, his interest in the life and disappearance of Amelia Earhart. An aeronautical engineer, he had researched information about her for years and had met her when he was a young boy.

Even before Dick could ask about Amelia, she projected herself into our session. But instead of relaying specific messages, she allowed me to enter—or I simply merged—into her consciousness. I was experiencing, in a timeless space, her last flight around the world.

"There's someone behind us, at the back of the plane—a man who is monitoring things. He's saying something, but we can barely hear him talk."

"That would be Fred Noonan, her navigator," Dick interjected.

"We're going down now! It feels like it's happening in slow motion, and not from as great a height as I'm accustomed to flying," I added quickly, trying to give Dick a responsible play-by-play account.

"Now we're in the water, and the right side of 'our' body hurts." I continued, "And there are round things floating in the water—they look like ping-pong balls!"

"Yes!" Dick again confirmed, "She had them in the plane for flotation!"

We went on and on like that for what seemed like hours, until we got tangled up in Dick's enthusiasm to have me put all that I was viewing and experiencing in reverse (on instant replay!), to try to fit my descriptions of the islands as we'd approached them quickly from the air (we *were* crashing!) to the maps he now held on his lap.

Months later, Dick asked me to do a special reading for him. He hoped that I could go back to re-experiencing Amelia's flight and give more details about her life and what had become of her. Dick later provided me with a transcription of the tape from that reading, nearly seventy pages of notes, which I referred to when putting together the remainder of this story.

Admittedly, at times Dick's enthusiastic responses to what I viewed and experienced through Amelia's consciousness may have been somewhat leading, as he was excited to have much of what I witnessed fit his theories about the disappearance of Amelia. But most of the information came so much in its own context and form—often "out of left field"—that I feel it can be trusted.

Knowing that Dick would want to pursue further explorations about Amelia after his first reading, I purposely avoided researching her or any other aviators. The most reliable and satisfying readings I do are those that come about when I come in "cold," with few connections to the subject or persons involved. Otherwise, interpreting and relaying the information given in the reading can become very confusing, foggy, and frustrating. I am able to disengage enough and come in from a different angle with friends whom I read as clients, but for projects such as this, I make a special effort not to influence myself.

My one connection to the world of aviation had been my father, who was an aerospace engineer at Lockheed Aircraft. He used to tell bizarre tales about meeting and running into Howard Hughes—the eccentric billionaire who dabbled in aeronautical explorations—but that is the extent of my background information concerning the world of aviation, at least that I'm consciously aware of. I even wonder if that slight influence of my father's occupation might have played some part in my path intersecting with Dick's.

REFLECTING BACK ON HER LIFE

I settled in again with Dick and, very soon, with Amelia, flowing easily back into her consciousness. She began by emphasizing the thoughts, over and over, that there was a far greater purpose in her mission than in all the intrigue and missing details regarding her last flight.

She projected information about a soul group of varied ages who had reunited in this incarnation. They had combined energies toward a greater purpose before, in other life spaces. She said that many in the group were very intuitive, and that their wonderful combination of talents has often created novel inventions.

I watched one shared life's experience of the group that had been a cumbersome, much less refined one, filled with hardships. There were many battles, wars, and the desire for greater ease in life. They developed a way to transport heavy goods (I saw cannons) from one place to another on rugged platforms—some sort of cart or buckboard with wheels. It looked as though the wheels had been carved by hand.

Again, she added, their mission this time went beyond the abilities of their good technological minds, and had to do with gaining a greater understanding about life. She hoped that our session would demonstrate that thoughts, memories, and curiosities go far beyond the death of the physical body.

She showed me another time when they had been fascinated by how things moved and had visions of heavy objects flying through the sky. There seemed to be a soulful agreement to come together in a time when that would be technologically possible. This time, they certainly had done so.

Amelia continued, saying that some included in the soul group were those like Dick, who was obsessed with uncovering the details about her life. Others were those who touched her life in seemingly minimal ways. Then she showed me a scene of her meeting Dick when he was eight years old, in a large building.

Dick confirmed that he was overjoyed at meeting her when his father had taken him to the Purdue University Armory Building. Amelia was a professor at Purdue, providing real-world leadership to the young women in the school. This meeting was just prior to her world flight, and the faculty of Purdue was invited to hear her plans for the trip.

She projected scenes from her own childhood, as young as three and four years old, trying to make something—it looked like a little rolling cart—work. She said that she came in that way—with curiosities, visions, and ambitions—and again said that it wasn't the first time, and, if my interpretation was correct, she added that it wouldn't be the last. Dick later verified that Amelia and her sister had built a wooden box roller coaster which they launched from their garage roof in Atchison, Kansas.

PERSONAL BACKGROUND

Amelia presented her life to me like a landscape, pointing out peaks of experiences that rose above others. Many of these events helped her to not take life too seriously and made her laugh. Those moments stood out to her because they seemed to be in such contrast to her customary intensity. She often emphasized that those were the times that pulled her out into life, not the events that everyone was so eager to know about.

She said that the intensity for her explorations enabled her to accomplish much, but at times that energy went inward and caused confusion about her identity. At one point she mentioned wearing men's clothing and dressing like her friend, Charles A. Lindbergh.

She projected memories of sitting at the feet of a father or grandfather whom she envied because he was a man, and the conflict she felt about all that her mother tried to teach her about being female. She said that her younger sister, Muriel, always understood her conflict. Although Amelia felt some unfinished business with her sister (and something left unsaid, about a boy lost or drowned in a river), she acknowledged that Muriel had been an example of one who easily accepted the prescribed roles available to a female, later settling in to a domestic role with a husband and children.

She shared her awareness that she could now see that she had accomplished many things in other life spaces where she had incarnated into male bodies. She'd been quite frustrated at the limitations of living a life in female form and never quite resolved others' expectations of how she should live and dress.

Then she projected memories of a white house in which she had lived, and how bored she'd get hearing about a woman who had been an aunt or family friend who lived in a rural area. Amelia laughed about a grandmother with false teeth, a string of dolls, and a tool shed. It felt like a rather "folksy" upbringing, and she reflected back with concern that she used to get quite bothered and distracted by much in her life that involved others.

It seemed that in her impatience and intensity, she hadn't taken the time to gain fulfillment from sharing in others' experiences, their differences and idiosyncrasies. They now intrigued her. Perhaps she had incarnated as a female in order to challenge herself to integrate those characteristics of sensitivity and compassion, to balance her more dominant male aspects.

She said that she had disengaged from the driving force that pulled her through this life. She still carried many curiosities about adventures in the physical plane that she yearned to experience in a new way, at a slower, more attentive pace.

There were also memories about living with her husband. She showed him standing by some books, as if in a library of the house (and a black dog somewhere in the house). She wished that he would turn around and face her, and I picked up on feelings that she longed for him to respond to her differently from all who thought her unique because of her unusual achievements.

It was difficult to sort out many of the memories Amelia projected, sometimes all at once. I watched scenes of her in a uniform, and something about Canada, and about the Red Cross. Dick said that she had been a nurse. Then she gave me the words "Ma-lo-lo."

I kept repeating the words, "Malo-lo-lo?" "Ma-lo-a-lo?" I started laughing, trying to get it right. Dick thought that I was trying to say Maloelap, thinking of the Maloelap Atoll in the Marshall Islands, an area which could have been the location of her crash.

"No," I insisted, "She's giving me Ma-lo-lo!" Months later, when Dick had transcribed the tape, he wrote me that on March 20, 1937, following a wreck from an attempted takeoff from Luke Field on Ford Island, Oahu, Amelia and her crew returned to the U.S. that same day on board the Matson Lines ship, the S.S. Malolo. The aircraft was returned as deck cargo on board the S.S. Lurline.

There were also thoughts about a group of women and a woman named "Nita" or "Anita." Apparently, Amelia had helped form a group of women flyers called the "99s," and the woman who taught her to fly was Neta Snook Southern. At one point in the reading, she kept referring to "Bobby, the little boy," and that she was aware of "the book."

Dick said that the book, *Stand By To Die,* had been written about Robert H. Myers. It is the personal account of Robert's experiences with Amelia when, as a little boy, he followed Amelia around the airplane hanger in Alameda, California. Amelia's husband, George Palmer, didn't like Bobby hanging around, but Amelia was kind to him and would give him milk to drink.

CHARLES LINDBERGH

The energy that was known as Charles Lindbergh also projected into the reading. He still carried and transmitted the sound of a screen door slamming, the image of a ladder leaning against a house, and beautiful gardens that had given him much peace. He conveyed that he'd had a premonition one day, as he walked in these gardens, that something would happen to his son. (His infant son was kidnapped and murdered in 1932.) He was very intent on relaying his greater perspective about the tragedy.

His was now very clear in recognizing the dualistic values we place on circumstances in the physical dimension, continually judging experiences as good or bad. He said, for example, that the loss of his son was thought to be a terrible misfortune, but what we view as a misfortune can also be something quite appropriate or opportune, because of all that it can lead to. He mentioned the inspiration that his wife gained, which flowed throughout all of her writing.

(Lindbergh's wife, Anne Morrow Lindbergh, was born in 1906. She is an author, noted for popular books about the environment, works of poetry, and writings that eloquently express her personal philosophy, gathered in two autobiographies and three volumes of diaries and letters (1972–1980). She has written many spiritually inspiring books, among them, Gifts From the Sea).

It's my personal feeling that the soul who came to the Lindberghs as their little son had signed up for a short "tour of duty," in order that his death might serve as a catalyst for the spiritual growth of many who mourned his passing.

Lindbergh said that our fear of death, believing that life ends with the physical, shades our judgment in all that we experience. He continued that when we can go beyond that fear, it will influence our perceptions of every experience. He indicated that part of the purpose of Amelia, himself, and others in projecting themselves forward was to assist in shifting people's focus in life, from living in response to all the fears of it, to the acceptance, exploration, and adventure of all that it offers.

Lindbergh mentioned a "Connie," as an example of one who lived or understood or had talked with him about experiencing life "just as it is," rather than judging it good or bad. (Dick later informed me that Dr. J. F. Condon had been a friend and physician who lived near the Lindberghs.) He added that that was quite an enlightened way to live.

(Charles Lindbergh was an aviator who lived from 1902 to 1974. He made the first solo nonstop flight across the Atlantic, in 33½ hours, on May 20, 1927, in "The Spirit of St. Louis." He became a hero overnight, worked as an airline consultant, and made many goodwill flights. The kidnapping and murder of his son led to a federal law against kidnapping, known as the Lindbergh Act. He was criticized for his pro-German, isolationist position from 1938–1941.

He later flew fifty combat missions in WWII. His autobiography, The Spirit of St. Louis, *published in 1953, won a Pulitzer Prize.)*

AND OTHERS

I told Dick that Lindbergh was saying that another in the group "over there" with him, included Eddie . . . Knickerbocker? Dick quickly corrected my interpretation of Lindbergh's thoughts, interjecting, "Rickenbacker!" Eddie seemed to have liked making airplane sounds as a child, or was trying to tell me that he became childlike in the end.

He was going on about some papers left to deal with at the time of his passing. Dick wondered if they might have had to do with business affairs with Eastern Air Lines. Eddie said that it sort of held up the time for his passing, and that he was relieved to finally "make it over."

(Edward Vernon Rickenbacker (1890–1973) was a US air ace of WWI, receiving the Congressional Medal of Honor for shooting down twenty-six aircraft. After the war, he became an automotive and airline executive.)

THE FLIGHT

Finally, we returned to re-experiencing Amelia's last flight and events that followed. I telepathically asked her what had happened with her last flight, but she first presented many details that took time to sort out: thoughts about tying down a plane on a ship going to Hawaii and waiting to communicate directly with President Roosevelt in Washington (and, she laughed, she remembered being as impatient to hear from FDR as Dick was to know all of these details!), concern about boxes shipped to Florida (where her flight began), and thoughts about being surprised about running into someone by the name of Robinson at a dinner she attended there.

Suddenly I was looking at numerous dials and knobs in front of me (us). I described the cockpit and didn't see anyone beside us, just a glove compartment and many papers. I could feel a man behind us, to whom she was passing notes. "Yes," Dick interrupted, "they passed notes back and forth with a fishing pole! That would have been Fred Noonan at the back."

He was blowing his nose (I think he had a cold), and I said that I thought he looked like a barking dog. Then I realized that his flying helmet looked like it had beagle ears. I was being told that a woman (his wife?) had teased him about his "dog ears."

We spent a while fiddling with knobs and dials, as I tried my best to relay Amelia's thoughts. She was thinking about a rough part of the trip: no land for a while, then one island, then a clump of a few more islands. She wasn't concerned, because she felt comfortable about the big leap, having done that type of flying for about that same distance without land.

Dick said, "That must have been her flight from Brazil to West Africa."

"Yes," I agreed, "Amelia's nodding, but she's referring to the time after reaching that first island."

"Well," Dick said, contemplating, "she felt very good about that first landfall; the navigator had done exactly what she had hoped he'd be able to do. My guess is that that's what she's referring to."

"Yes," I said, "she's nodding."

Then I watched something on the instrument panel that looked like a black ball, rolling back and forth. "There's also something that she's pulling that looks like a ball, like one from a pin-ball machine."

"That would be the turn and bank instrument and throttles," said Dick, rolling his eyes.

Now we were back to the point in her consciousness where we were flying over the coast of West Africa. We watched the trees and the beautiful craggy coastline, then the thought, *Fuel!* I asked Dick if she stopped for fuel there.

"Yes," he answered, "she was north of her intended landfall by about 120 miles. She needed fuel, so she landed."

"It seems to be dusk now. I can see the sun coming down."

"Yes." Dick, having made a similar flight, reflected, "It really lights up the coast, the sun shining on the land from the west!"

By now we had landed and were joking around with someone at a gas stop, one I had seen before in Dick's first reading, that looked like an old desert gas station. Then came thoughts about flying south and watching the control panel. "Well," said Dick, "she and Noonan had argued about where they were located. Noonan had told her that instead of flying north, she should have flown south! She was always flying north of her intended course. As a navigator, Noonan would have known that pilots tend to do that."

I said, "There are thoughts about someone named 'Thompson.'"

Dick later found that commander Warner K. Thompson, U.S.C.G., was the skipper of the Coast Guard Cutter "Itasca," which was waiting for her at Howland Island.

"Now we're flying over a large land mass, then a memory or connection about something to do with ice or Iceland, then something about China."

Dick replied, "Icing on the wings was always a big problem—no way to remove it. And Fred Noonan had navigated the China Clipper. He would have also been worried about the wing ice."

"Things are getting a little 'touchy' now, and I'm seeing Fred reading some magazines! Would there have been time to read magazines?" I asked.

"Oh yes, I'm sure," Dick responded, reveling in all the details.

"And now, lots of thoughts about the cold, about the scarf around her neck, feeling very tired, when we'd be stopping, then the next direct shot to another coast."

"It would probably be in reaching and leaving India, after the cold desert," Dick reasoned.

Then I saw those kites again! "Yes," Dick confirmed, "they had kites on board, two of them. They were to be used to lift an emergency radio antenna!"

I said, "She's just done something with the kite, and now we're coming around and are about to go down. Now there's a feeling of concern, something is shifting or sliding around (fuel?), and thoughts about someone else's decision about us going down. I don't think she was in favor of the decision, but she's thinking, 'Oh what the heck!' and about doing something she's been asked to do, off and on. Does this make any sense?"

"Yes!" Dick exclaimed, *"Go on!"*

"Well," I continued, "now she's doing something with a wire that does something to the wing, and Fred's fiddling around with something back there, er, would he be taking pictures?"

"Yes. That might have to do with the reconnaissance mission I mentioned before, the one that FDR insisted upon, against Amelia's wishes," Dick said, speaking slowly and deliberately.

GOING DOWN

"Something is going wrong, and Amelia is saying, 'Well, here goes!' And now we're going down! I see a crescent-shaped piece of land. I don't know how much time has passed since that location where it was cold, but she is taking me to this scene now because she knows that there's a lot of energy on this."

"Yes, there is!" Dick confirmed, again rolling his eyes and now rubbing his hands together.

"First we went to the right, now to the left, and she's doing something again with the wire and the wings."

Dick asked, "Is she afraid? Is she angry?"

I answered, "This wasn't her doing, and there's a lot of ambivalence about it."

"Now there's a concern about the control wires and the left wing, and we're losing control of the plane! She's pointing to Dick, saying, 'You know! You invented something years later, that improved something about these wires!'"

Dick verified that yes, he remembered inventing a "fly-by-wire" system when he worked at Ling Temco Vought Corporation.

"Well," I said, confidently, "She was there *helping!* She was transmitting helpful thoughts to you!"

I said, "We're coming down, and there are thoughts about a Tom who may have worked on the plane, and about a 'Mac.'" (Dick later learned that Bo McKneely was a mechanic whom she knew in San Francisco.) "I see palm trees, and we're looking at something over to the right that sticks out into the water from the land, like a jetty—I think it's a bridge or a dock. It looks white, maybe concrete."

"I know what that is!" said Dick, excited, "That's the ramp that the Japanese used to bring their seaplanes up out of the water!"

"We're approaching the dock, and I can see tanks, like small army tanks. It's all starting to get a little confusing. And now we're at that jetty thing and we're coming down!"

"No!" Dick yelled, "You're still too low! You'll have to go OVER that!"

"I don't think we do," I answered.

"Oh boy, you'd better!" said Dick.

"It's kind of like stubbing your toe," I added, trying to not omit any important details.

"Yes, it *would* feel like that," Dick laughed.

"Now we're down—I think we're in the water—and we're feeling something about a shoulder and leg, and concern about the one at the back of the plane. I can hear a sort of 'glub glub glub.' I see that box again and feel the concern about it, and there's that long piece of the plane, a wing. Now we're losing consciousness, but still foggy thoughts about the box, someone lifting it out, shoulder hurting." (Dick suspected that the box held the camera, a Fairchild K–3, which Roosevelt had sent with her.)

"Does she know where she is?" Dick asked quickly, as if trying to catch me before *I'd* lose consciousness.

"Yes, yes, and she was afraid of this," I replied, "and she's thinking something about 'half,' something like 'and we'd just gone half-way!' She knew she should have trusted her instincts."

Captured

Now I found us in a room that looked like an office, with many cardboard boxes around us. Men in uniforms are questioning Amelia, but she's not paying much attention to them. She's more angry at herself than she is at them. "Darn it," she's thinking, "I *knew* this would happen." She had a premonition about this, whatever or wherever it was that she did or went that was against her wishes.

"Can you see the building that you're in?" asked Dick.

"I can't describe the outside now because we're *in* it! We're on the first floor; I think there's another one above us. It's a concrete building. There's a huge steel door that's very distracting when it slams shut. We passed some concrete blocks with cables hanging out of them, like materials used for construction."

(Dick later said that this description of the building correlates exactly with one he filmed on both the Atolls of Maloelap and Wotje. There was also an identical building on Jaluit and Mili Atolls.)

"Someone is bringing something in from the left, and there's a scent of oranges. They're showing her a map. She seems to know where we are or where we're going, and she's not surprised. There isn't much that they need to know from her, as they seem to know all about her. It's almost as if they were expecting her.

"Now we're being moved out of the room, through the steel door. There's a circular stairwell. It's feeling a little scary, like walking through San Quentin prison. Outside, we're passing something big and round, like a water tank. Amelia's feet are dragging. There's the smell of fish or squalor, and still that smell of orange!

"We're now in a small dark room, an old blanket thrown around or under her. A wooden bench—something wooden in the room, and the sound of two contrasting voices. One is gruff, abrasive, and very irritating; the other is soft and kind. Something metallic sounding, like a bicycle chain. Then the soft voice, and the name Mary or Marianne."

"Can you see outside the room?" Dick asked.

"Yes, she's thinking more clearly now, and there are trees, the water, a sand bar—the sand bar and a clump of trees just beyond it. She can hear and see boats. Now she can hear planes, and for some reason, she's thinking 'eight or nine months.' There's a transport that goes back and forth regularly. She's gotten used to the sound of it. It gives her hope."

"Are they treating her at all?"

"Yes, there was something put on her skin. I think something was broken—her hand, her finger or something. Feels like right shoulder, left leg.

"She's grieving for the plane and for a person in it. That must have been Fred. I didn't see him in the water. Maybe he was shot. Maybe that was the sound of heavy shifting or sliding that I heard before we went down. Maybe that was Fred! She's thinking about a good luck charm, medallion or coin in the plane—something shiny."

Finally, as I started to "burn out," there was awareness of a tanker or large boat that may have taken her somewhere else, something about China, steel balls (a hint about something) and lots of people and voices, like a prison.

Amelia ended her projections to Dick, concluding this long session with the thoughts, "And you know the rest."

According to Dick, many sources believe that Amelia was taken to Saipan, was transferred to a Japanese prison in China for the remainder of the war, and was brought home at its end by her aviatrix friend, Jacqueline Cochran. They maintain that she lived in New Jersey as Irene Craigmile, and later became Irene Bolam after another marriage. Robert Myers claims to have met with her there in a limousine.

They believe that Amelia had lived uncomfortably with all the notoriety before her last flight and enjoyed anonymity until her death in 1982.

Dick later shared more connections with me. He had spoken with First Lieutenant Jim Harmon, one of six men who parachuted into a prison in Weihsien, China, at the end of the war to keep the Japanese from killing their prisoners. Jim and his men set up a communications system so that all could notify their families of their condition and whereabouts.

He said that Amelia had been transferred to that prison where he himself saw her, looking very thin, in a cell similar to the one described in the reading. He said that all that she had in the room was a wooden bench and an old blanket, which was wrapped around her. Dick felt that her awareness in the reading went from her initial questioning on one of the islands mentioned, to her incarceration in the prison in China.

Jim connected the gruff voice to the Japanese "Counselor" who was in charge of the prison but tended only to Amelia. He oversaw her "welfare," giving her drugs, possibly morphine. He said that this man left immediately when Jim and his men arrived. He added that the soft voice belonged to the name which had come through Amelia's consciousness, Marianne, the nun who had looked after her in the prison.

Dick showed me a copy of a "speed letter" sent from Amelia through the State Department to G.P. Putnam, which passed (and was logged) through its communications system. Dated August 28, 1945, it read: "Following message received for you from Weihsien via American Embassy, Chungking: 'Camp liberated; all well. Volumes to tell. Love to mother.'"

Like Amelia, I was less interested in the quest to unravel the mystery about her disappearance. I was more impressed with having experienced so many details, still existing in her consciousness. To me this was more evidence that memories, thoughts, and emotions of all that we have ever experienced go with us, in and out of different physical bodies and incarnations, whether consciously remembered or not. They make up the sum total of who we are. None of it is ever lost, as we continue to evolve.

(Amelia Earhart was born in 1898 and died, some believe, in 1937, but quite possibly 1982 in New Jersey. She was the first transatlantic female passenger (1928), first solo transatlantic female pilot (1932) and made the first ever solo flight from Hawaii to the US mainland (1935). She disappeared over the Pacific Ocean on an attempted around-the-world flight in 1937.)

One soul may simply need to be heard or to be visible to influence others (and himself) in a meaningful way. Another soul may have the belief that if he had a crowd loving him, he would feel more loved and be worth more. So he may need to experience fame, to live out that notion as the rock star on the stage with a large audience applauding, but actually feeling quite empty and cynical about his following—that they couldn't love him or really know him.

Inevitably, he would come to the realization that he needed to know, to accept, and to love himself first. And if we do have the God-power within us, then that is loving

God. When you love yourself for the light that you are, so much more love can then flow through you to others.

So the illusion of fame and fortune—that because one has a following or has amassed greater fortune, he is therefore greater than the rest—is another way we separate ourselves from each other. When we revere or emulate another and give our power over to that soul, we vacate our own sense of wholeness.

The Guru

Judy is a friend and client whom I respect a great deal, especially for the sincerity and integrity with which she leads her life, and the example of those qualities that she presents to her yoga students. She and I used to muse over how it is that many "gurus" or purveyors of wisdom can still have remaining earthly lessons to which they have yet to attend. It seems that enlightenment can still come through *in spite* of their ongoing challenges.

I had never heard the name of a particular guru before the day that he made a visit to (projected his energy into) one of Judy's readings. I said to her, "We have here now someone whom you knew as, what, Nana? Nunu? Bana? Booba?"

"Oh," Judy interjected, "I think I knew who this is."

"Well," I continued, "he has a connection with you. In reflecting back on his life, he would like to acknowledge something that you know, some issue, and confirm your thoughts about it; he's looking at other, wiser choices that he might have made. He also has some regrets about a conflict that has transpired since his passing, involving a brother and a sister and a fight for the throne."

Judy nodded, silently, lowering her head. I went on with her reading, leaving it for her to discuss, if she wished, at the end of our session. We covered a variety of areas about her life and purpose, then I concluded as I usually do, going to yet another level of consciousness for a parting message. I finished, grounded myself, opened my eyes, and looked at Judy.

"Years ago," Judy began, "when I was studying in India, I became involved with the 'inner circle' of a large following who were learning from this guru. I became aware of immoral activities, and subsequently returned home, feeling very disillusioned and unhappy about it all. I promised myself that I would not speak of it, unless asked." She looked down, saying, "He was sexually molesting young girls who were among his followers. I knew one of them personally."

The guru found his way to several more readings. He would join in whenever I'd be reading a client who happened to be involved in the subsequent drama. I trusted that these clients had been guided to readings with me to facilitate some sort of understanding or resolution with this guru, because I had not been involved with, nor even aware of him, or of the circumstances involving his followers or successors. I chose to keep it that way.

Judy and I did discuss the positive aspects of "taking a guru." A guru provides a clear reflection of your own

God-self, while teaching enlightening information. Also, when disillusionment results from the realization that another cannot hold your truth, it draws you closer to trusting your own process and direct connection to the God-force, and to your potential to attain Christ consciousness.

I've since had other great teachers appear in readings, some more radiant than others, but all certainly seemed to be "well lit." Just as we carry that same light, many of them, like ourselves, have also accumulated excess baggage on their reincarnating journey here on the earth plane. Some will have yet to return to balance karmic residue with wiser choices.

I respect all that great teachers take on in signing up to guide others. They are continually challenged to stay mindful of their own issues, which have separated them, like ourselves, from Home and often from their followers.

Human frailties and enlightenment co-exist, and it's possible to learn much from one in whom both are revealed. The challenges of the human condition don't have to negate all the light that comes forth through others. Our tendency to judge someone all one way or the other is only a mirror showing the lack of acceptance of our own personal shortcomings.

Fritz Perls

It felt like a game of charades, trying to guess what personality a particular soul had been from the image of the physical self that he was projecting. He came in beside Carol, toward the end of her reading. Carol was an old client and a student in one of my classes. She had asked about problems with her husband, whom she was about to divorce.

I described to her, "This soul is showing himself with a white or grey beard, sitting in a rocking chair on the front porch of a cabin in a densely wooded area. I think this was in Canada. He's sure you'll figure it out."

She thought for a moment, then said that she couldn't imagine whom it could have been. She asked for more hints and he gave me more details, which only eliminated the possibility that it might have been a grandfather.

The next week in class, I was distracted by the image of this same entity coming in around Carol again, grinning. I interrupted class (they were used to this) saying, "Carol, are you *sure* you can't place this soul with the beard, sitting in the rocking chair? He's saying that he knew your husband!" She shrugged and shook her head no, indicating that she couldn't make any connection.

The following week it was Carol who had the grin on her face. She had hesitantly asked her husband about this entity, and he promptly replied, "Oh, *that's Fritz Perls!* I was sent to Canada to spend time with him when I was a teenager. I gave my family a lot of problems, being pretty much a delinquent."

(Fritz Perls was the founder of Gestalt therapy. He died in 1970, and lived his last years in Canada.)

Identifying him now, again around Carol, he nodded, yes, that he had been there to help her husband and wanted her to know that he was still assisting him. He still cared; that's why he was presenting himself, hoping to influence her husband to get back into counseling.

Ernest Hemingway

Another well-known personality who came to assist was Ernest Hemingway. He projected himself into a reading that I had been hesitant to give. The temporary landlord where I lived when I moved to the Bay Area was having a very rough time getting along with people, particularly women. Chuck was the epitome of a "macho man."

It was difficult to converse with him without expending a lot of energy dodging his sexist, insulting innuendoes. Few women, when dropping by to pay the rent, escaped the inconvenience of his tiresome conversation. The usual reaction was, "Is this guy for *real? They* still *exist?*"

I tried the direct "tell the truth" approach with him, saying, "It makes me feel very uncomfortable, Chuck, when you talk to me this way, asking me to give you a hug and to walk on your bad back, when I've only come by to pay the rent." He didn't hear me. He talked right over me, and reached for more than a hug. I tried ignoring his comments, but they didn't go away.

Then Chuck called one day, having picked up one of my brochures at the local bookstore. This time he cut the macho remarks and sexual puns, and asked to schedule a reading. I told him that I would drop an Intro Tape into his mailbox and then he could schedule, if he still felt that I could assist. The tape may have accessed a better part of Chuck, or encouraged him to relate to me from his more whole self, as opposed to the sectioned off, false projection of himself. Anyway, he called again to schedule a reading, and we had a decent conversation.

I wasn't surprised during Chuck's reading of all that I viewed in his childhood, abandoned by an alcoholic father, dominated by his mother, and left to figure out life skills that amounted to no more than survival tactics. He was playing life by rote, responding to it by what he saw on the big screen, in *Playboy Magazine,* and much that he'd learned in the military, rather than by what he felt.

He had married and divorced once or twice, and had a son, somewhere.

When I went into great detail about the patterns I observed in his life, I sensed a very different Chuck. He let down the facade that was so "off-putting," and revealed a very vulnerable and sad individual. He responded to my observations, and spoke from the heart.

About the time I began discussing Chuck's life and beliefs, Ernest Hemingway showed himself. I sensed him more by his presence than his appearance. His energy felt dense, concrete, without (the best way I can describe it) any spaces in between, not porous.

Chuck jumped when I mentioned the name of our visitor. He had recently had a dream in which Hemingway spoke to him, and was surprised to connect with him because he hadn't read many of his books. In addition, another psychic had once told him about a past connection with Hemingway.

"Hmm," I thought, "where to begin."

"Well, Chuck, I think he can really relate to you, to where you now find yourself in life. He'd like to save you some grief. I guess he's learning a lot about balancing his own male and female aspects. He seems quite enlightened about this, and is anxious to try it again, back in the physical dimension—I'm not sure, but possibly as a female. He's reminding me that he cut short his last experience with suicide.

"He's saying that he wasn't a very happy man," I continued, "and so much had to do with his fears. He says that he projected a fearless image, but that simply masked his fear of feeling the vulnerable, soft, and sensitive aspects of life. The way that women responded to his behavior only helped perpetuate a false, strong image of himself. He's adding that that kind of strength didn't run very deep.

"Chuck, now he's 'talking' about the alcoholism in both of your families, saying that it goes back as far as fathers and grandfathers have feared their feelings. He'd like to help you, as a guide, if you will. He'll be around, while continuing to reflect back on his life, choosing his next conditions. He also wants to help you with the writing you might be doing, if you choose. He's saying, 'Let's do it together.'"

A fitting guide for Chuck, I thought, as I brought the reading to a close. We *are* all in this together, and when one helps another travel towards home, we all move closer to it. There's a lot of assistance available for men in these times, if they have the courage to open up to their vulnerable, sensitive side—and so much more of life for them to feel.

"How about a hug?" Chuck asked softly, as he opened my door to leave.

Chapter Sixteen

Caught Between Dimensions

Some Stayed Behind

"Hi, Louise, it's Terry!" I hadn't heard from Terry since we worked together years before, as therapists at a hospital for the developmentally disabled. She was an Assistant Director of Rehabilitation Therapists, and a very grounded person whom others liked to approach for honest opinions and objective perspectives. She had moved to northern California a few years before, transferring to work as a program director at another hospital.

"You're going to think this is really weird," Terry continued. Probably not, I thought. People often called to alert me to unusual events, happenings, programs, or movies, thinking because my work doesn't come under traditional, conventional guidelines, that I have a natural magnetism towards anything peculiar, bizarre, or outrageous. So it didn't seem unusual for Terry to be calling with something extraordinary to report. Her call began one of the most delightful adventures I've ever experienced through my work.

Terry reported that her office was in an old Victorian building on the grassy grounds of the hospital where she now worked. It had been the home of a hospital administrator years ago, and now accommodated Terry, her assistant Bruce, and a few other staff members. The downstairs living and dining rooms were used as conference areas, and the upstairs bedrooms had been converted into offices.

She said that it had all begun one cold winter day and vividly remembered darkness falling very early that day. Everyone having adjourned from an important meeting upstairs, three remained downstairs to review the meeting—Terry, Bruce, and a visiting bureaucrat from Sacramento. As they were getting ready to leave, all three heard a thumping sound upstairs, followed by footsteps, and they assumed someone was still lingering after the meeting. Terry went upstairs to check, but found no one.

Terry and Bruce didn't think too much about it until they started hearing the noises regularly over the next few weeks, always at about the same time of day, when everyone but herself and Bruce had left. The upstairs noises began sounding as if they came from inside one of the walls. Terry tried to identify the noise as something comprehensible, such as a mouse scratching in the wall. Finally, at one point, Terry impatiently called out, "If you want to talk, talk, but stop making noises!"

Terry had half-jokingly brought an old ouija board to work, and it had sat there for a month or two. About this time, she and Bruce decided to wait until they were the only ones left in the house, then pulled out the board. (I usually discourage the use of ouija boards, simply because they open people up to whatever energies, often prankful or negative, that might be around.) In this case the board became a useful communication tool which helped to unravel quite an interesting mystery.

From the beginning, she continued, the messages came through strongly, with a distinct difference between two transmitting energies. One was that of a number of children, with garbled, misspelled words and with a desperation for each individual entity to be heard, for each to tell his story. The other energy came through with a sense of clarity, loving, higher-mindedness, and much better spelling! At times, when trying to decipher the children's words, Terry would call out in frustration, "Isn't there someone here who can *spell?*" Then the other seemingly older entity would communicate.

She continued relating the story to me, saying that the children kept talking about "apple, fire, help." She finally called me because the presence of these lost souls in the house was becoming distracting. As she mentioned this, I felt the projection of an entity beside me, to my right. It was the image of a woman in a bibbed dress or uniform, her body slumped and accustomed to moving in a shuffling manner. She seemed to have come to relay a message on behalf of the lost children she had personally known. She transmitted the thoughts, "They're in the back room, carrots and apples, by the radiator; fire in the orchard; some who drowned in the lake." She mentioned several names of the children, and said that her name was (had been) something that sounded like Mabel.

Terry took note of this message, and of my mention that this kind of information usually makes more sense with the passage of time. A week later she called to tell me that she heard a noise under the stairs on the enclosed back porch of the house. She went back to investigate, and saw, by an old radiator, a box marked "carrots and apples" and intuitively felt that this is where some of the lost children were playing. She also talked to an elderly female patient, the oldest at the hospital, who identified several of the names that Mabel had mentioned. She also gave Terry the full name of May Belle Stone. She added that sometimes, in the old days, bad things happened to patients, and a few had drowned at the lake.

In the following months, Terry checked with the fire department and old newspaper reports, and found that there had been several fires in that valley in 1936, and that some had occurred on the hospital grounds, one in the apple orchard behind the hospital. Meanwhile, among the many messages she continued to receive came one from the clearer, older source: "Find the key, the key is at the lake." Terry, her husband David, and Bruce took this literally and went often to the lake, looking under hundreds of rocks for a key, which they anticipated might unlock some valuable treasure.

In frustration, they finally took the ouija board to the lake. Then the pieces to the mysterious puzzle began to be revealed.

They asked, "What is it about coming here to the lake?" Their source answered, "It has the gift to help. Go there or send someone." Every once in a while, the message came through, "Prayers, right has to be done." The "key" at the lake was the information that the lost children had remained earthbound because of their feelings toward a grave injustice that had been committed against them. They had been falsely accused of setting fire to the orchard. This sense of having been unjustly judged and betrayed, plus the deep resulting emotions, had kept these souls from going to the light.

At the lake, the energy of a deceased administrator who had falsely accused the children, in whose past residence Terry's office was housed, presented himself from the Other Side, to admit and announce the children's innocence. Terry had been reached by lost souls, facilitated and monitored by an older soul, to reach another who had gone to the light, in an attempt to bring about resolution, vindication, and release for the lost children. After that moving occurrence, Terry felt the noticeable absence of most of the earth-bound presences, but sensed that a few still lingered.

A year later, after I had moved to northern California, I received another call from Terry. She asked me to come up to give a presentation and do a few readings for some friends. She mentioned that she and David had received a lovely collection of messages from the entity at the lake. She and her entourage would wait until other staff had gone home, change into old clothes, and surreptitiously trek out to the lake with "the board." They sat on rocks and received many messages from the older, wiser soul who had by now identified himself as Watap, an old Native American whose tribe, the Miwok, had lived near the location of the hospital, one of several tribes known to have settled in that area.

As she told me this, I viewed a scene of Watap, from which I could only interpret that "he had stayed behind." Of course, these scenes are only left up to my own inter- pretation, and I deduced that Watap must have stayed behind when his tribe had moved on, possibly closer to the coast. I told Terry that I knew I would understand the meaning of his message by the time I came to meet with her group.

The day of my presentation for Terry, I stopped at my mailbox on the way to have lunch across the street, where I planned to review what I would present that evening. A new Time/Life Series book entitled *Psychic Voyages* had arrived. Ordinarily, I would have dropped it off, along with my other mail, back at the house. But I felt compelled to tuck it under my arm and take it with me to the restaurant.

After I'd placed my order, I pulled out the new book and opened it to a page entitled, "Lives of the Dalai Lama." My eyes went right to the paragraph that said:

> The advanced soul may choose to post-pone Nirvana and remain on the wheel of reincarnation in order to help other souls toward enlightenment. Such a being is called a *bodhisat-tva,* a Sanskrit word meaning awakening warrior. Bodhisattvas vow not to enter Nirvana until all other souls have preceded them.

It was then that I understood why it was that Watap had chosen to stay behind. He had, through his love, helped to release several lost, earthbound souls who had been left behind.

Months after my presentation, I made another visit to Terry's office, in order to investigate the remaining lost souls. As I have mentioned, I don't do "ghostbusting," but I was too involved in this adventure not to see it through to the end. I walked throughout the house and felt drawn to an upstairs back room which the staff had been using for storage. I could see the etheric bodies of several young girls, crying on their beds, believing that they were still in the sleeping porch/dorm of the hospital where they had been sent to live, years ago.

My daughter, Adrianne, Terry, another friend, and I formed a circle. I asked them to visualize these lost souls and to surround them with a circle or cylinder of white light, then to telepathically send them the thoughts that they were no longer here in the body, that all they need do is to turn to the light, where loved ones would receive and help them over. I sent additional thoughts to one of the lost little girls that her beloved grandmother, the one who had given her the gold bracelet, was waiting for her, with lots of love.

Suddenly, we felt a "whoosh"—a feeling of energy moving upward and out. And so, a few more lost souls were released to the light.

Terry and David compiled a lovely assortment of messages from this wise old Native American, which they gave to friends for gifts. The following are excerpts from Messages From Watap.

June 30, 1988: From little lambs peaceful wool is taken, but lambs do not fear because peace is within. If they can lose their coat, you can lose material things and still survive—even better without excess. In fact, riches smother you. Why not share excess to help others. Also, they have a secret for all. They live in harmony and follow their leader without fighting his will. They also give a gift of their wool to help other kinds and it comes back to them just as it was before, and they have no regrets and don't expect to be thanked. Be kind in this way.

July 14, 1988: Life is climbing a mountain. From low there is no depth and you see little. But the higher you are, the more the spirit is elevated. When you are on flat ground, everything is one-dimensional, but from high [ground] the world is in view. The struggles in life are like your climb—the higher, the more difficult, but the more spectacular the view and the fresher the air. If you look for God's help, remember that his view is even greater. If you trust, then you know that He will not let you fell. Having trust means not having fear. If you stumble, simply get up and determine what happened. There is need to look a little ahead but do not look too far because you will lose sight of your mission. As you climb your path, knowledge follows because you become aware of those obstacles and how to overcome them, including the obstacle of fear. Goals are here in front of you, if you just learn to identify them. Others can benefit from your climb, because they can see what trust did for you. The climb up puts you in touch with nature.

Zorro

Zorro was standing beside me. At least he looked like Zorro, only without the mask. This entity was incensed that he had been accused of mischievous haunting.

"That was *my* ranch!" the entity protested, projecting his energy in the form of what now looked like a very misunderstood Zorro. "Why would I want to hurt it? I've been helping you!"

It was Rory's reading. I had met Rory and his family months before when I worked at the Newport Beach magic club. After I did "mini-readings" for his family, he asked me if I did "dehaunting." I replied as I usually do, that I did not. He then asked if I would try to help if he were to come for a private consultation. He wanted to bring something from his ranch near Santa Barbara, to see what information I might be able to pick up on.

He said that his ranch was haunted, that the ghost would appear to houseguests in the middle of the night. They would report seeing the "visitor" looking like a caballero, dressed in hat, boots, and black cape. Terrified, the guests would leave before dawn, hesitant to accept future invitations. He had also lost two fearful caretakers. Rory added that his daughter would often wake up screaming at night, always at the same time.

Rory said that things were getting worse. The horses were plagued with a rare disease, and he was experiencing bad luck with the ranch in general. He was afraid that the ranch was cursed.

He said there was an old tale about the ranch, and he was now beginning to believe it. Apparently the original owner, an early Californian from Mexico, had borrowed a large sum of money from a gringo. There was an understanding among *ranchero* owners who shared a common

Mexican heritage that, when money was borrowed, no interest was charged.

When it came time to pay off the loan, a large interest charge was added to the amount due. The story went that, in his fury, the owner buried his gold coins, the money owed, and put a curse on the ranch. He then hanged himself.

Before Rory came for his reading, I asked him to make sure that he sincerely desired to be done with this entity. People often hold on to lost souls, enjoying the attention they receive from having a good story to tell. Some even admit that they would feel a loss, should their "friendly ghost" move on. "We're absolutely sure!" Rory was quick to answer. "Whoever he is, he's become a terrible nuisance!"

A few weeks later, Rory came for his scheduled consultation and brought with him the original door knocker from the ranch. I was holding it when "Zorro" appeared. Believing himself to have been misjudged, he projected the thoughts that there were other lost souls around the ranch who were causing mischief, but *he was not!* Then he wanted Rory to know that he knew about the water problem.

"Water problem?" I asked Rory.

"Yes, it has to do with irrigating the land. There's a dispute with a woman whose property is below ours. We're trying to get the water up to our property."

"Well, now he's showing me a windmill." I continued interpreting. "What would that mean?"

"Hmmm," said Rory, thinking. "Oh! A few years ago I had a dream—a very clear one—about a windmill, and later I found that the original one still stood on the property!"

"Ah hah," I said, making the connection. "He wants you to know that *he* was projecting that image of the windmill to you in your sleep. He says that it worked for him; it would work for you. There's something about the windmill that will help with the irrigation problem."

(Rory later informed me that when it came time to dig a new well, the water source was found to be under the original windmill.)

Adding to his self-vindication, "Zorro" said that there were some who lingered behind who were responsible for the misdeeds. I asked him, telepathically, how he had died, but he seemed more interested in answering questions about the ranch.

I sent Rory home with instructions to help send any of the lost souls to the light. I advised him to bring the family together and to form a circle in a room where they customarily gathered. Then he was to instruct everyone to surround themselves with white light, each one visualizing a cylinder of bright light around their self, and then around the group. This light would protect them and would raise the vibrations of the group, thereby facilitating the implementation of their higher intentions—to send earthbound souls to the light.

Next, I suggested that they call in the lost souls, telepathically inviting them into the center of the circle, trying to imagine or visualize them as they did so. At the point that any of them started to feel the souls' presence, they should then send the message, lovingly but firmly, that they no longer belonged here, that they needed to turn towards the light. They were to assure the souls that when they faced the light, they would be met by loved ones who would be there to help them over.

Most often, I have found that these souls do not want to be here, and they are simply lost and bewildered. Imagine, being caught between dimensions without awareness, with only the misperception that you are still on the physical plane. In my experience, lost souls are grateful, relieved to be released, and they leave quickly.

Rory took the message from "Zorro" to heart, feeling a kinship with one who had also labored hard with the difficulties on the ranch. Rory and his family had the little ceremony, but he was driven to uncover more information that might explain all the bad luck and mischief that plagued the ranch. He became obsessed with finding answers.

He researched the history of the ranch and found that it was originally owned by Francisco Cota. Cota lived in Santa Barbara and entrusted the care of the ranch to a relative, who eventually lost it. The property was then divided and syndicated by a Santa Barbara entrepreneur and was eventually sold to the son of a famous Hollywood director. The owners experienced many hardships on the ranch, including terrible droughts, which forced them to cut oak trees to provide grazing land for the cattle.

Rory invited an anthropology professor to the ranch. The man had been researching haunted dwellings up and down the west coast and was glad to respond to Rory's plea. He discovered that the ranch had been built over Indian burial grounds, and that it was a powerful vortex of negative energy. Along with other entities, this man also saw the one who looked like Zorro, but wasn't able to confirm that he had actually hanged himself.

Rory also enlisted the assistance of a local psychic/ healer, who said that the ranch had been a place of much misery and pain, which still enveloped it. She pinpointed areas where souls still lingered in their grief, sensing it very strongly in the guest room. There existed so much foreboding negative energy on the ranch that Rory finally concluded that it could be moved around or pushed into the corners, but could not be extinguished or dissipated.

He finally sold the ranch, and in retrospect, Rory identifies the whole adventure as a meaningful catalyst that opened him up to his own spiritual awareness. The psychic whom he had called upon became the teacher who helped him identify and develop his own gifts. He eventually went on to become a spiritual teacher.

Rory came to realize that the ranch did have a hold on him, and that it was through his own spiritual awakening and the resolution of many of his own "dark corners" that he was able to disengage from its pull. At that point, the ranch finally sold. Rory added that he sold it to a family who, at last report, were enjoying having seances in the attic.

PART THREE

The Light and The Homeward Journey

Chapter Seventeen

White Light

Higher Level of Resolution

White light is pure energy. It may be used for protection and healing, and assists in telepathic communication, and is extremely useful in raising the vibrations of a person or a situation. Visualizing a cylinder of white light around oneself and others will lift the level on which one is operating in the physical world. It will also raise the potential for challenges and issues to be resolved to a higher level.

I used to have students bring other souls, whether in or out of the body, into their own private gardens in meditation. They would invite one with whom they had issues to resolve to join them in these gardens. Then they would see the other soul start to appear on a white bench across from where they found themselves seated, also on a white bench. Sometimes their bench had a red "X" in the center, marking the student's special, significant place in the universe.

I guided the students to surround their guest with brilliant white light, as they had done with themselves when they entered the meditation. Then they would begin to feel the light raising them to a higher vibratory frequency.

At this point I would encourage them to have a conversation with the other soul, on this higher level of resolution, staying receptive and open to allowing new thoughts and perceptions to come through, rather than making this an opportunity to impose their wills on the other. It was common for students to report in class the following week that they'd received a call from a relative that resolved a past issue, or found themselves in an unanticipated moment, speaking spontaneously to a surprisingly receptive employer.

It's only after a person has acted out enough of one's own misperceptions about oneself in one's reality, frustrated at the inability to make things go one's own way, unsuccessful in the attempts to force the world and everyone in it to fit into rigid concepts and beliefs, that one will be ready to take the next step.

That step frees one from a need to be "right"—no longer compelled to prove that one's own rigid beliefs are true for everyone else, a position that leads only to failure and unhappiness. Taking the next step ushers a person into a new, open, vital expanse of life where being "wrong" is acceptable, where "not knowing" is an enlightened place to be, a place that leads to happiness and fullness of life. In turn, one can gain a new sense for all of life that can now flow through. The ability to surrender to that perfect flow is what allows a person to release any of life's issues to a higher level of resolution.

Surrounded

Cynthia and I decided to explore the Big Bear mountain resort area in search of a pleasant location for our next class retreat. She and I worked well together, and we had long since discovered that this wasn't the first time. We had both experienced past-life overlays of another life space when she (he) had been my priest. I had been shuttled off to him when my family didn't know what else to do with me. Having a child with "the sight" was an embarrassment and carried the risk of exposing the family to ridicule and harm.

What my family didn't know was that *he* also trusted that kind of knowing and was a bit of a church renegade. We had seen that we had gone on a long journey together in that lifetime, both riding very uncomfortable mules on the way to some sort of celebration to the north of our village. I was thrilled to be able to go, and it was only with someone such as this holy priest that a young woman would have been allowed to do so. Many long days of our journey ended with suppers in taverns and with me putting my responsible priest to bed after consuming too much wine. Many of those days were mixed with warm, loving talks and with his irritating complaints about the discomforts of traveling by mule.

We made another journey, in this current life space, up the coast to Santa Barbara on highway 101, the old El Camino Real trail along which the California missions were built. Driving in my comfortable BMW, I got a strong "deja vu" feeling, but it was more a sensation of two time periods merging. I knew that I had once promised my priest a trip in a more comfortable mode of transportation, and here it was, as promised.

Cynthia had attempted to visit the Santa Barbara Mission a few years before with a boyfriend, but felt physically ill, disoriented, and upset as they approached the entrance. At her insistence, they went elsewhere. This time I encouraged her to confront whatever it was that repelled her, talking softly to her as we toured the mission.

She knew it was here that she had lived another episode as a priest, in an attempt to balance emotions of scorn and bitterness which she carried against the church. When the tour ended at the cemetery, Cynthia also knew that the body of that priest-self had been buried there.

We now found ourselves—again on a journey— going to Big Bear to find a cozy cabin for our retreat, located an easy walk to a forest clearing where I could "go deep" with the group. We began making plans, her Virgo "nuts and bolts" approach complementing my Aries "go for it" style. (At times I seem to surround myself with Virgos, who help me pay attention to necessary, grounded details, back here in the body.)

The day of the retreat arrived, and class members from one of my very first classes began arriving, having made the trip up the hill through heavy Friday afternoon traffic. After food and friendly conversation, I guided them through meditations and exercises, then adjourned for an early bedtime in preparation for a dawn rising and meeting in the forest.

The next morning I sat cross-legged on the ground, my back against a tree. With my eyes closed for over three hours, I delivered a message from "us"—higher energies and my higher conscious' ness. (I feel that guides represent a personification of our own higher consciousness. However, I feel that when the projected personalities of our inner guides are given too much emphasis, they can give the guided one the impression that guidance comes from external sources, rather than as a reflection and augmentation of one's own internal God-source). I concluded with individual readings to help apply the information received to each one's personal life. Everyone took a turn sitting in front of me with tape recorders in their laps.

Sandy was the last one to sit before me. She and I had acknowledged a very loving bond between us, having cared for and supported each other in past life spaces.

The deep emotions resulting from that bond caused us to nearly avoid each other in this life, feeling that to open up to the extent of our connection would be overwhelming.

Toward the end of Sandy's reading, the Light came. I'd had other "Light experiences" in my life, once at another of these retreats. This time, the Light came down, and . . . the only way I can adequately describe it is. . . it *zapped* us! It surrounded both of us and the tree like a band of energy. I felt overflowing joy and quiet peace, and a feeling of secure openness and oneness with the entire world and everyone in it.

At the end of Sandy's reading I opened one eye to look for some evidence of what had happened. Birds had come closer and sat on the perimeter of this circle of light. I looked at Sandy and we both shivered with deep, confirming emotion, then looked away. Later that night, I asked her if she had seen or felt the Light, and she motioned for me to follow her into an adjoining room. She said that she had something she wanted me to hear.

Sandy rewound the tape from her reading, saying, "Listen to this part, when the Light came." All I could hear on that portion of her tape recording was static, so much that it blocked out all else; no words were audible. We hugged and looked at each other again in silent agreement about what we knew and needed no words to confirm, then turned from each other and again went in separate directions. Sincere, higher intentions and an open heart can pull that kind of light towards you, at times more dramatically than any other way.

The Light also came three years later, while I was conducting another mountain retreat. This was during the Harmonic Convergence, a time prophesied to signal the beginning of shifts in our world order, and to pull us back into alignment with spiritual values and the earth.

We all met at sunrise, Saturday morning, on the upstairs deck of another mountain home we had rented, cradling mugs of coffee and tea, with sleeping bags draped around shoulders and under bottoms. I had just guided the group through a meditation. While everyone sat, deepened and quiet, I looked up and focused on the top of a majestic pine tree.

I felt so much gratitude for being able to be a conscious part of this perfect plan that I gave thanks in the most profound way that I know, by slowly, softly reciting the Lord's Prayer. I personally believe that this prayer is a very powerful mantra which vibrates at a high frequency and thereby raises the vibration of anyone who meditates on it.

As I continued, whispering to myself, "Thy will be done, on earth as it is in heaven," the Light came again. This time I stared right into it. It was so intense that I wanted to look away, but resisted. I tried to bring the group into the experience by saying out loud all that I was experiencing. In that Light, I *knew*. All was so very clear—the illusion, the drama we live out, pretending that there are good guys and bad guys, that there isn't a much bigger picture. I distinctly knew that when living in the light, I would not be able to pretend or give power to what I saw, in that moment, as shadowboxing on the wall.

By this time my body had begun to vibrate as it rocked back and forth. I sometimes rock gently like that in readings, much like a blind person does in sensing his space, but this was more of a pulsating rocking motion. Someone who sat on my right pried the coffee cup from my hands and later told me that the cup was sizzling hot and the tea inside was cold.

There are many interpretations and explanations about Light experiences, but what is important to me is that they always remind me, in a flash, of all that I once knew, before I started pretending in this illusion. The Light always pulls me back for a quick visit to Home and lets me know that it will be there for me when my tour of duty is finished here.

White Light and Chuck E. Cheese

We stood in front of the school, making the customary arrangements that mothers make for this sort of occasion: I would take my son, Dylan, to her house for her son's birthday party the following Saturday. Donald's parents would then drive the boys in the fourth grade class up to Chuck E. Cheese's Pizza Time Theater.

My husband and I decided to use this opportunity to go to dinner that same evening, further up the coast. At 8:00 p.m. I would call the mother of the birthday boy at home to verify they had returned, and we would then pick up our son on our way back down the coast.

We dropped Dylan off that Saturday evening, and I remember noticing, as he jumped out of the car—looking so grown-up in a blue and green rugby shirt with blue pants—how tall he was getting, and that it was again time to lengthen his pants. Dylan is one of those children who wakes up in the morning with a smile, and a "what's in store for today!" grin on his face. He has his lessons here, like the rest of us, but his lovely spirit always radiates a sparkle, recognition that he's back here for another adventure and knows the role he's playing.

Dylan has never had trouble attracting friends. Both times that we have moved, once to a new courtyard, the other to a new town, he sat on the front stoops of the new residences as the last of the boxes were being brought in, elbows on knees, chin in hands. The first time, I asked him what he was doing. "Waiting," he replied.

"Waiting for what?" I asked.

"For someone," he answered.

"Who?" I pursued.

"A friend," he concluded, deep in concentration.

And, sure enough, one or more would always appear to make his acquaintance within an hour or so. The second time I saw him do this, I didn't need to ask. I knew that he was manifesting a friend.

My husband and I went up the coast to dinner that night, enjoyed a seafood meal by the water, and browsed through a dockside gift shop specializing in outrageous cards. It came time to call Donald's mother. Donald's father answered the phone, saying that the birthday entourage hadn't returned yet, and could I please call back in twenty minutes. Something didn't feel right, I thought, as I hung up the receiver in the phone booth.

First my mind reasoned that things felt peculiar because both of Donald's parents were to be at Chuck E. Cheese's. Why was the father already home alone? But the feeling was something stronger, outside my mind's reasoning, more on the perimeter, over to the side. That's where my most intuitive flashes usually come in. I walked back into the gift shop, updated my husband, then went back and sat impatiently on the bench beside the phone booth, checking my watch for the passing of twenty minutes. Finally, I called again.

Donald's father began hesitantly: "The reason I asked you to call back is that my wife is still back at the party place. They can't find Dylan. He's been missing for over an hour. She had me come home to catch your call. You'd better meet us there." I hung up, still processing what he'd told me, understanding it all mentally, and waiting for it all to hit me on an emotional level.

I was numb when I returned to inform my husband about our lost son. We hurried to the car and, as we began driving down the coast, I noticed that his reaction to this crisis was to whistle loudly. I took a deep breath and looked out the window. The sky was growing darker over the ocean, and I heard the familiar sound of the waves, which always seemed to mock any urgencies or anxieties

I might feel, reminding me that the tide goes in, the tide goes out, life goes up, life goes down.

I did notice that my first mother-instinct reaction was to imagine the worst possible. I remembered a time when my children were babies and we were driving over the Golden Gate Bridge in San Francisco. I thought I was crazy because I was picturing them falling off the bridge, calculating what I would do. I wondered if there's an emotional defense/preparation system that runs scenes of worst-case scenarios on the mind screen to accustom parents to first-stage alerts. I don't even want to recall all that appeared on the screen as I thought about Dylan and what might have happened to him after he disappeared.

Then I shook myself and remembered to practice what I often emphasized in my classes. I took a couple of deep, cleansing breaths and pulled in the white light. I imagined it flowing in through my crown—down in through the top of my head—and flowing down through the rest of my body. As I surrounded myself with the light, I extended it to my husband and all who were involved in this ordeal. I also visualized a cylinder of this light around my son. Then I got an idea.

I remembered the powerful exchanges with souls and guides on the other side which I interpret in readings. Why not also call on them, or the energy that they represent, which is closely aligned to earthly, mortal beings and doings. "All right, all you guys," sending my thoughts telepathically, "I relay a lot of messages for all of you! Now it's time for you to help *me* out. Any who know or love Dylan, please surround him, wherever he is. Keep him safe and send him back to us!" That was at 8:30 p.m.

As we approached the kids' party place, I thought, "Yuck," when reminded of this franchised children's depository for sensory bombardment and sugar highs. The location of this particular pizza restaurant was a few miles inland, quite remote actually; the fact that it was past dark was of no comfort to me as I thought about my missing child. We walked into the front door and were met by the manager and the security guard. They pointed us towards the office and, as we proceeded, I suddenly knew that Dylan was safe. An incredible calm came over me. It was just something I knew.

I greeted Donald's mother, who was beside herself, seated at the manager's desk, talking on the phone to a policeman. "Blue and green stripes," she was saying. It hit me, feeling very unreal, that she was giving a description of my son and his clothes.

The security guard pulled up a chair beside me, my husband watching from the doorway in which he was leaning. The man asked me about Dylan. I told him that he was a very responsible child, that he had been cautioned about the customary things since he was little—about talking to strangers and about getting help from men or women with badges. I smiled at Donald's mother, who had just put down the phone and turned towards me. Whatever happened, I knew that I couldn't blame her. How easily I could be in the same position.

Donald's mother said that she had escorted all the boys out to the car, noticed Dylan was missing, then came back in and searched all over—through tunnels, behind video games, and under picnic tables. She had no idea where he could have gone. Just then, the phone rang. The manager answered, smiled, then hung up. "That was a woman who lives about five miles from here. She has Dylan at her house. I've got the directions."

We drove there in separate cars, Donald's parents in one, my husband and I in the other. When we reached the house, a pleasant, sporty-looking mom was waiting for us at the entrance to the side of the house. We walked in and found Dylan engrossed in a video game with the woman's son. Then she told us what had transpired. She and her son were leaving the pizza theater and were driving along the main thoroughfare, a very busy two-lane highway, towards home.

She said that she passed a young boy who was walking alone on the same side of the road. She drove on by, but as she approached the next intersection, something told her to go back and get that boy. She made an illegal U-turn in the middle of the intersection, and turned back to pick up Dylan. She said that she had to talk him into coming with her, convincing him with, "It's okay, I'm a mom and I've told my kids the same thing your mom has told you. But it's okay to come with me, please!" I asked her about what time that occurred, and she said that was around 8:30 p.m.

On the way home, Dylan calmly related what he had experienced. He said that Donald's mother had left without him; he saw that all the boys had left, then went out onto the sidewalk to find her. He looked where she had parked her car, and it was gone. Then he looked across the intersection and saw a toy store. Being a bit disoriented from low lights, cokes, and too many video games, he mistook that store to be one of the same name that was a mile from our house. Thinking that he was close to home, he just started walking.

That night, as I tucked him in bed, I had to inform my son about potential dangers out there, from which loving parents try so hard to protect their children. Now I had to reveal some of the unpleasant possibilities which exist in our world. Although I believe that violence and dastardly deeds are on a vibration that oscillates at a very low frequency—and therefore aren't drawn to higher frequencies where more light exists—I had to make Dylan aware.

"Sweetheart, some people who don't think straight get pleasure from hurting others, because *they* are hurting so much," I began.

"I know," Dylan answered, hiding his face in his pillow.

"And sometimes these people take children into their van or car, and those children aren't found for days; and sometimes when they are found, they have been hurt or killed."

"I know!" he protested, embarrassed.

"So what would you have done then, if someone had tried to pull you into a van?"

"I would have just run!" he whispered, turning his head towards the wall. So I hoped that my son had learned something.

But we both learned something else. Dylan and I discussed how Donald's mother had handled things, and I told him that I had observed that she was under a lot of pressure from a very demanding husband. Out of fear and her own embarrassment, she had probably told her version of the story to protect herself, maybe not even so much from us but, heaven forbid, from her own husband. I told him that as long as he could stand behind what he believed to have taken place, and could leave things in a truthful place with himself, that's what mattered, and that we both should surround Donald and his parents with love and light, and release the whole incident.

Two years later, I received a call from another mother of one of Dylan's classmates. This was the day after another of those delightful birthday roundups: this mother had taken two classes of boys from Dylan's school on a rented bus to a miniature golf course. She said that before they left their house, where parents were dropping off sons, one mother approached her, pointed to Dylan, and cautioned, "You'd better watch that one! He wanders off!" She said that had seemed strange, particularly when she took notice of Dylan playing around with the other boys. He seemed quite together and responsible. Just in case, she assigned another boy to keep an eye on him, as she made a mental note to do the same.

As the afternoon progressed, the mother's warning made less and less sense. Finally, on the bus heading home, she said that it all started to become clear: Donald, sitting toward the front of the bus, had turned back towards Dylan and yelled "Dylan! When you came to *my* party, *you* ran away!" She said that the boy seemed to be testing the water about something of which he was uncertain.

"Yes," Dylan answered, *"that's* because your mother *left* me."

The mother added, "And everyone heard him." Long after it mattered, feeling no need for vindication, Dylan had already resolved the situation within himself. I'd seen it time and time again: when one's security no longer depends upon another's perceptions, a gift comes in sideways.

White light had helped to protect my son. It had also helped us to release negative feelings about the role Donald's mother played. That release had allowed the entire situation to rise to a higher level of resolution, beyond any outcome that our personality-selves could have anticipated.

Chapter Eighteen

What Keeps You From Going Home

The Challenges and the Gifts

The more awakened you are, the more alert you become to the purpose of challenges and all you have to gain from them. When you trust that the most difficult experiences offer the greatest growth potential, you start to identify them as opportunities and the people involved in them as your greatest teachers.

Many of the experiences you face in life are a cumulative collection of unfinished business, reflecting back to you all that has yet to be balanced within you. So when you step back and look at the bigger picture (or pull the camera back, as I like to say) to estimate the nature of the lesson and what new perception it presents to you, you increase your ability to move through old barriers that have held you back for lifetimes. This allows you to balance and be done with those challenges forever.

To do this, you have to move through the challenges, rather than run from them. Our behavior becomes more and more compulsive in our attempts to deny the emotions stirred up by the challenges which have yet to be healed. Denying all of those feelings is like frantically trying to spread putty over any cracks through which they might seep.

The wonderful thing about meeting challenges is that you find that, yes, they can feel painful and intense, but you notice that it costs you far more grief and energy in devising ways to avoid them than it does to experience them. I have two personal examples of this.

The first was a few years ago, the night before I was to go into the hospital for surgery. I went into the kitchen for a glass of water and ended up foil-lining the burner pans on the stove. I stopped myself, realizing that I was compulsively attending to a project that had not been my intention when I came down to the kitchen. I asked myself, "What am I not wanting to feel?" "Oh yes," it hit me. I was scared.

I was scheduled for surgery in the morning. I felt alone and scared. So I paused, took a deep breath, and identified that fear was present. I wasn't fear, and fear did not own me. It was simply present. Then I let myself experience the fear. I tried to observe it, explore it, give it a color, to feel it as a sensation. As I let the emotion of fear move around me and through me, I noticed where it hit me—in the solar plexus. My body registered it as a loss of power. I was going to surrender my tolerant and forgiving body to the abilities of some surgeon.

This whole experience—identifying and releasing the emotions—lasted maybe seven minutes, a small amount of time to allow myself to feel those emotions which might have taken much more energy to escape from.

Early the next morning, while being admitted to the hospital, I had the thought, "I *just* don't want to be on the operating table during an earthquake!" I got my wish. The San Francisco earthquake came the next day, October 17, 1989.

The second time I was aware of stopping myself dead in my compulsive tracks was the night of the day that my son left to live with his father. Dylan and I are very close, and his light-hearted spirit and sense of humor blend beautifully with mine. I had been trying to prepare myself for his departure, saying over and over to myself, as if repeating a mantra, "Parents are to give their children roots and wings. Parents are to give their children roots and wings."

I knew there comes a time when a boy needs the close proximity of his rather. I had encouraged it after my divorce, but Dylan's dad didn't have/make/wasn't able to take the time to spend with the children. The night before Dylan left, I "happened" to turn on the TV just in time to catch one of the interviews with Bill Moyer and Joseph Campbell.

Joseph Campbell was saying, at that moment, that primitive tribes have a ceremony wherein the mother gives up the fourteen-year-old-son to the father. She pretends that she is weeping beside the son, and the father creeps in and steals him away. We have no such ceremonies in our culture. But that's exactly what was taking place with my son of fourteen years.

Dylan left late in the afternoon the next day, after he and his father had loaded all of his things into a rented van. As they pulled away from the curb, headed for southern California, I watched Dylan watching me in the large side mirror of the truck. I will never forget his look nor how I felt, letting go of my son. I knew that by letting him go, I would never lose him. We had been through a lot together, and he needed the freedom to explore his own life without feeling that he had to take care of his mom.

In trying to be both mother and father to Dylan I often projected onto him what I felt I would be missing in his situation. And I'm sure there were heartaches he did feel that I couldn't have imagined. One day I decided it was time to teach him the maneuvers of tying a tie. I had recently cleaned out my drawers and happened to find a little Nordstrom department store booklet, "Ways With Scarves." Leafing through it, I thought, "How perfect! And here are diagrams showing how to tie a man's tie!"

I planned that when Dylan arrived home from school that day, I would conduct The Tie Ceremony. "See?" I thought to myself, quite pleased, "Somehow, there's always a way." I heard him come in and yelled down for him to come up to my room.

"Hi, Mom, what's up?" he greeted me, standing in my doorway.

"Hi, Sweetheart!" I began with obvious great anticipation. "I have something to show you!"

Dylan stepped beside me in my bathroom dressing area where I'd been practicing in the mirror. He put my tie-scarf around his neck, looked at the diagram on the counter, and said, "Oh, I get it!" He tied a perfect knot, first try, smiled at me, and walked out.

The night Dylan left I sat at my computer for hours. I reached for a glass of wine that wasn't there. I no longer drank wine, my evenings alone, and felt a little silly when I caught myself in the middle of this automatic response. That's when I noticed I was reflexively going towards behaviors that would numb my pain. So I turned off the computer and let the feelings of sadness and loneliness flood over me.

I had a good cry, a wonderful release of emotions that lasted maybe fourteen minutes. In fact, when no more tears would come, I felt a little disappointed that I couldn't pull out more to punctuate such an emotional event. I went to bed that night feeling weary, empowered, and deepened by the experience which I had taken time to feel.

When my parents died and I finally allowed myself to embrace and live with the deep emotions of loss, abandonment, and sadness, I received the gift of experiencing life on deeper levels. It pushed down the floor in my life (bottomed out?), but it also raised the ceiling.

When I surrendered control of my children's paths, I received the gift of peace in aloneness. Another time, when I challenged myself to hold my cat Tao, dying in my arms, while the vet gave him the shot to release him, I allowed myself to grieve openly with sobs that came from a very deep place in me. It felt as though I had been scooped out. And I was given the gift of truth behind the illusion of death, as I watched his etheric body rise up, shake itself, and follow me around for days.

My greatest life challenges, which I refer to as "Very Life Situations," are always my greatest teachers. When I allow myself to integrate the feelings from those situations, I always receive their gifts.

Finding the Pain

I had left my Sunday morning Tai Chi class, pleased that more practice had earned me a little less admonition from my teacher. It was too soon to return to my closet-office for more writing, so I dropped off the freeway to explore one of the little northern California hamlets between Pleasant Hill and Oakland. I found Orinda with its short street of shops, pleasantly receptive to Sunday wanderers, with a coffee shop and bakery and a lovely Italian restaurant next door, open for brunch.

Sunday brunch isn't as exciting for me now, with my vegetarian preferences, but I stuck my head through the door of the restaurant to ask about menu alternatives to Eggs Benedict and three-egg stuffed omelettes. A pretty, attentive, young waitress responded that yes, they could fix me up with a Caesar salad.

"Fine," I thought, settling myself into an airy booth by the window that opened out onto the sidewalk. I took in the ambience of the place, unpretentious but California chic with the crisp blue and white and light wood decor. A modern semi-circle of a bar invited folks to sit and visit beneath rows of sparkling hanging wine glasses. I officially ordered my Caesar, then pulled out a paperback from my purse. It was Natalie Goldberg's second book, *Wild Mind.*

Her first book, *Writing Down the Bones,* had gently and simply, in a clear-thinking, Zen sort of way, given me permission to ignore the critic on my shoulder who used to scoff at my writing attempts, "Now *who* would want to read this, and *what* makes *you* think that *you* can even *write,* huh?" She had metaphorically told me to hang these thoughts, the critic, out on the clothesline to blow in the wind, to let someone else bring him in off the line.

In *Wild Mind,* she encouraged me to write about something painful. This was just one more nudge, pushing me toward a similar notion to get at some undefined gnawing feelings that had been "bubbling up in the bucket" for the past few days. I thought that now, finally, I might be approaching a breakthrough. I even tried a ten-minute non-stop writing exercise that Natalie swears by, right there on the butcher paper covering the blue table cloth.

I thought that I might write about all that I used to feel when confronted by the unloving, intrusive words and deeds from fearful "born again" Christians. Opening up to those feelings did not bring forth the flow of words I had hoped for. The sentences that I scribbled went one direction, but other thoughts still pulled me in another.

I finished my salad, ordered more tea, and quickly slipped out to the bakery next door to buy a hazelnut/chocolate chip biscotti cookie, with the permission of my accommodating waitress. I returned and began dipping and munching, while crossing out my futile writing attempts. I decided to release my mind thoughts, which were trying too hard to figure out what it was that was itching to be written about. I dipped the last scrumptious chunk of biscotti, losing it to the bottom of the cup. I was successful in a rescue attempt with my spoon, and it was well worth the effort.

I drove home, trying to think of other painful experiences in my life. The obvious ones were the loss of my parents, divorce, a fire, a surgery, putting beloved cats to sleep, and living with physical distance between me and my two children earlier than I'd ever anticipated. I decided to lie down and present it to my Higher Self, opening myself up to receiving insights through meditation, or to fall asleep and let my subconscious give me direction.

Sure enough, before I'd taken a third cleansing breath, I found myself intensely involved in a revealing dream. I had walked into a jewelry store, looking for the owner. A young, good-looking man greeted me as I stood by one of the glass cases mounted on the wall. He said that he worked for the owner and his wife, that they were out to lunch, but he was competent to help me out. I found him attractive and full of energy.

I showed him a charm held in my hand, saying it had been given to me several years before but that I would like to exchange it for something eke. I looked at it, as did he, a little gold charm of a stork lying in my open palm.

I pointed to the glass case on the wall which displayed three necklaces. One was of silver Indian beads, one of chubby amber balls, the third made of rose quartz stones. The silver one looked like a necklace I'd bought in Santa Fe, New Mexico, several years before when I was on a trip there with my ex-husband. The amber beads reminded me of the handle on an antique purse that be-longed to my grandmother. And the rose quartz necklace was identical to one that a student in one of my first classes had given me, years ago.

Meanwhile, the owners returned, the wife relieved the young man of his duties, and then approached me to ask what I was doing. I explained about the exchange and tried to tell her that I'd rather not deal with her, but preferred to continue with the young man. She said that would be impossible, that I'd have to deal with her.

I turned back around to look at the necklaces in the glass case. While trying to decide which to choose, I was also conscious of the meaning of the exchange and what the dream was communicating. My subconscious was presenting a short play in which I was acting out one of my most painful challenges: letting go of my children— trading in the stork charm for a necklace. Circumstances had forced me to surrender my plans to live with and care for my children while they finished high school, and to adjust to living alone, without them.

The emphasis was shifting from my role as a mother, and I was trying to choose where I would now direct that energy. One choice was to pursue my spiritual work in new ways, symbolized by the silver beads, which were purchased on the trip where I underwent the past-life cleansing at the Light Institute in Galisteo, New Mexico, a center connected with spiritual pursuits.

The amber beads which reminded me of my grand-mother spoke to me of the expectations that family and others had of me in my life. Would I choose to put my energy into meeting others' expectations? And the rose quartz beads, representing love and the heart, enticed me to choose endeavors that would encourage me to live and speak from the heart.

I was fully conscious in my dream of two levels of feelings with which I live: one maintenance level, where I make the best of things—who wants an old charm bracelet, anyway?—and use unanticipated events as catalysts for greater awareness; and the simultaneous, deeper level, where sadness still exists in trying to live happily within the necessary alternatives.

I was also aware that the shopkeepers who were "out to lunch" were my ex-husband and his new wife, who had not been supportive of my daughter, Adrianne. She was living on her own, very determined to find her own way. Each time I let go, she did something positive with the loosened reins.

The new wife interceded and ran a campaign that greatly challenged both Adrianne and me with ominous "speaker-phone confrontations." It was painful for me to watch the wife orchestrating a symphony (with my ex-husband standing way back behind the kettle drums) compared to the duet I had tried to play in my marriage. Then they invited my son to come live with them, discontinuing child-support for both children.

The whole situation is working out, but the dream reminded me of the sadness and pain I feel when I think about missing those years with my children. It wasn't hard to figure out why I preferred not to deal with the shopkeeper's wife.

Finally, I was able to approach the painful experience I'd been searching to write about. My hand never stopped during the ten-minute writing exercise that followed, after my subconscious reminded me of the subject on which to write. When the intention is set forth from the heart, everything in your life will help you to reach what it is that you seek, that which needs to be healed.

Believing the Illusion

I was really down in the dumps one night, having momentarily forgotten every truth I know and trust about life in this dimension. I'd forgotten that it's all an illusion and was very depressed, tired of making my own way, rising to meet every challenge in a positive, higher mode, and really just plain tired of this life. I wanted a sign, some neon indicator that I was on the right track with all the choices I was making. I wanted a miracle.

I felt lonely and tired of getting myself enthused about having learned to "live with the depth and peace of aloneness." Yuck. Ready or not, I wanted *the* relationship, to give and receive from, to play with, to love and grow from. Just *how* "whole" did I have to become before meeting a great partner? *Forget this "Becoming Whole" business!*

And I was sick of trying to become "sovereign" with my finances. Double yuck. Yes, I knew that somewhere in my evolution I must have called out for the opportunity to venture into all this unknown territory, where Woman has "feared to tread," but I'd had enough.

Feeling exhausted, I went to bed early. I lay there and prepared to surrender, but first contemplated my options. I no longer pray-bargained ("Dear God, if you'll just . . . , then I'll . . .), ever since I'd developed a working relationship with my Higher Self. Pray-bargaining felt like I was talking to some elevated entity who would bestow a great favor, if I could make a good enough case. I couldn't have begun to make a good case, because I couldn't think of what I should be doing that I wasn't already doing in my life. I was very tired of trying to figure it all out.

When I contact my Higher Self, it's easier for me to turn it all over, to release my concerns; my Higher Self feels like an accessible link between my short-circuiting little self and God, The Force. But it felt annoying and tedious to ask—one more time—to understand that which was out of my grasp, to be shown that which I needed to know. I didn't want to understand.

I couldn't even look sideways at ending it all, or asking to be taken. By now it was too ingrained in me how pointless that would be—all that I'd have to return to and repeat. Besides, I couldn't stand to think of missing out on the ending. Or the middle, for that matter.

So the only remaining option that I felt was available to me in my despairing frame of mind was to call out, "*Help!*" And that's what I did. I then tried to recite my ultimate surrender and miracle maker, The Lord's Prayer. But I fell asleep just after "in Heaven," trying to picture a much better place to be.

Evelyn, my client the next morning, arrived several minutes late. She had lost her way, having turned onto the wrong freeway. She had to stop a couple of times to ask directions, but no one she approached spoke English. I could see that she had been crying.

I helped her get comfortable on my couch and encouraged her to take a couple of deep breaths to calm herself. "Don't forget, it's all an illusion," I offered, smiling, handing her a box of tissues. After giving my invocation and deepening myself, I viewed several aspects of her life and waited until I could communicate it all in some clear fashion. It's like trying to pull infinity down through a very small-mouthed funnel.

"Well, my goodness, it looks like you've had it and are about to give up!" (My words to her felt vaguely familiar.) I could see that much of the frustration she was feeling was actually the positive sign I often see in readings. She was moving through a lot, processing new perceptions, grieving the loss of old beliefs and safety nets. (A common one with many female clients is, "If I become powerful, I'll no longer be a candidate to be taken care of.")

Evelyn still had the tip of her toe into old ways, while the other foot nudged open a new door. At the same time, her analytical mind registered "tilt," like trying to balance huge bundles piled high in both arms—determined to know it all, present *and* future, and to do it all perfectly, while attempting to stand on her two opposing feet.

She hadn't seen any outward manifestations of all the inner shifts coming about within her and said she didn't think she could hold out much longer without a sign, some encouragement. She thought she was doing something wrong because she was feeling so much pain, and she didn't think she could handle much more.

The sentiments I picked up on were feeling even more familiar.

Then I realized that Evelyn's reading was the answer to my last night's plea for help. Excluding her thoughts of suicide, she mirrored back to me, almost word-for-word, every thought that I had taken to bed with me. The answers that came for her were a gift to me.

I saw a scene of her in another life space, wherein she had contemplated and followed through with suicide. It was during the Great Depression, in the 1930s. She was born into her current incarnation in 1956. I described the pain and despair she (then a "he") felt, sensing no way out of humiliation and financial failure, while shouldering a tremendous burden for his family (her present mother was in there somewhere). He believed that without his money or success, he was worthless, and so was life. Believing nothing but the illusion, he exited that life, feeling exactly (and more) as she now felt.

She'd chosen to shape her whole life thus far to create the circumstances that would rearouse those same thoughts and beliefs, that same feeling of futility. When reflecting back onto the life she had left behind, she had been eager for another opportunity to do it again, to make new choices that would teach her (and remind her) of greater truths about life. And that's where she now found herself, tempted to "check out" again, but now with the awareness of alternative paths available.

To my far left I viewed an overlay of a much more remote, but no less vivid, past life space, wherein Evelyn, as a woman, was a very courageous and powerful guide for hundreds of people, drawing from profound inner wisdom and well-developed intuitive skills. She was leading the crowd to a river (it felt like the Nile).

Her present self laughed, saying "hat despite losing her way this morning, she did have a gifted sense of direction.

The warrior-woman I saw was named Nema. Her hologramlike image actually turned around to talk to Evelyn. She said that she was still part of her, and encouraged Evelyn to draw from her later in the day, when she knew she would be having a difficult meeting with her new boss. "You don't have to feel helpless any longer," Nema said, gently and lovingly. "Allow me to tell the little girl in you that she is safe and strong and doesn't have to hold on to the old ways anymore. You are about to mature into your adult spiritual self. Let me help you."

Then, over to my right, another hologram appeared. This time it was the image of a man, already existing in Evelyn's future, one I had seen before in her first reading. He also turned to talk to her.

"Please try to remember," I interpreted his thoughts, "that we planned it this way. You needed to face your dark shadows alone. We've known each other in many ways. There's a very loving bond between us, but I wasn't able to make you happy. You never knew what caused you so much sadness and desperately wanted to find out—to face it all. I'm also finishing up some issues. You wouldn't want our relationship before it's time. We've already done it that way, before."

Then he showed me the same (future) scene I'd viewed before, walking with her up a dirt road. They were looking at the spot where they were planning to build a house together. He was wearing a plaid shirt and corduroy pants, and his arm was warmly embracing her as they walked and talked.

I ended Evelyn's session with a short, true story, which took place just a week before. I was returning from BART (the Bay Area's equivalent of a subway) from an evening in "the City" (San Francisco) with Cindy, a dear friend who was visiting from southern California. It was close to 0:00 p.m., and we were waiting on the lower level of the station where we'd jumped off to transfer, halfway between the Powell Street and Lake Merritt stations. The station was in one of the roughest areas of Oakland.

I was sitting on a wooden bench, leaning back against the wall, talking to Cindy who was standing, facing me. I looked to my right, and noticed two black girls sitting next to me. One wore a dark leather jacket, and the other, who sat closest to me, hair pulled back into a pretty topknot, looked as if her front teeth had been knocked out and glued back in. Both girls looked right at me as I turned towards them.

"Where are you two headed?" I asked, making conversation.

"We're going to an NA dance at the Coliseum," they answered.

"NA?" I asked.

"Narcotics Anonymous," they answered, in unison.

The conversation became the delightful connecting of four "old" friends in passing, our essences hooking up outside the illusion, over to the side of the very different staging of our individual plays. I felt so close to them, so interrelated, that it was hard to know where I ended and they began.

They talked about how they were finding strength in letting life flow through them. They said that we "normies" (pointing to Cindy and me) take for granted how we have faith that things will work out. The girl with the broken teeth said, "When *you* can't pay the rent, you save what you've got, and have hope that you'll get what you need in time. We take what we've got, and go get drunk to forget that we've got to pay the rent. You size up the worst that can happen, but we look at jail, prison, or death. We could tell you stories that would curl your hair more than ours!"

We laughed and shared ideas, and the girl closest to me turned to her friend, saying, "Hey, she talks like us about life!" She turned back to me, smiling, and said, "Sometimes the only thing that keeps me here is the thought that I could be just *five minutes* from the miracle!" We stood up to board the train that had just arrived. Without hesitation, all four of us exchanged quick hugs and best wishes, then stepped back onto the train and back into our dramatically different lives.

The more we can live and move through the rough spots in our lives, remembering that we're simply projecting the challenges that we've wanted and need to resolve, into this "holographic universe," the closer we'll get to Home. Believing the illusion is what took us so far away.

Chapter Nineteen

The Rewards

Just What You Asked For

I was laughing, saying to Ann, a long-time client who was having an in-person reading, "I don't think that you're going to want to hear this!" She had asked me for insights about her financial challenges.

"Hear what? Go ahead, you can tell me!"

Sometimes clients think that I might hold back information from the scenes that I view. Nothing is ever given in an ominous or foreboding way; there's never a reason to hesitate in presenting all that I see.

"Well," I continued, "it looks like your plea has been heard—one that you put out there over one hundred and fifty years ago. I'm watching an overlay of you in Victorian garb, lying on the grass beside a close friend whom you now know as Helen. It's a lazy afternoon. You're under a tree and you've been reading to each other. You've just put down the book beside you.

"One of you is engaged to be married in a fairly prearranged affair, and you're trying to settle in with what life is presenting to you. You're spending a lot of energy in trying to adjust to what is expected of you—what is simply *done*. There is little sense of enthusiasm for your choices in life.

"You're both day-dreaming—the kind of dreaming that's charged with emotion, dreams that seem out of reach, ones that you think you can only hope for. You're talking about the day that you might have something to say about your own finances, to be independent enough to earn your own money, like your fathers and brothers. You're longing for the opportunity to determine what you might do with money—how to handle it, where it could take you and what important decisions it would allow you to make.

"So, Ann, it seems that one of the challenges with which you are now wrestling is the very experience you longed (died?) for—to incarnate into another time period with a theme that would point you towards sovereignty and independence, the reclaiming of your female-goddess power and the balancing of your male energy. You now find yourself in a time when you've not only been granted the opportunity to handle your own finances, but are being forced to!"

I view such irony in many of my client's readings. The situations that are grating on them the most are the very ones which they have prayed to experience. They're feeling frustrated and overwhelmed because they simply haven't had experience with this kind of opportunity before. It's all new. Therefore, I encourage clients to be patient with themselves while exploring new and unfamiliar territory. Many of us, women and men, are blazing very new trails and we don't have many models.

I also advise clients to monitor the mind-thoughts that convince them that they ought to be able to perform "perfectly." That notion of unattainable perfection misleads one into believing that if he can just do it without blundering, he'll have control over his life, its circumstances, his fears, and of what others think of him. Striving for that rigid control doesn't allow us to expand from our choices—the wise and less wise ones—and into life. Compassion for and patience with ourselves gives us more elasticity and freedom to explore and learn. It also makes us more allowing for the circumstances and the people in our lives.

I caught an example of this in my own life one day. I was feeling my loneliest, all out of steam in the midst of this potentially empowering life adventure, and very frustrated at my inability to control it. I'd caved into the illusion that if there were a man in my life, right now, I'd be "home free." I could relax from all that is stretching me. In retrospect, the weak moments in which I've indulged in mind thoughts coming from fears would have been the most disastrous times to receive a relationship—I would not have been coming from my whole, true identity, but more from a sort of formless ball of energy.

So I happened to wake up in the middle of one of those moments and realized that the very thing I was bemoaning was the very answer to a prayer I had repeated endlessly during my unhappy marriage. I'd whisper into my pillow at night, "Get me out of here! Don't ever let me get into this powerless position again!" I had received what I'd asked for. I was alone now and well on the road to becoming whole. Challenges were only forcing me to find my God-given power which is part of that true identity.

Donna is a client who also received what she'd asked for. She has always attracted handsome men with great ease. Her father, a physician, left her mother for another woman when she was about eight years old. For years, her mother said, over and over, "He'll be back. He'll be back." She would take Donna window-shopping for new bedroom furniture, picking out what she would choose when he returned. Many of Donna's challenges definitely centered around her need for a man and in trusting her own feelings within a relationship.

She has been married twice, both times adopting the lifestyle and values of her husbands unconditionally. Her second marriage, which bore her two adorable little girls, ended when her husband became restless and was seeing another woman.

Donna was forced to move out of the house, which the husband had owned before he met her. Married eight years, he had never put her name onto the deed, and was successful in camouflaging his income and his ability to help her more graciously through her transition from being a dedicated, full-time mother, to a full-time working mother. So Donna and her two daughters moved into an upstairs two-bedroom apartment.

Shortly after her separation, Donna starting dating Nick, a warm, congenial fellow, who was kind and gentle to her and the girls. He worked as a furniture mover, having retired early from the trucking business. The humor they shared and the comfortable, undemanding way about him gave Donna much more freedom to express and accept herself in many new ways. Those attributes seemed to overshadow any differences in background, education, or lifestyle.

Nick, for all appearances, had the best of both worlds—a warm, loving home to come to, with no commitments. He could leave, and did a few times, whenever he tired of obligations that Donna would attempt to impose on him. The last time he left, she said she was done, and would definitely move on to someone who had matured beyond the fear of committing to a relationship. She meditated on it and listed her affirmations, her new beliefs about herself in relationships, and taped them to the door of her medicine cabinet.

As she started settling into the feelings of what she was desiring, Donna accepted, reluctantly, to go to her first singles party. She had been a teacher before her marriages, but found little opportunity to re-enter that profession. When divorce necessitated her return to work, she moved up quickly into the ranks of management and training with a large department store. One of her coworkers invited her to the party. She was hesitant, wondering what she might encounter "out there" now, new to her forties.

As the party progressed, Donna found herself seated between two men, both of whom were vying for her attention. One was an attractive, very successful banker, separated but not divorced, and the other was an equally attractive physical education teacher. Both of them asked for her phone number. She wrestled with that. Which one to date!

She felt that the universe had challenged her to follow through with her intentions, and to not be rendered unconscious by the glamour of the banker, whom she knew from her own experience from divorce, still had much to go through. She doubted that supporting a man through divorce would be compatible with her determination to take care of herself.

True to her assumption about the seduction that his lifestyle posed to her, the banker surprised her by showing up at her desk the next week, wearing a formal topcoat over his three-piece-suit, with an offering of flowers and a luncheon invitation. She was proud that she stayed focused on her intentions and held her ground.

Brett, the physical education teacher, wanted many of the same things as Donna—travel, good communication, and the safety and trust of a relationship within which to open up to deeper levels of himself. Although he had two grown children, he was still the custodial parent of an adopted thirteen-year-old son, and was therefore quite supportive of Donna's parenting priorities. They became involved and very soon into the relationship were discussing moving her and the girls into his home.

About this time, Nick came back on the scene, wanting to re-enter Donna's life. He had recently returned from the east, where he attended his mother's funeral. Donna wondered whether all of the changes he professed to have experienced and was eager to reveal might have been the inevitable realizations that come with the loss of a loved one.

She agreed to meet with him, much to the consternation of Brett. She saw evidence of some new deeper shifts in Nick and could see that he desired to make new choices in his life—one among them, to commit to becoming an official family with Donna and the girls. She became increasingly confused. *Now* which one to marry]

Donna was additionally confused because of a reading I had given her a few years before. I had seen her interacting with a man in a future scene. The description I gave her fit Brett perfectly, down to specific mannerisms and certain words that came into a conversation I had observed (which had already taken place outside of time and space), which simply hadn't yet come into this dimension at the time of her reading. I reminded her that a few years before I had also viewed a few clear vignettes of her with Nick, whom at that time she had yet to meet.

I'm forever reiterating that it's the emphasis and interpretation that we project onto these future scenes that
shade their meaning. I'm shown significant scenes, but
it's often difficult to capture their nuances or importance.
It's not unusual for clients to place a certain emphasis on
the neutral information I give, an emphasis influenced
by their own, sometimes desperate, needs. They often
interpret, *"He* (or she) must be *The One!"* Only by being
fully present in our experiences and listening to our inner
guidance can we find these answers.

This is such a challenge for clients. I've had clients
who don't want to go for pizza with a new acquaintance
unless I can tell them (they wish!) that, "he (or she) *is*
The One!"

Donna found herself in the middle of an experience that was exactly what the soul called out for—this
time, with a built-in safety mechanism that wouldn't let
her revert back to the old pattern of letting herself get
absorbed into the life of another man. She was forced to
go slowly, as both men waited and watched.

In facing a proposal of marriage from two sincere,
loving men, the only path that would lead her towards
the solution to her dilemma lay in staying fully conscious.
She had to continually come back to the center of her
emotions to discover *what* she felt, to trust those feelings,
and then to act on them.

With the help of a counselor, Donna began to learn
which of her feelings came from fear, which came from a
sense of guilt or duty, which ones came from the rational

logic of the mind, and which ones came from the heart. When she sorted them out, she did know which feelings she could trust. Exactly what she had asked for.

Donna is now happily married to Brett, the teacher, and is enjoying the stability of a loving, healthy relationship. She is preparing to return to the teaching profession, and is growing from the challenges involved in merging two families.

Epiphany

Years ago, a message came through for one of my classes that has only recently become meaningful to me. It said, "You may wonder why you have all been traveling the path for so many years, when others will awaken and come to understand so quickly. You will see that you were paving the road to help others travel Home."

I'm astonished and gratified to witness the evidence of all to which the message alerted us. Understanding is coming instantly to those who open themselves—even just a pinhole—to let the illuminating Light filter into their lives, to those who simply reposition themselves to perceive themselves and others from a new angle. Incredible gifts await us in the new realities that are being created by every individual's new perceptions.

I guess I would call it "non-linear healing." It does not take as long to pull yourself out of the goo—in which you have become so stuck—and to resolve and balance past conflicts, as it took for you to create it. Healing comes in a moment of epiphany: a comprehension or perception of reality by means of a sudden intuitive realization. A shift occurs that can rearrange your whole molecular structure—and change your present, past, and future. Those moments are among the greatest gifts you receive as you begin to awaken.

I imagine that when those moments occur, we inadvertently step to the side of our temporal, physical selves and thereby gain an expansive view that is far greater than the limited one by which we are accustomed to perceiving ourselves and our world. For a brief moment, we drop the costumes we wear and the scripts from which we act out our plays, and see a flash of how life *really* is.

It's a moment of truth that confirms the perfection of the bigger plan, the greater design and purpose of our life here. For that brief moment, all that seems senseless and random in this reality suddenly has order. You can't put that understanding into words, but you just know it, comprehensively and completely. There's a "nothing but" quality to the feeling, a very peaceful knowing.

A moment of epiphany can sometimes include a glimpse of life beyond this dimension and, more often, an awareness that goes beyond time. Time does not exist when you sense such a moment, and it conveys a comforting assurance that all the experiences in our lives come at their proper time, with no rush, no fuss, in an even, flowing rhythm.

Finally, in these moments, which do increase with our awakening, there is a truth that blatantly contradicts the illusion of ourselves as separate from each other. You lose any sensing of yourself with your temporal, physical boundaries. You don't know where you end and another begins, and a wave of warm, unconditional love sweeps over you and all others that you see and know in your world.

Once I experienced a moment of epiphany while standing in line in a store. I glanced over at a woman, first noticing her very poor teeth, oily hair, soiled clothes, and the excess pounds that weighted her down. She looked nervous and distracted. As our eyes connected, I could see nothing but a bright light within her. I felt so much love for her that it felt awkward to be pretending that we didn't know one another. Suddenly it felt like we were part of each other. Then I pulled back into myself and felt very sad.

I wished that the woman could know within herself all that I had just seen and felt in her. And I felt alone because in having snapped back into my individual awareness, perceiving from within my own physical borders, I instantly felt a gaping expanse between myself and that other person.

I was separated once again by all the beliefs, attitudes, and misperceptions that we acquired early in our evolution, the ones that pulled us both back into this dimension where we perceive ourselves as separate from each other, and from Home. But having experienced our true interconnectedness, I was left feeling assured that in having experienced that moment, I was a step closer to Home.

Another time I was looking out my living room window, appreciating a gorgeous, pinkish-purple sunset over the skyline of Oakland, behind the peaceful water of Lake Merritt. I looked down at some joggers and brisk walkers and, in an unexpected moment, felt overwhelming love for every one of them. I loved them and myself for being such good actors in our myriad of challenges and dramas. I appreciated our foibles, traits, and the different ways of seeing things that make us all so unique, all so different, but at the same time so much the same. "Aren't we all so dear!" was my quick thought, as I took in everything in this scene.

I was part of everything and everyone that I was watching and experiencing through my window—the people, the trees, the ducks and birds in the water, even the cars driving along Lakeshore Avenue with the bass turned way up and vibrating through the stereo speakers. In that moment I knew the perfection of my own and everyone else's life plan. The little annoyances, like bills to pay, and even greater challenges all seemed to fit in the bigger scheme of things that I momentarily had within my grasp.

Then I pulled back into my own life and all that I've set before me on this tour of duty, trying to hold onto the moment of epiphany that had just slipped away. I was back into my own play once again, but felt comforted in knowing that in some other unpredictable moment up ahead, I would be given another gift of a few seconds of intuitive realization about how it all really is.

Free Time

When you're traveling your spiritual path, you begin to gain a more accurate appraisal of who you really are. Through every experience that you encounter, you're able to cancel out old perceptions about who you thought you were, and to discern that which you are by recognizing that which you are not.

We are presented with situations that allow us to make choices, some of which will take us closer to Home—towards our own wholeness. Others will tempt us into more adventures that become the detours that take us farther from Home. As we make better choices, we become lighter beings—less weighted down from all the debris and false perceptions that brought us back.

I'm discovering something very interesting as I observe and participate in the tremendous awakening of souls who have set forth their intentions to become whole, integrated, free-choosing individuals, in contrast to the old way of evolving by being pushed and pulled through life by karmic vignettes.

I can sense a definite point in many of my clients' lives, ending the need for the soul to attract karmic drama for necessary learning, beginning a period of free time. I see this as the time left; to experience the physical plane as never before, while still inhabiting a physical body. Unfinished business lacking closure and the need for resolution and balancing no longer dominate their lives.

At the same time, this turning point signals the beginning of new life experiences which become available in response to the clearer, more focused, conscious choices made by these awakening souls. All the determination and attention paid to healing personal issues result in the brilliant illumination of dark corners, now leaving space for the free time. There is time to create, way beyond old expectations, and to discover the nature of one's true identity, as a whole, integrated self, connected from one's own center to the center of all that is—to God.

I watch the lives of my clients as I observe my own. Most of us have set forth our intention for expansion, healing, resolution, greater knowledge and insights, and for the recognition of our spiritual selves. We are experiencing dynamic responses to that intention. We're able to see every person and situation that comes upon our path as part of the response that guides us more directly down the center. The following list includes some of the gifts that we receive as we become more awakened travelers on the journey. The gifts are available to any of us who open ourselves, even just a pinhole, to receive the light.

New Life Experiences in Response to Clearer Choices

Greater Ability to Make Clearer Choices

Being more conscious and present enables you to choose more freely and courageously in the moment. Your choices become more consistent with your personal truths and higher intentions. Compromising them brings you instant, clear indicators that you are doing so. A contradictory choice will not be in resonance with the frequency on which your true being vibrates, and nothing will feel right. That prompts you to make a different choice. Then you no longer need external structures and rules to guide you.

You will make choices without guilt, allowing full expression of yourself in the moment rather than with hesitation. Choosing with hesitation from guilt promotes distrust in yourself. It splits you off from yourself and from the experience. One part of you is determined to go on with the experience to make new choices, and the other part of you—separated off in guilt or fear from the past—pulls you away from choosing in the present and forces you to fall back on old unconscious choices. That creates what we then experience as negative consequences. Staying present lets us choose freely and intuitively, facilitating more positive outcomes.

FREE TIME TO CREATE BEYOND OLD EXPECTATIONS

No longer motivated by guilt, fears or "others' voices," which reflect your own doubts and hesitations, a new voice now announces and reminds you, *"It's your life!"* You can now choose freely, beyond the limitations of all that you were taught (and which you believed), as to how much joy, love, abundance, trust, and fulfillment you are worth receiving in life.

FREE TIME TO DISCOVER THE NATURE OF YOUR TRUE
IDENTITY

You become aware of your natural intuitive gifts. They can now come through, no longer blocked by all the issues, drama, beliefs, and doctrine that distracted you and separated you from the gifts. Every healed emotion aligns you more directly to your Higher Self, the part of your consciousness that connects you to God. Making that connection opens you up to higher consciousness and creative energy.

The sensations become clearer as you receive information from higher consciousness, off to the side or in the periphery of the mind. You become increasingly adept at trusting that which the analytical mind cannot reason. You again return to operating as the multi-sensory being that you once were.

You begin to identify and connect with others who are also becoming aligned, sharing similar information and insights, often beyond words. You begin to accept an awareness of your normal telepathic abilities.

FREE TIME TO WATCH AND EXPERIENCE FROM A
GREATER VISTA

Expansion gives you a clearer view, from a higher, wider, and deeper perspective. You know, in the moment, why and what you're experiencing, rather than making sense of things in retrospect. You're able to detach and gain an objectivity that lets you understand what the experience is bringing you.

You're no longer astonished at events which you used to perceive as miracles. In your spiritual maturity, you come to understand that "miracles" implied positive outcomes that were the exception, different from the norm. A more complete acceptance of self has made you more accepting of all that is in your life.

This opens up your connection to the whole. The whole is perfect. It always was. You had only separated yourself from it with your beliefs and fears. Perfection is now becoming the norm. Things working out and wonderful adventures occurring no longer seem miraculous. Anything experienced as separate from the whole becomes the exception.

You start to experience the freedom from being owned by anyone or anything, from old ways by which you used to define yourself. You flow into the experiences created from the new choices you make in an awakened state. You feel peace from the healing of your dark shadows. That provides more room in your consciousness for new thoughts, which then create new pathways.

You feel enlivened from the energy that is no longer spent on deception and the need to make you or life situations other than what you/they are. You sense joy in the stillness of the peaceful acceptance of situations and people as they are. And in accepting your true identity and all the love that it can give and embrace, you feel so much more love for your life, and for everyone in it.

I wish all of this, for all of you—with love—on your continuing journey.

"Let me light my lamp," says the star,

"And never debate if it will help to remove the darkness."

Rabindranath Tagore from "Fireflies"

About the Author

Louise Piatt Hauck was born with the gift of being able to sense, interpret and read the vibrations of the Universe, to gather its intelligence, translate it, and make sense of it in a meaningful way in her life and the lives of others. She is committed through her counseling and teaching to helping others find and use their own power and gifts, which come from one's own awakening.

Louise is a native Californian with a background in music therapy and psychology. Her experience includes work at Milledgeville State Hospital in Milledgeville, Georgia, the Psychology Research Department at Patton

State Hospital, and as a Behavior Modification Specialist at Fairview State Hospital in California. Additionally, she has served as a consultant to various schools, agencies and special programs.

Louise has been guided on a spiritual path since her childhood and later began the study of metaphysics. For the past ten years she has effectively combined her psychology experience and spiritual awareness in readings and lectures.

Information on presentations, readings and tapes by Louise Hauck may be obtained from:

> Illuminations
> P.O. Box 10942
> Oakland, CA 94610
> (510) 763-2729

Made in the USA
Middletown, DE
14 March 2021